# Water Sheikhs & Dam Builders

# *Water* Sheikhs&
# Dam Builders

**Stories
of People
and Water
in the
Middle East**

# Francesca de Châtel

**Transaction Publishers**
New Brunswick (U.S.A.) and London (U.K.)

Library of Congress Catalog Number: 2007011681
ISBN: 978-0-7658-0377-1
Printed in the United States of America

Library of Congress Cataloging-in-Publication Data

Châtel, Francesca de.
  Water sheikhs and dam builders : stories of people and water in the Middle East / Francesca de Châtel ; with illustrations and maps by Michael Durran.
    p. cm.
  Includes bibliographical references and index.
  ISBN 978-0-7658-0377-1
  1. Water resources development—Middle East. 2. Water-supply—Political aspects—Middle East. 3. Water-supply—Planning—Middle East. I. Title.

HD1698.M53C43   2007
333.9100956—dc22                                    2007011681

# Contents

# List of Maps

# List of Illustrations

# Glossary

al hamdu lillah, hamdu lillah: Praise be to God, thank God

aliyah: the return to the Land of Israel, literally "the ascent"

aquifer: an underground bed or layer of earth, gravel, or porous stone that yields water and transmits it to wells, springs or surface water bodies

arak: a strong alcoholic drink of the Middle East usually distilled from fermented date palm sap

Coastal Aquifer: a layer of porous rock that runs from Gaza to Israel's northern border

galabiyya: loose cloak worn by Arab men

ghusl: in Islam, the large ablution that is mandatory after sickness, intercourse and menstruation among others

goy, pl. goyim: non-Jew(s)

Hadith: a body of traditions relating to the deeds and words of the Prophet Mohammed

hammam: Islamic bathing house

huerta: irrigated plain

insha'allah: God willing

khettara: see qanat

mikvah: Jewish ritual bath

Mountain Aquifer: a layer of porous rock that lies mainly beneath the West Bank

muezzin: a Muslim crier who proclaims the hours of prayer, usually from a minaret

mufti: a Muslim legal expert empowered to give rulings on religious matters

qanat: (also karez, falaj, foggara, khettara, madjira) network of tunnels and wells that taps the groundwater and leads it to crops and villages

sura: a chapter or section of the Koran

Talmud: As a supplement to the Bible, the Talmud is the basis of religious authority in Orthodox Judaism. It consists of a collection of ancient rabbinic writings: the Mishnah and the Gemara. The texts included in the Talmud were written between the second and fifth century AD. The word Talmud literally means "study" or "learning."

Torah: the first five books of the Hebrew scriptures

wadi: a rocky watercourse in the Middle East and North Africa, dry except in the rainy season

wudu': in Islam, the small ablution that is required before worship

Yom Kippur: the Day of Atonement, the most solemn fast of the Jewish year, eight days after Jewish New Year

# Acknowledgements

In the five years I worked on this book, countless people provided invaluable support, advice and assistance.

I would first of all like to thank my father Peter de Châtel for his endless patience and help in structuring, writing and editing the book. His unconditional support and encouragement over the past five years have been wonderful.

Many people helped me during my trips through the Middle East and North Africa, by pointing me in the direction of water stories and people. I would especially like to thank Mr. Robin Twite and Dr. Clive Lipchin in Israel; Dr. Shaddad Attili and Dr. Nader El Khatib in Palestine; Dr. Mauwwia Sheddad, Dr. Abdel Monim Artoli, Dr. Farouk Habbani and Dr. Mart Durieux in Sudan; Dr. Heba Raouf Ezzat in Egypt; Joshka Wessels in Syria; Her Highness Sharifa Zein Bint Nasser and her husband Mr. Omar Shoter in Jordan and Mrs. Fatiha Bellioua in Morocco, and of course all those who were willing to speak to me about water in the region.

Dr. David Brooks of Friends of the Earth Canada was infinitely generous with his time and advice. He read the manuscript in detail and provided invaluable comments and corrections on all aspects of the book. His kind words about my research and writing were also extremely encouraging.

I would like to thank Professor Haim Shaked at Miami University for introducing me at Transaction Publishers and supporting the English-language publication of this book. Professor Irving Horowitz at Transaction Publishers stunned me with his out-of-the-blue letter in which he accepted the manuscript of this book. I cannot thank him enough for his trust in my work and his good advice for the finalization of the manuscript.

Thanks are also due to my editor Laurence Mintz, whose help in removing all flaws and inconsistencies from the text was invaluable.

Dr. Jonathan Chenoweth of the University of Surrey read and corrected many facts and details in chapters five, seven and eight, and also provided valuable explanations and advice on several complicated aspects of water management in the Middle East.

Dr. Julie Trottier let me in on her vast network of contacts and introduced me to many wonderful people and stories in the Middle East and North Africa. From the first day I met her, she was even more convinced than I that this book would one day be published.

I am also indebted to my editors at Contact Publishers in the Netherlands, Bertram Mourits and Sander Blom, who helped structure the book and spent many months working on the manuscript with me. I would like to thank them for all their help and for their faith in this project.

I would also like to thank my father Peter de Châtel and his wife Csilla Almási for their great hospitality from 2001 to 2003, and my mother Denise Blondeel for putting me up for several months in 2005 and for supporting me throughout my research and writing.

Michael Durran, the best travel companion and friend anyone could wish for, made the beautiful sketches in this book. Karin Kamp was another fantastic travel companion in Syria and Jordan; she also helped structure the book and provided constant moral support. Nicola du Pisanie repeatedly helped solve logistical problems from a distance when visas or permits didn't come through. Mitzi Angel and Robin Hunt helped shape the first ideas for this book and encouraged me to undertake my water journeys. Finally I would like to thank Maud Isacson, Katie Pisa, and Marina Castrinakis for simply being there.

## Map 1
## The Middle East and North Africa

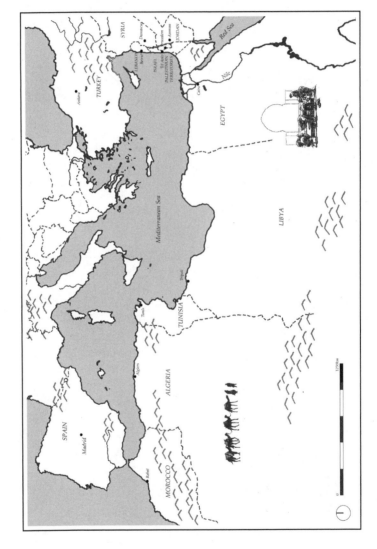

# Prologue:
# Abundance

*"A nomad had told me: 'Walk north to the dunes and walk along them. Count twelve dunes and walk three days and there will be a well.' We walked and we found the dunes, we counted the dunes. I tied knots in my scarf to remember the number of days; in the desert you lose all notion of time, the only thing you think about is thirst."—Abderahmane Naamani, talking of his journey from Timbuktu to the Moroccan Draa Valley, M'hamid Ghizlane, Morocco*

### Keeping the Fish Happy

The rain fell from the sky in torrents, washing down the Rock, turning the steep streets into rivers and sending jets of water spurting up from the drains—the heavens had opened over Gibraltar. On Main Street, heavy drops clattered on the cobblestones. The town was deserted except for the occasional lone figure rushing by, hunched under an umbrella.

Huddled around the gas stove in Cannon's Bar, locals were discussing the merciless rain—it was the wettest winter on the Rock since 1914. Cannon's Bar was run by Ahmed, a Moroccan from Tangier. He had been in Gibraltar for twenty years now, and spoke English with a strange lilt—a mixture of Arabic, Spanish, and East End cockney. John, a Scot and a regular at Cannon's, sat at the bar. He worked in the port of Tangier and hated all Moroccans. Except for Ahmed, who was serving him his pints. John was drunk. He was propped up against the bar, dangerously leaning into the row of empty pint glasses in front of him. "Every five years," he said, looking over to the Australian woman sitting on her own by the window in the corner. "Every five years, it rains here. I've been here twenty years and every five years, it's a wet winter." He looked vacantly into his nearly empty pint glass as if looking for another thought.

The Australian woman nodded and smiled politely. Suddenly he looked up again: "You see," he said, "I do a lot of fishing in the lakes. The lakes in Spain." He nodded as if to emphasize his point. The Australian woman nodded too, pretending to see the point. "It's like this every five years," he said again, looking a bit lost. "You get nothing for five years and the water, it's all gone," he said with a sweeping gesture. "Right now—well, not *right* now because it's raining now—there's only about this much left," he indicated with his thumb and index finger. "But with this rain it will fill up again. It fills up every five years."

1

He looked at the woman with satisfaction, pleased to have brought this piece of reasoning to a logical conclusion. She still said nothing. As he fumbled for a cigarette and lit it, John started waving his hand at her again: "It's important, you know. It keeps the fish happy. Very important, keeping the fish happy." A short pause as he took a drag of his cigarette. "You see, I do a lot of fishing up in the lakes in Spain and it's important to keep the fish in water. Keeps them alive."

"Yes," said the woman. "So are the lakes really threatening to dry out?" she asked, perhaps in the hope of moving the conversation on a bit. He hadn't been listening though, and was staring into his glass. The woman turned away, shrugging her shoulders. She took a sip of her drink and looked out at the rain.

It had been relentless and constant, a Spanish monsoon. Seven days and seven nights it had rained: I had traveled south from Valencia to Gibraltar, visiting Granada, Cordoba, and Seville on the way and all the time hoping the rain would stop. Instead it got worse. I had never seen so much rain, unbelievable amounts of water pouring down from a seemingly never-ending supply in the sky. In Seville, I stayed in a little room that had been built as an annex on the roof of a tall nineteenth-century building—it was the cheapest option, a little hut hidden behind washing lines and satellite dishes. The roof was of corrugated plastic, which amplified the sound of the rain beating down, and, of course, leaked. My clothes were permanently soaked, and my interest in Andalucia seemed to veer more and more towards the warm interiors of tapas bars and their wine lists. I slept fitfully, dreaming of stormy seas and floodwaters swallowing people and houses, whole villages and all the lands around. In my dreams I was saving drowning people from rafts. I saw my little room perched on top of the high building like Noah's Ark, the only dry refuge left in Seville while the rest of the town had been swept away by apocalyptic floods.

I left Seville by bus, driving through a landscape of flooded fields and swollen riverbeds. It was ironic: I had set out on this journey, a journey that was to take me to countries that lived with growing water scarcity, and here I found myself caught in a Spanish deluge. I had planned to cross the Straits of Gibraltar and travel across North Africa to the Middle East, ending my journey in Turkey. It was neat and seamless, at least that's how it appeared on the map: a broad arc around the Mediterranean that would take me from the Sahara desert to the banks of the Nile and then north through Israel, Jordan, Syria and Lebanon to Turkey. It looked wonderful in that two-dimensional light-pink and light-green hue of the map, but I would soon find out that pencil marks on maps do not always translate into travelable routes. From the closed borders between Morocco and Algeria to the Libyan visa that arrived a year and a half later, and the unrest in Israel and Palestine, my smooth line was cut into loose strands that had to be bridged by airplanes, the gaps filled in later when visas were finally granted or turmoil had subsided.

It was of course an unusual route, not India or the Inca trail, but through countries to which most people would never dream of going: Arab and Muslim countries, countries at war, full of Islamic terrorists, fundamentalist zealots and unexploded landmines—or so many people told me. I knew from other trips that this was not true: traveling through the Middle East had never brought any problems—as long as you survived crossing the street in Cairo, haggled for every cup of tea in Tunisia and put up with the leering of Syrian men. One of the paradoxical attractions of traveling in the Middle East is that many of the countries—Lebanon, Syria, Iran, and Sudan—are virtually free of tourists and the industry that comes with them, mainly because Western preconceptions have labeled them as unsafe. Western imaginations seem unable to grasp that people in Iran and Lebanon are people just as we, that they have lives with jobs and families, and that there are cities with cars, roads and shops.

My obsession was water. I wanted to find out how water is perceived and valued in places where it cannot be taken for granted, how people think about water when it does not flow freely from a tap and hardly ever falls from the sky. I wanted to learn about people's relationship to the arid land on which they live and the water they use, about the history, beliefs and customs that lie at the core of water's use in the Middle East and North Africa today. And I wanted to know the meaning of water's absence.

## The Meaning of Water

When I think of water, I think of my childhood in Holland, the water land. I was born in Holland, and I grew up surrounded by water, without ever really noticing its presence. It was a relationship that went beyond thought, for water had imperceptibly crept under my skin and become part of me. Water flows through my childhood memories: I was the last in my class to learn to swim when I was six years old. I had to take extra lessons before school to catch up with my classmates, these water children who had taken to the deep end like fish. Dutch summers were synonymous with water, with going to the beach to build sand castles that were then slowly eaten by the tide, with learning to sail and capsizing dinghies on the lakes near Amsterdam, and with watching other summers being washed away by endless rain.

Even when it is not raining, water is everywhere in Holland: it washes up on the 450 kilometers of coastline and streams into the broad estuaries; it covers 7,643 square kilometers, or one fifth of the country in the form of rivers, canals and lakes, while a quarter of the land has been won from the water and lies below sea level. Water shapes the Dutch landscape: the flat, green fields that stretch to the horizon, the low polder lands that have been reclaimed from the sea, the huge expanse of sky with the towering clouds that are reflected in the canals and lakes. Even the Dutch language has been permeated with countless expressions related to the sea, the rivers, the dykes, and the surging floodwaters; from letting God's water run over God's land, to getting one's sheep onto dry land and carrying water to the sea—the Dutch equivalent of carrying coal to

Newcastle—the language reflects the landscape in which it evolved: a man-made water land.

Water's presence is deeply embedded in Dutch culture, the element that has been most decisive in shaping the land, its history and its identity. For more than a 1,000 years the Dutch have been finding ways to live with water, first merely trying to survive, building artificial mounds to keep their feet dry, and then gradually devising more and more sophisticated methods of keeping water out and winning land from the sea. The medieval dyke masters applied their knowledge of tides, sands, clays, and willow boughs to the construction of dykes and the reclamation of new lands. Piece by piece, they dammed the polder patchwork that now makes up Holland.

The endless struggle against rising waters, the perpetual cycle of winning and then losing new land, that for centuries dominated life in the Lowlands, was seen as a divine trial. By surviving these ordeals—the breaking dykes, the floodwaters, and the fierce winter storms—the Dutch believed themselves to be redeemed in the eyes of God. Inspired by the biblical Deluge, they believed that those who survived the flood were God's Chosen Ones, the Elect. Sixteenth-century Calvinist preachers depicted the new, hard-won land as not just reclaimed, but also redeemed, as purified by floodwaters, which wiped clean a sinful slate to reveal the young Dutch nation in new-born innocence.

But the Calvinist God was strict and would not tolerate luxury, material abundance or excessive wealth in his Chosen People. What the flood had granted in the form of divine favor, it was believed, could just as easily be taken away. Thus the Dutch lived in fear of abundance: torn between the fear of drowning in an abundance of water, or of drowning in an abundance of wealth and sin, which would bring down nemesis on the whole nation. It was a permanent struggle, a physical struggle to redeem the land, and a moral struggle to resist the temptation of excess and sin and thus redeem one's soul.

I thought that in the deserts of Africa and Arabia it must be the opposite: here the struggle is not with abundance of water, but with the lack of it. Here it is water's scarcity and absence that defines people's perception: I imagined their water thoughts were tinted with memories of drought, of thirst and parched land, and that their water beliefs would always remain ultimately ungraspable to me, a Dutch girl to whom water's absence was so inherently alien.

Before embarking on my journey, I had read countless books on the "water question" in the Middle East. Written by political scientists, economists, geographers and engineers, these books saw water as an economic resource, as the "blue gold" that would soon replace the black gold, oil. Water was therefore a political weapon to be wielded against, withheld from, or sold to, neighboring countries. Water would be the cause of the wars of the twenty-first century some authors affirmed, while others believed that water scarcity would lead to peace and collaboration between nations. Here I was in the realm of facts and figures, of clearly delineated problems that were sliced into chapters and handed to the reader in clear analytical order.

There were, I learnt, three main types of fresh water: groundwater, that is the water in underground reservoirs which are known as aquifers; surface water, the water of rivers and lakes; and rain water. There were three main river basins in the region through which I was to travel—the Nile Basin, the Jordan River Basin and the Tigris-Euphrates Basin. The Nile is the longest river in the world, covering a distance of 6,825 kilometers between its source at Lake Victoria and the Mediterranean Sea, and flowing through nine countries. The Jordan River—a much smaller river that is compared with the others only because it has been the source of so many political tensions—flows south from the Sea of Galilee through Israel, the Palestinian West Bank and Jordan to the Dead Sea. Finally, further north, the Tigris and Euphrates flow from the Anatolian highlands in Turkey through northeastern Syria, and on into Iraq where they sprawl through the vast marshlands of the Shatt al Arab to finally drain in the Persian Gulf.

Yet none of these facts answered what it was really like to be that Saharan nomad who has to survive for weeks on the water he can carry with him. Or what it feels like to be that Moroccan farmer who rises each morning to pray for rain that never comes. These books had numbers, but no human voices that transmitted what it meant, day to day, to survive on ten liters, or two liters or a cupful.

## The Meaning of Absence

A few weeks later in the south of Morocco, at the edge of the great sand dunes of the Sahara, I heard the significance water can take on when its poignant absence means it is the only thing you think about. I had traveled all day from Marrakech, driving through eerie rock deserts, landscapes of desolation and loneliness. At dusk I arrived in M'hamid Ghizlane, a village of ten houses at the end of the road. From here, there was nowhere to go but the desert. I stayed in a former French army barracks, and met the Naamani family, Saharawi nomads who were originally from Yemen and had lived on the caravan routes between Sudan, Libya, Mali, and Morocco for countless generations.

I listened to the stories of the ninety-year-old Monsieur Naamani, who sat wrapped in a black woollen cloak and took my hand in both of his as he smiled warmly. He told me he was old and could not talk too much about the past. It made him too sad, thinking about the time when he was still young and strong. His son translated as he spoke: "I went from Gao, near Timbuktu, to M'hammid. I had 900 sheep with me and 100 camels. There were twelve of us. We walked from Gao for days without knowing exactly in which direction we should head. A nomad had told me: 'Walk north to the dunes and when you get to the dunes, walk along them. Count twelve dunes and walk three days and there will be a well.' We walked and we found the dunes, we counted the dunes. I tied knots in my scarf to remember the number of dunes and the number of days; in the desert you lose all notion of time, the only thing you think about is thirst.

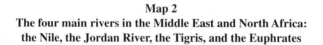

**Map 2**
**The four main rivers in the Middle East and North Africa:**
**the Nile, the Jordan River, the Tigris, and the Euphrates**

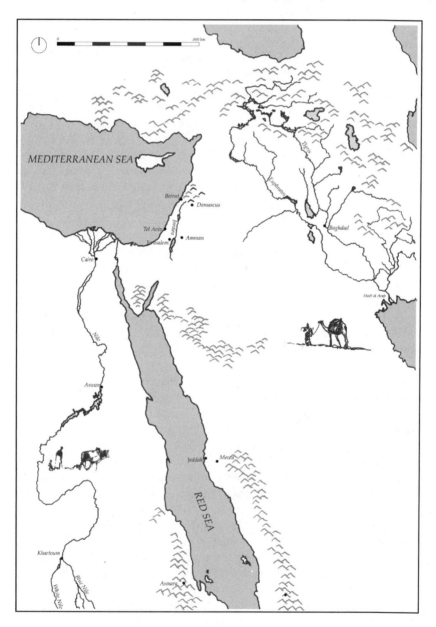

"We got to the twelfth dune and there was no well. I didn't know what to do; without water the animals would die and so would we. We walked on, and at the thirteenth dune we found the well. We uncovered it and some men went down to clear the sand out. We rested for four or five days, for the animals to regain strength, then we carried on north. I always walked in front by four or five hours, to make sure there were no bandits who would rob our caravan. We walked for three months."

The nomads of the Sahara desert are known to have a sixth sense for water. Just as seamen are said to be able to smell the approach of land, the desert dwellers can sense the proximity of water. In a paradoxical way, they have lived with absence for so long that it has become an integral part of their life, and the search for water becomes instinctive. There are even several accounts of desert caravans that were led by blind guides who—according to a certain Major Denham who traveled through Libya's Great Sand Sea in 1939 for the British Royal Geographical Society—knew "by smelling the earth where the springs lay and are never known to mistake the spot." Leo Africanus, who traveled with a caravan between Morocco and the Sudan in the sixteenth century, also relates that when his caravan lost its way, it was saved by a blind guide who "riding foremost on his camel, commanded some sand to be given to him at every mile's end by the smell whereof he declared the situation of the place."

Naamani looked into the distance with a mournful gaze as though tracing the slow progress of the caravan over the scorching dunes. Then his eyes lit up and he resumed, waving his stick: "When a nomad digs a well in the desert and then moves on, he covers it up with a piece of camel skin, to avoid it getting sanded over. To find it again later, or to find a well someone else has dug, you follow the camel droppings: a place with many camel droppings indicates a well. Then you take a stick and you poke at the ground to find the well. It can take two or three days to find it. When it is uncovered, it needs to be cleaned out by going down into it and clearing the sand out. When a family leaves a place, they will leave a trace in ash, pointing in the direction of the well." He stopped abruptly and said he could not speak anymore. It was making him too sad. "I am living on borrowed time," he said, "my life ended twenty years ago; all this is just extra time from God."

Naamani had talked of a world that no longer existed, of caravan routes that were slowly fading off the map and Saharawi traditions that had become obsolete. His stories were like fairytales, words woven in the realm of the imaginary. They were however also testimonies to a culture that has been shaped over the centuries by water's absence. Here, no one had a memory of abundance; these deserts had been created many thousands of years ago and man had adapted to their harshness. But elsewhere in the region, a new scarcity was rearing its head, forcing farmers to abandon their land, making water a rationed good, and transforming ancient oases into deserts.

# 1

# The Death of the Garden of Eden

*"There is no more rain, but there are more and more people. We forget that we are living in the desert here and that more than a quarter of the Syrian population now lives in Damascus. We have no water anymore and our Barada River cries. In the plain, in the Ghuta, it's the same thing: there used to be five large springs there that fed the crops. They have all dried up."—Nizar Hussein, agricultural engineer, Barada & Awaj River Authority, Damascus, Syria*

## The Paradise of the Orient

Dawn was slowly breaking over Damascus, one of the oldest cities on earth. I stood and watched the silence over the city. It was Friday, the holy day and the city was still sleeping even as the sun rose. A layer of haze—or was it smog?—hung over the sprawling capital. From where I stood, on the summit of Mount Kassioun on the northern edge of Damascus, I could barely make out the walls of the old city with the rectangular shape of the Great Omayyad Mosque at its heart. Faisal sucked at his water pipe and as he blew the smoke out through his nostrils, he said: "Did you know that the Garden of Eden once lay here?" I nodded, though looking at the haphazard urban mess below, it was hard to picture a biblical paradise here. The city was like a vast sea of stones and concrete that stretched beyond the horizon. "It was paradise on earth. A town with many streams, beautiful gardens, large orchards…. The best fruit in the whole Middle East," Faisal said. "This place here, where we are standing now, is where the Prophet Mohammed stood many centuries ago. He looked down on the town and saw paradise. He even had to look away, to leave; the temptation to stay and indulge in an earthly paradise was too great. And he knew his real quest was for heavenly paradise."

I had met Faisal and his friends Nabil and Hassan on Mount Kassioun. It seemed they had been there all night. They had set up stools, a small gas stove for preparing tea, and Faisal was nursing an early morning glass of arak and water, which probably accounted for his poetic mood. "This is a very old town, maybe the oldest in the world—rich in history," he continued, pausing for a moment to suck on his water pipe. "It was the crossroads between East and West, the political and cultural center of the Islamic world…whole poems have been

9

written about this city. People called her the 'Bride of the Earth,' 'the Star of the Wind'.... It was like a miracle in the desert, the most fertile land in the Middle East..." He sighed and gazed dreamily into the distance. As Faisal wove a more and more fanciful picture of Damascus, my mind wandered. I started thinking about the past four years of travel through the arid countries of the Middle East[1] and North Africa and the many water stories I had listened to.

There was Mr. Naamani in the Moroccan Sahara, who had explained how he had found water during his long treks across the desert; Heba, the earnest young woman in Cairo who had spoken passionately about the meaning of water in the Koran; and Nisan Tzuri, the old man in the Negev Desert who had told me about the Jewish settlement of the Land of Israel in the 1940s and how the first settlers had made the desert bloom....

From Morocco to Sudan and from Israel to Iran people had spoken about water as a cherished good: the source of life, a divine gift and a resource with the power to transform the desert into a paradise. But I knew that although water was cherished on the abstract level of storytelling and tradition, in everyday life it was treated as an expendable resource. All too often its presence was taken for granted, and people used it unquestioningly, as though supplies were endless. More and more, I sensed that there was a gap between reality and people's perception of the resource, and while water scarcity formed a growing threat throughout the region, few people were aware of its implications. There was a discrepancy between the way people talked about water as a sacred and treasured resource and their wasteful behavior.

In many places the scarcity was not yet tangible and instead of acknowledging present realities people were still able to comfortably avert their eyes and continue believing in past realities. Faisal also seemed blind to the sprawling reality at the foot of Mount Kassioun. Instead, he still believed in the paradise that the Prophet Mohammed had seen in its place. I too had looked for the Damascus of storybooks and poems, to no avail.

The journey to Damascus had taken longer than planned. The rickety, over-crowded mini-van that had brought me over the Lebanon Mountain Range from Beirut had to wait for an hour at the border. It was a cramped journey: I shared the van with several Syrians, and three peasant women from Dagestan who had filled the back of the van with huge bales of clothes and other goods. None of them spoke any language that the border guards understood, so there was the necessary delay in clearing the women—heavily wrapped in layers of skirts, scarves and shawls and armed only with scruffy looking bits of paper for identification—and their belongings. Eventually though, the sight of a handful of dollars, extricated from a hidden pocket beneath a shawl, made all translation and negotiation unnecessary and we were waved across the border with a happy smile from the guard.

I had passed the time reading *Eothen,* the journal of the British traveler Alexander Kinglake who visited Damascus in 1834. Like his Arab counterparts in the

Middle Ages, Kinglake was enchanted by Damascus: the sight of this Oriental city was like a romantic idyll to him. He wrote that it was "a city of hidden palaces, of copses, and gardens, and fountains, and bubbling streams." The Barada River that flowed through the city was "the juice of her life," a "gushing and ice-cold torrent that tumbles from the snowy sides of Anti-Lebanon."

It was dark when we arrived in Damascus, but even then I could see that the city Kinglake had described no longer existed. The twelfth-century Moorish traveler Ibn Jubayr had said: "…gardens encircle it like the halo round the moon." The only halo I saw now was a wall of high gray housing blocks, bisected by a four-lane highway that ploughed into town.

Today Greater Damascus is a capital of an estimated 5 million inhabitants. After 1948, when Damascus had a population of just 700,000, the population exploded. Not only did the city have to cope with a large influx of Palestinian refugees; over the years it has also attracted a growing population of disillusioned farmers who abandon their land to seek a better life in the city. Damascus was not designed to cope with such a swelling population and its infrastructure rapidly deteriorated. Today it is a grubby, thirsty city that is slowly being stifled by its soaring population.

It was late when I finally found a room in a small hotel near the old city, an old Damascene house with a fountain in the middle of a vine-covered courtyard. At the reception a small sign read:

> DUE TO THE ACUTE WATER SHORTAGE IN THE COUNTRY
> THE WATER IS CUT EVERY DAY FROM 17:00 TO 5:00.
> PLEASE TRY TO HAVE YOUR SHOWER BEFORE THIS TIME.

The realities of modern-day Damascus, bereft of any of the romanticized images of "gushing and ice-cold torrents," were rapidly forcing themselves upon me.

As I sat in the courtyard and ate some leftovers of bread and cheese I had bought in Lebanon, a distinguished elderly man in a white suit came over to talk to me. I had noticed him when I came in, sitting in a corner by a table, sipping a can of strawberry soda. He was small with a big mop of brown hair, which I suspected was dyed. In flowery public school English that had undercurrents of French or Italian, he told me it was his eighth trip through the Middle East in eight years. He had fallen in love with the region, Israel and Egypt in particular, and went back as often as he could. There was something of a nineteenth-century traveler about him, a gentleman on the Grand Tour of the Levant, taking his time to soak up the sights and reflect on their meaning. He had several large boxes with him, filled with stone statuettes and copies of relics from the Egyptian Museum in Cairo. With a flourish of the hand he asked one of the receptionists to carry them upstairs, ordering him about as if it were a five-star hotel instead of a budget hostel in a back street.

He turned to me again and said: "Where were we? Ah yes, sights…. Have you been to the Lebanon? I've heard it's awful, terribly Westernized and vulgar…." He loved going to the Christian monuments in the region, and asked whether I was Church of England. When I told him I was Dutch, he immediately said: "Ah, then you are Reformed." I said nothing. His name was Frederico Gutierez, Costa Rican aristocracy, or so he said. At length he left me to go upstairs to his room. "But we shall see each other again, I trust," he said. I never did for some reason, but the brief meeting stuck in my mind. Like Faisal on Mount Kassioun, the nineteenth-century gentleman Gutierez seemed to see only the Damascus of the past, the Paradise of the Orient.

The next morning I set out to discover that legendary city and the source of its prosperity, the Barada River. Described by medieval writers as the "Nile of Damascus," the seasonal Barada River springs forty kilometers from Damascus in the Anti-Lebanon Mountains. Before it dried out in 2000, it flowed from there through the narrow valleys of the Anti-Lebanon to the Damascus plain. Fifteen kilometers from its source it received the waters of the Aïn el Fijé spring. While this is a more regular and abundant source, its water flow has also declined by 42 percent since 1947. At the foot of the Anti-Lebanon at the village of Rabwe, the river divides into seven channels that fan out over the plain and flow through the city to the orchards and gardens around, to finally drain off in the Ateibeh and Hijaneh lakes. The origin of the channels is unknown but it is certain that they date back to pre-Christian, if not pre-Roman times. The oldest written manuscript recording their existence comes from the Gallic bishop Arculf, who traveled to the Holy Land in 670 AD and recorded "*IV magna flumina*," four large rivers, in Damascus.

Situated in a zone of low rainfall on the edge of the Syrian Desert and sheltered from coastal rains by the Lebanon Range, Damascus would never have become such a prosperous city without the constant flow of the waters of the Barada River. Simple gravity and the creation of seven canals with their countless side-channels allowed for the development of the most fertile and productive agricultural region in the Near East. This was the Ghuta, a plain around the city that covered 8,000 hectares in its early days, and later expanded to 25,000 hectares as more canals were dug and the irrigation network grew more sophisticated. The oasis was disposed in concentric rings around the town, the most intensive irrigation and fertile grounds being near the city. Cultivation became less intensive and water less abundant as one traveled away from Damascus.

In the fourteenth century, a Damascene sheikh from the village of Rabwe counted 110,000 gardens of orchards and vegetable plots in the Ghuta: apricots, pomegranates, walnuts, cherries, peaches, figs, aniseed…. Beyond the gardens was the Zor, a less irrigated area where vines, cereals, and olives were cultivated, followed by the Marj steppe land, a green pasture in springtime and a dusty dry plain during the rest of the year. This was where cattle were kept. Covering less than two square kilometers, the old city was a mere speck in the midst of this dense greenery. Yet by the tenth century Damascus had become an economic, cultural and political center, a crossroads of desert caravan routes from India and Persia, the Arabian Peninsula, East Africa, Anatolia, and Central Asia, and a meeting point of nomadic populations from the East and settled coastal populations from the West.

Today the old center of Damascus is surrounded by the crumbling remains of the medieval city wall. The eight gates still stand. Counting these gates one poet affirmed this *must* be paradise, as in medieval Islamic cosmology paradise was made up of eight levels, each with its separate entrance gate. Stepping inside the walls is like being transported into a medieval painting: small houses with tiny doors, plastered white or brown and built haphazardly along the narrow lanes. Sometimes the first floor juts out over the street below, nearly touching the house opposite. Covered archways and small side lanes trail off, leading further into the warren or simply ending at a front door. Vines hang down from the carved wooden balconies; horse-drawn carriages and small pick-up vans navigate through the narrow lanes, and boys zoom past on their bikes. I could almost have believed that I was back in the Damascus of Kinglake, but as I passed the citadel on the northern side of town, that illusion soon faded. I crossed one of the seven canals of the Barada, the Banias. Today its riverbed, which winds between and beneath the medieval town and skirts the thick city walls, is little more than an open sewer. A thin sliver of water trickles between garbage and rotting vegetables, and a foul stench rises up from the river.

When these canals were still the main source of water for Damascus they were regularly cleaned. Each canal was managed by an elected committee of

Umayyad Mosque
22nd June 2001 4.30pm.

users who organized the yearly cleaning session. This usually took place after the rainy season, so that the land was moist enough to cope with several weeks without irrigation. Teams of workers from each village were sent to do the work: the canals were drained and cleaned out one by one, silt and mud were removed and the banks rebuilt. When the water was let back into the canals, a procedure known as *fath al taqah*, "the opening of the hole," a torrent of spring water and hundreds of fish would come gushing down, to the great delight of local fishermen who threw themselves into the floods armed with nets and baskets.

Clearly, this tradition has disappeared today: the canals are not only filthy, there is also hardly any water flowing in them for fish to survive in. The abundance that the city was once famous for is now a myth of the past. Today, only untreated sewage flows through the canals to irrigate the remains of the Ghuta.

At the Damascus drinking water authority Dr Shalak, the head of planning, explained that today almost all the water from the Barada is tapped at the source and led through a pipeline to satisfy the growing demand for drinking water. This means that there is almost no water for irrigation and the canals are dry. Tracing the course of the river on a large map that hung on the wall of his office, Shalak explained that today the water doesn't even reach many of the villages in the Ghuta. The Ateibeh and Hijaneh lakes, into which the Barada used to drain, dried out in 1969 after excessive pumping from the canals, general wastage of water and frequent droughts in the region.

Shalak commented: "It is a terrible situation. The water deficit grows every year and the Barada and the Aïn el Fijé can no longer provide sufficient water for domestic use. Since the mid-1990s the water deficit has risen to 40 percent; each year it gets worse. Nine well-fields have been created southeast of the city to make up for the deficit, but it is not enough. So now we have special regulations cutting water for twelve hours a day in Damascus." I asked him how the Ghuta Oasis was irrigated if there was not even enough drinking water. Where did the water for irrigation then come from? He looked at me and sighed: "That's a different story, a bad story. For that you should go and see my friend Dr Faluh."

Dr Jameel Faluh was the director of the Barada River Authority, the office that deals with the distribution of irrigation water in the region of Damascus. His offices on the outskirts of the city were surrounded by high gates. Outside it was a scene of chaos: dozens of farmers stood queuing in front of the building, clutching forms and documents—applications for subsidies, requests for permission to drill deeper wells and appeals for compensation for yet another failed crop. Throughout my meeting with Faluh people came in, asking for favors, approval of documents or money to help their farms survive. Faluh spoke in a halting mixture of English and French, apologizing as he mopped his brow: he said he was more comfortable in Russian as he had studied in Moscow.

"*L'eau est une question difficile à Damas* [Water is a difficult issue in Damascus]," he started off. "The population keeps increasing and reserves are very limited. We have been suffering severe shortages for ten years now.

Farmers are worst hit." Rainfall levels in the Damascus plain have always been low at around 200 millimeters per year—a fifth of the yearly rainfall levels in larger U.S. cities like New York, Chicago, Seattle, and Houston—and less in the eastern areas of the Ghuta Oasis. Agriculture has therefore always depended on irrigation, using water from shallow wells in the plain and from the Barada. Recent fluctuations in rain- and snowfall levels in the Anti-Lebanon have further aggravated the situation. "All the people you see coming in here are asking for permission to dig new or deeper wells. Usually they get permission; otherwise they will sink them anyway. This way, we can at least control them."

Faluh explained that the government has launched a long-term and large-scale modernization of the irrigation system, introducing new techniques that will mean significant amounts of water can be saved. In Syria, 90 percent of water goes to agriculture, and traditional irrigation systems are often very inefficient, wasting more than 70 percent of the water before reaching the plants. Modernization is therefore a high priority for the government which is introducing sprinklers and drip irrigation systems throughout the country. In addition, water for irrigation is virtually free in Syria and farmers only pay a nominal fee that doesn't correspond to their usage levels.

New technologies like sprinkler and drip irrigation can offer huge water savings compared to the traditional method, flood irrigation, which is still widely used in Syria and other countries of the Middle East such as Egypt, Morocco, and Yemen. However, observers describe the scheme as ambitious and overly optimistic: the new irrigation systems are partly subsidized, but even then the installation of a drip irrigation system will require a considerable investment from farmers. Yet Syrian water policy makers believe that by demonstrating the new technique to farmers and holding awareness campaigns, they will convince them. Dr. Georges Somi from the Ministry of Agriculture admits that not charging for water makes it hard to limit wastage, but he believes communication with farmers can also raise awareness of the issue. "If it is free, you don't feel the shortage, it's human nature," he says. "Here in Syria there is a certain awareness but we also need to encourage the people to participate in water management: we now organize field days for farmers to come and see the advantages of new irrigation techniques."

Even with more efficient water use, Damascus and its Ghuta will suffer shortages. Transfer of water from the Euphrates and Orontes Rivers in the north of Syria and treatment of wastewater are now being proposed as long-term solutions, though none of these projects have been implemented as yet.

### The Barada River and its Seven "Magnificent Canals"

A few days later, I witnessed just how much local farmers are suffering when I visited the source of the Barada River and the Ghuta Oasis beyond Damascus. Dr. Nizar Hussein, an agricultural engineer who worked in the area and knew the history of the Barada and its Ghuta Oasis, drove me there in his beat-up Lada

Jeep. He was a shy man, initially. Each time I spoke to him he looked shiftily at the ground behind me. But gradually he opened up and spoke more. He used few words, but said a lot.

We drove out of Damascus towards the Anti-Lebanon Mountains to the source of the Barada. The landscape was arid; mountains of sheer ochre rock—I wondered how there could be a spring anywhere near here. But when we turned off the highway, we found ourselves in a green valley, filled with cherry and apricot orchards. Young boys and men wearing the traditional chequered heads-carves were working in the fields, watering the crops with hoses. We drove to the source of the Barada. The twelfth-century writer Al-'Umari, wrote that the upper valley of the Barada was one of the "most admirable spectacles that one can see" and added that "the water from the heavens and the land are plentiful here, the sun and the air are full of dew...."

We came to a shallow stagnant pool where foul green water lay festering in the hot July sun. "In a week it will be dry," said Nizar. The Barada is a seasonal spring that flows part of the year depending on the rain and snowfall in the mountains above. Besides the pipeline, which taps its water at the source and leads it to Damascus, decreasing precipitation levels have also shortened the period during which the Barada flows each year. In the past, there was abundant water for at least six or seven months of the year, but now there is only a small trickle from December to March, barely four months. The Wadi Barada, the valley through which the river used to run to Damascus, is now a dry riverbed strewn with garbage. Spring water has been replaced with untreated sewage water that irrigates the crops in the valley. To supplement the sewage water, farmers dig wells up to seventy meters in depth to reach the groundwater levels. "Until five or six years ago there was water in the river all year round," said Nizar as he looked blankly at the slimy green water. "Now, because the government takes all the water to Damascus, the river runs dry in summer. And as there is less and less rain, the period that there is water is also shorter each year."

We drove back to Damascus along the riverbed through the Wadi Barada. Here Nizar pointed to three workmen who were dismantling a row of greasy black motor pumps: "The pumps used to bring water from river level to the fields above. But now there is no water to pump, so there is no use for them." Further along he pointed to a set of abandoned buildings on the riverside. There was a fence around the precinct and a gate with a heavy lock. "That was a fish farm. It closed five years ago. There was no water to keep the fish in." As we drove down the valley, we passed through villages that looked prosperous. Though it was dry, the riverbed was lined with trees and crops. It ran like a sliver of greenery through the harsh mountainous landscape. Poplars, fruit trees, walnut, and fig trees grew in abundance.

But further down the trees that lined the valley floor were dead. Clusters of withered poplars stood sadly between the houses. The green serpent that wound itself through the valley further up, was thinning to a green thread here.

It looked as though the rock was creeping down, aridity eating away at the oasis. We passed riverside restaurants with cheerful red and yellow awnings and fairy lights strung along their façades. The Garden Restaurant and the River Café had large terraces overlooking a gray trickle of sewage. Ironic if it were not so tragic. "There is no more rain," said Nizar, "but there are more and more people. This is a problem. We forget that we are living in the desert here and that more than a quarter of the Syrian population now lives in Damascus."

As we re-entered Damascus, the traffic grew heavy, as did the heat; it was past noon and the temperature was rising above 40 °C. We were going to Rabwe to see the point where the Barada canals fork off and flow to the oasis. We turned off the main road and pulled into a parking lot. On either side, slimy canals lay languidly in the scorching sun. On the left was the Barada, a stinking pool of black water with empty plastic bottles and other rubbish floating between the duckweed. On the right was an even more miserable and putrid little trickle; this was one of the seven Roman canals, the Mezzeh. A smell of rotting eggs hung in the air.

We walked up the hill and came to a white building with a fenced door where a group of children were playing with empty plastic bottles. As we turned around we saw a big burly figure in a striped *galabiyya* striding up the hill on flip-flops. This, Nizar explained, was Abu Fares, the supervisor of the canals—and also, he hastened to add, the manager of the best teahouse in the area. We followed Abu Fares up a set of steep stairs to his terrace café where I was shown more canals. By now I was only thinking of the putrid smell and the depressing sight of this sickly liquid which locals still insisted on calling water. "From here the channels go to different areas and there they split up again into many more branches that go to the villages and the fields," Nizar explained as I sipped a 7-Up in the shade of the vines on Abu Fares' terrace. As I sat below a turquoise fountain—which was no doubt also spewing sewage water—I listened to Abu Fares who had just joined us. He was now in his work outfit: a pair of blue terry cloth shorts and a white vest. He was sweating profusely after filling the fridge with bottles of Coke; his fat hands gesticulated energetically as he talked about water.

He told me he had grown up here at Rabwe, living to the rhythm of the Barada and its canals. "I used to drink this water, we used to wash in it. Once I even caught a fish this big in that canal over there," he said, first indicating the size of the fish (big) and then pointing to one of the canals behind us. "Five kilograms it was," he said proudly. I asked what he thought of the state of the canals now, but he was laconic. "God decides." After a short silence, he added: "People don't love each other enough, that's the problem." As I failed to see the link between neighborly love and the filthy canals all around us, Abu Fares explained: "If we would be more tolerant of each other and love each other, then God would be merciful, and he would give us water." Behind him, his assistant, a sultry looking boy with greasy hair and bloodshot eyes, was noisily stacking

crates before lying down in the shade and dozing off. It didn't look like Abu Fares would have many customers today.

## The Desolate Oasis

We drove through Damascus to the Ghuta, the oasis of fairytales and legends. Turning off the highway, we drove through a slum-like area: workshops and garages, factories and dusty truck yards. As Damascus' population grew after independence, the city sprawled uncontrollably, swallowing the Ghuta and its orchards, and expanding from 1,900 hectares in 1945 to 8,500 hectares today. Thus the oasis was gradually eaten away from its grand 25,000 hectares to just 10,000 hectares, destroying some of the most fertile lands in the region.

Housing shortage and lack of government housing policy led to uncontrolled and illegal development; in the 1960s low-income households could not afford developers' prices and took the law and the shovels in their own hands. The results were disastrous: high-rise blocks were slapped together along narrow streets and basic facilities such as sanitation, electric power, water supply and ventilation were virtually non-existent. During the 1980s more than 70 percent of housing belonged to this category and even today more than 50 percent of Damascenes live in this type of accommodation. The construction of this concrete ring around the old town was the last step to destroying the link between the old city and its oasis. Further uncontrolled urbanization has engulfed the small villages around Damascus into the urban fabric and thousands of trees were felled to make space for the small workshops and light industries.

The authorities have long been aware of the threat of Damascus' uncontrolled growth: several urban plans have attempted to address the city's chaotic and voracious spread into the oasis. The last urban scheme dates back to 1968 when the French urban planner Michel Ecochard was hired together with the architect Robert Danger to solve Damascus' problems. Their plan had little regard for the social and cultural realities of the Middle Eastern city and was eventually discarded, but they did voice concern over the state of the Ghuta and the threat the advancing city posed to its survival. "If this illegal mode of settlement is allowed to develop," Danger warned, "the gardens will disappear and with them the green belt that surrounds the city. In just a few years we will be surprised to see that in their place there is a collection of shoddy and unhealthy huts spreading the worst diseases." The Ecochard scheme also addressed Damascus' ever-growing water requirements, by proposing the creation of a series of dams and reservoirs along the course of the Barada, the Awaj and the Aïn el Fijé.

Nothing came of the plan though, and the Ghuta is suffering, losing an estimated 200 hectares each year to the advancing city. Groundwater levels have dropped severely and the water, both on the surface and in the underground aquifers, is heavily polluted with sewage, pesticides and industrial waste that is dumped without treatment or regulation. The government is starting to take the case of Damascus seriously and is trying to impose measures to limit further pollution and wastage: used waters are to be treated, irrigation systems modernized, wells to be regulated and industries that consume too much water will be banned in future. These measures may go a little way in preserving what is left of the Ghuta, but by the time the policies have been implemented, it will be hard to reverse the damage, both to the city and to its ecology.

As we drove out of the slums I saw trees, more and more of them, lining the road, in large orchards, all planted in neat rows. The only thing was: most of them were dead. Fields and fields I saw; barren, dry trees, the branches brittle and sad. Poplars, beech trees, apricot trees, cherry trees.... Some orchards were still alive, but the leaves on the trees were yellow and sickly. In some fields, only amputated stumps of trees and roots remained, the trunks and the branches lay chopped up and swept to one side, ready to be used as firewood. We drove through a small village. The streets were deserted and dust flew up between the houses. Nizar pointed to an empty water channel on our left. "Five years ago, this was a good spring, Deir Asafir. It flowed at 200 liters per second. Now it is dry." Further up, it was the same. The Fayed spring, which was as big as the Barada, lay dry: a huge crater on the edge of the village where there used to be a lake with freshwater welling up bountifully. This is the result of years of massive over-pumping of groundwater, which has also caused many shallow wells in the Ghuta to dry out.

We drove out of the village and found ourselves in the desert. A few houses were dotted around, slapped together with rough concrete blocks and splatters of cement. They lay in a wasteland: flat, gray soil, barren and infertile. A few pumps could be seen in the fields. But there was no water to pump. "This was the middle of the Ghuta Oasis," said Nizar. "These were all apricot orchards. As far as the eye could reach. Look at it now!" I asked what the farmers here did now, as there was nothing to live off anymore. "They go to the city to find work. Anywhere. And in the winter they hope and pray for rain." I was speechless, it seemed unbelievable: acres and acres of desolation, punctuated only by gnarled tree stumps.

We drove on to a farm that belonged to Nizar's friend. It was a large wasteland. "This goes on for about five kilometers that way," Nizar said, waving in the distance. "This farm was twenty-five hectares, all apricot trees. Now, there is nothing." We turned off the main avenue into a side lane. On the left stood a dying apricot tree in the middle of an empty field, on the right a green field of vegetables and crops. Maize plants, courgettes, aubergines, even a few timid apricot trees stood here. "This is irrigated; that isn't," said Nizar. "That's the difference." His friend could afford to irrigate four hectares, enough to plant the vegetables he needed to sustain his family; the rest lay fallow, waiting for some miracle or for the desert to take over.

Nizar then took me to another farm. Only it was not a farm, but a private house, a holiday home, with some trees and vegetables. It was surrounded by a high stone wall. The Sudanese housekeeper let us in and as soon as we stepped through the gate, we had left the desert and arrived in Florida. A rich, soggy lawn surrounded the large house, while climbing roses and jasmine blossom crawled over a small folly at the back of the garden. Behind the house the water in the large swimming pool (with attached Jacuzzi) shimmered seductively in the mid-day sun. And there was a small orchard: peach trees, apricot trees, cherry trees and some small crops. All carefully watered every day by the housekeeper.

But where had this water come from? Why was there abundance here and desolation and ruin next door? The answer, of course, was money. "If you have money, you have water," Nizar said dryly, as he strolled along checking on a small cherry tree. "As long as you have the money to dig deep enough, you will find water. The well here is at 200 meters. Ten years ago, more than 90 percent of the wells in this area were no more than twenty meters deep. Now we have to go down to 200." But not everyone, in fact, very few people, can afford to dig to 200 meters and pump from that depth. And that means their land will dry up. I wondered how much bribing went on around the digging of wells. At the Barada River Authority Dr Faluh had told me that 87 percent of the 25,000 wells around Damascus were illegal and that the government was trying to legalize them. But legalization also means restriction: the government then controls how deep you dig, how much water you draw from your well, and what you use the water for. And surely there could be no provision for lavish English lawns in the water quota?

On the way back to Damascus I asked what the government was doing about the situation in the Ghuta. Surely there were measures to help farmers here in some way. Nizar did not understand my question and seemed to imply that the government was doing nothing. Then he hesitated, and said fervently: "I will tell you a secret: the Arab governments have no idea about long-term planning. They have no vision, no plan. In Syria, we are all sleeping. And maybe, just maybe, the day when the water really runs out and we face a disaster, we will wake up."

Damascus is Syria's worst case: in other regions rainfall levels are still higher and urbanization does not pose as much of a threat. Still, high birth rates and a changing climate are leading to increasing water deficits throughout the country. The problem is how to address this deficit as it is not just about water, but also about society and culture. Dr Somi at the Ministry of Agriculture confirmed this, when he explained the scope of the problem facing the Syrian government today. "The question of managing water, a scarce resource, goes further than plain water issues. To deal with water, you have to deal with related issues like population growth. Limiting Syria's high birth rates has to be one of our main priorities. This is not a straightforward task though, as we have to confront traditions and religious beliefs which have been engrained in our society for centuries," he said.

Dr Jamal Jamaleddin at the Ministry of Water Resources also emphasized the importance of limiting the birth rates in Syria. "It is not that water levels, that is, rain levels, have gone down so drastically; the population has gone up. It is the same everywhere; the whole region is suffering acutely," he said. "Every year, the water situation worsens; and every year the population increases by half a million. Given the internationally recognized minimum water supply per person per year is 1,000 cubic meters, it means we need to provide half a billion cubic meters of extra water every year. This is impossible. There is no way we can provide this. We can't even satisfy current demand."

## Notes

1.     The term "Middle East" often leads to confusion. It was coined in the nineteenth century when European geographers divided "the Orient" into three regions. The Near East was the area nearest to Europe on the eastern shores of the Mediterranean and within the limits of the Ottoman Empire, thus including present-day Turkey, Syria, Lebanon, Jordan, Israel, and the Palestinian Territories; the countries of East Asia were the "Far East," and in the middle, in the area from the Persian Gulf to southeast Asia, lay the "Middle East." This geographical division shifted during World War II when the Middle East came to denote both the "Near" and "Middle" East, thus covering the area of Northeast Africa and Southwest Asia. Today there are still no clear delimitations of the "Middle East," as some authors exclude the countries of North Africa and consider Egypt the only "Middle Eastern" country of Africa.

Similarly the term "Arab world" is not always clearly defined. Logically it should denote Arabic-speaking countries—Egypt, Jordan, Syria, Lebanon, the Palestinian Territories, Iraq, Sudan, Libya, Tunisia, Algeria, Morocco, and the countries of the Arabian Peninsula (Saudi Arabia, Kuwait, Yemen, Oman, Bahrain, the Arab Emirates, Qatar, and Oman)—but cultural, religious and political criteria are often confused so that non-Arab Muslim countries like Turkey, Iran, and Pakistan are included.

# 2

# A Gift from God

*"The Prophet said that water is the best scent. He meant that to be clean and pure is more important than using perfumes and luxuries. Water is the purest scent that shows real cleanliness. Cleanliness is half of faith, it completes faith." –Heba Raouf Ezzat, political scientist and writer, Cairo University, Egypt*

In today's Middle East, where religion is central to many people's lives, water has a very strong spiritual value. Ancient rituals and symbolic meanings may have been forgotten, but the reverence for water that transpires from Mesopotamian and ancient Egyptian mythology still survives in the region's three main religions: Judaism, Christianity and Islam. This reverence stands in sharp contrast to the perception and usage of water in everyday life, where it is often wasted and undervalued.

## Rivers of Water Unstalling

Heba met me on Al-Tahrir Square in downtown Cairo. I was waiting in front of the British Airways office as we had agreed, and saw her from a distance, walking towards me with her two children, carrying a large pile of papers under one arm and a bag of books in the other hand. She wore a long grey *abaya,* the wide overcoat worn by pious Muslim women, and a white silk headscarf that covered her hair and her shoulders. "I am taking you for lunch," she said smiling warmly as she helped her children into the back seat of the car and cleared away piles of books and papers from the front seat and the floor. "It's a special treat I promised the children as it is a holiday." It was May 1 and Cairo's streets, usually a seething chaos of cars, taxis, and buses honking their way through traffic jams, were strangely quiet and deserted. As we drove through the empty streets, Heba said: "I know it is a bit late for lunch, but I guess we could call it 'linner' or 'dunch'—like an afternoon brunch," and she laughed.

A friend in Oxford had given me Heba's name. "You'll like her, I'm sure," she had said. "She is a political scientist working at Cairo University." So I had e-mailed Heba before setting off on a thirty-six-hour bus journey from Libya's capital Tripoli to Cairo, telling her I was on my way and asking whether she would have time to meet. Her reply came the same evening:

"Dear

Salam

Of course! I would be happy to meet you.

Please call me when you arrive so we can arrange to meet.

Keep well

Salam 🖋

Heba"

And now we were having linner or dunch at Tawa Fast Food Chicken. We carried our orange plastic trays up to the first floor, to the area reserved for women and families, and found a table away from the television that was showing another noisy episode of Arabic *Who Wants to Be a Millionaire?* As we ate the greasy grilled chicken and fries and sipped at our Cokes, we talked about Islam, Heba's belief and way of life, and water, this ungraspable substance that had become my passion in the past four years. Her intense brown eyes radiated thoughtfulness, serenity and warmth. "Water is a very important element in Islam; it has great symbolic value in the Koran and in the descriptions of paradise," she said as she tore small pieces of chicken off the bone and gave them to her children. "You read about the rivers of paradise, the rushing streams, the fresh bubbling rivers and the greenery—it's all about water…"

The next day, I went to Cairo's university library and found a bilingual copy of the Koran. The green leather cover was inscribed with elegant golden letters and read: *The Bounteous Koran.* As I paged through the book, I saw that water flows through the text like a subtle undercurrent, ever-present but constantly changing in character: now it is the symbol of God's mercy and benevolence when it falls from the sky in the form of precious rain, now it is an angry, seething liquid that punishes sinners in the afterlife. On earth it is God's gift to the believers, a reward to the faithful that the Almighty bestows at will; in paradise it is the symbol of plenty and abundance, flowing through lush gardens with a soothing freshness. Poets and writers throughout the Islamic world have been inspired by the Koranic descriptions of this heavenly garden, *al janna*, underneath which rivers flow and where there are "rivers of water unstalling, rivers of milk unchanging in flavor, and rivers of wine—a delight to the drinkers."

The many Koranic descriptions of the gardens of paradise also inspired theologians and philosophers who tried to map them. Based on this, the powerful rulers of Islamic empires in Mughal India, Persia, Arabia and Andalucia sought to create their own pleasure gardens and hunting parks. Water was an important feature in these designs, an essential component in the harsh climates of the Middle East and Arabia. These gardens were often arranged around a fountain or a water tank, which symbolized the sources of paradise, while four watercourses symbolized the four rivers of paradise: Jayhan, Sayhan, the Nile and the Euphrates. These rivers of Koranic paradise are inspired by the rivers that flowed from the Garden of Eden and which are mentioned in the Bible as Pishon, Gihon, Tigris, and Euphrates.

## The Mingling of the Waters

The Koran conceives of water as the first element, the primary substance from which God—whose "Throne was upon the waters"—created all else: "Allah has created from water every living creature." The Koranic account of creation shows many similarities to the Christian and Judaic stories, which can in turn be traced back to the much earlier Mesopotamian creation myths.

Thus water also plays a key role in one of the oldest written myths in existence, the Babylonian Epic of Creation that was written around 1700 BC. Preserved on seven clay tablets that were retrieved from the ruins of the Babylonian capital Nineveh in 1850, the *Enuma Elish* describes the creation in two phases, a primeval creation with the birth of the gods and from there, the creation of the universe as it was known to the Babylonians.

The first step in the creation is a chaotic "mingling of the waters," the mixing of saltwater and freshwater, respectively represented by the fierce mother-goddess, Tiamat, and Apsu, who was identified with a deep abyss below the earth. The Babylonians believed that all springs flowed from this single divine source. Divided into male and female parts, the prime element water thus lies at the core of creation. It represents chaos but at the same time, its "mingling"—a kind of primeval intercourse—brings forth order and an offspring of gods who represent the horizon, the sky and the earth.

But as the number of gods increases they become a burden to Apsu: "their clamor reverberated" and he "could not quell their noise." Despite Tiamat's protests, Apsu plots to kill them all. But the clever god Ea hears of the plot and kills Apsu himself. Together with his lover, Ea then sets up his dwelling in the watery abyss Apsu, becoming the god of freshwater and wisdom. Here he creates the god Marduk, the "highest among the gods."

Tiamat for her part is furious and promises to avenge her husband's death. She creates an army of monsters with giant snakes, ferocious dragons, demons, rabid dogs and scorpion-men. "Whoever looks upon them shall collapse in utter terror! Their bodies shall rear up continually and never turn away!" she warns. The terrified gods turn to Marduk for help and convince him to face the angry Tiamat. The battle is short: Marduk defeats Tiamat by shooting an arrow through her gaping mouth. He throws down her body and slices it in two "like a dried fish," lifting the upper watery part to the roof of the sky and placing the lower part below him to form the earth. He then places the sun, the moon and the stars in the sky, thus creating days, months and years. And with the blood of his last enemy, Marduk creates mankind, a race that will serve the gods.

Water is also a central feature in the Jewish account of creation that is recorded in the biblical book of Genesis. Like the *Enuma Elish*, it begins with a description of Primeval Chaos and Emptiness, Tohu and Bohu. God's spirit hovers over "the face of the Deep," a bottomless waste of water. In Genesis II, life on earth is also related to the presence of water: "When the Lord God made earth and heaven— when no shrub of the field was yet on earth and no grasses of the field had yet sprouted, because the Lord God had not sent rain upon the earth."

There are many parallels in this account of the creation and that recorded in Mesopotamian stories like *Enuma Elish*. Thus the Babylonian god finished the work of creation within the span of six tablets of stone, just as Genesis records six days of creation. In the *Enuma Elish*, the seventh and last stone praises the beauty of creation and the gods' ingenuity, while Genesis describes the seventh day as God's day of rest. Both cosmogonies also begin with a primeval watery chaos and the emergence of earth from it, probably a metaphor for the annual appearance of dry land after the retreat of the winter floods along the Tigris and Euphrates Rivers. Creation is thus described as the first flowering after the flood, a first spring.

Water features in many other biblical passages, including the story of the flood, the crossing of the Red Sea and the Jordan River. Springs, wells and rivers form an important theme in the stories about Abraham, Isaac, Lot and Moses and are often described as social gathering places, but also as sources of conflict. The Hebrew Bible dedicates extensive passages to the Land of Israel and its harsh desert environment. The importance of water, and rainwater in particular, is reflected in the rich vocabulary the Hebrew language has for rain. *Yoreh* designates the first rains of autumn and *malkosh* the late rains of spring, while there are several words for different types of floods and drought. Water is also the subject of prayers such as *Tefillat Hageshem*, the Prayer for Rain that is recited in the winter and *Tefillat Tal*, the Prayer for Dew that is recited in the summer. In the Hebrew scriptures rain is deemed more precious than the Torah and creation itself, as this rabbinical saying shows: "The day of rainfall is greater than resurrection...than that whereon the Law was given to Israel...than when the heaven and the earth were made."

But this life-giving gift from God is not accorded freely and if the believers turn away from their God they will be punished as the Book of Deuteronomy warns. "Take heed lest your heart be deceived, and you turn aside and serve other gods and worship them, and the anger of the Lord be kindled against you, and he shut up the heavens, so that there be no rain, and the land yield no fruit, and you perish quickly off the good land which the Lord gives you."

The poignant story of Hagar and Ishmael—or Hajir and Ismail, as they are known in Islamic tradition—who are sent into the wilderness by Abraham, is recorded in both the Jewish and Islamic tradition. Abraham's second wife, Hagar, an Egyptian slave woman, bears Abraham's first son Ishmael, as his wife Sarah cannot conceive. After Ishmael is born, Sarah also falls pregnant and gives birth to Isaac. She grows resentful of Hagar and her child, and asks Abraham to send them away. The Hebrew Bible records that heeding God's words, Abraham sends Hagar and Ishmael into the desert with some bread and a skin of water.

Hagar roams through the wilderness until she runs out of water. She is desperate and fears that her son will die. God hears the crying child and speaks to Hagar, revealing a "well of water" so that she can quench the child's thirst.

The Islamic story tells that Abraham accompanied Hajir and Ismail to Mecca. Here he leaves them in a desolate valley, assuring Hajir that God has ordered him to do so. When her water runs out, she anxiously runs through the valley in search of water, running seven times between the mountains of Safa and Marwa until she hears a voice. Then she sees an angel digging the earth with his heel and water starts flowing from the ground. Hajir's desperate quest for water is today remembered during the yearly hajj when pilgrims walk back and forth seven times between the two hills.

The source that was revealed to Hajir also still exists. Water from the Zamzam spring is considered to be especially holy, and has the ability to satisfy both hunger and thirst, and cure illness. Visitors to Mecca drink Zamzam water and sprinkle it on their head, face and chest, while some also dip their pilgrimage clothes in the spring water. The white hajj robes are then preserved and used as burial clothes. Zamzam water is also a popular gift for pilgrims to take home to friends and relatives. And despite the fact that Saudi authorities have prohibited the commercial export of Zamzam water, bottles purporting to be filled with the holy water can be found on sale in many countries around the world. More often than not, these are fakes. The British government environmental agency recently tested purported Zamzam water that was on sale in London, and found high arsenic levels in much of it, making the water not only fraudulent, but also dangerous.

Besides being used by pilgrims and believers, the holy Kaaba, the large granite structure inside the mosque in Mecca that forms the holiest place in Islam, is also washed twice a year with Zamzam mixed with rose water. The ritual is led by members of the Saudi royal family and attended by prominent representatives of the Saudi government and ambassadors from Islamic countries.

## Cleansing Waters

Beside its symbolic role in Islam and in Judaism, water also plays a very important physical role. In Islam, this is reflected in the compulsory ablutions that form an integral part of prayer rituals. "Water is part of daily life for us," Heba explained. "Much more than in Christian religion: we have to perform *wudu'*, ritual ablution, five times a day before each prayer. After intercourse or illness we have to perform full purification, *ghusl*, before we can pray, read or even touch the Koran—so you see water is inseparable from our everyday life, it is part of our cultural identity." She told me that the Prophet himself attached great importance to purity and cleanliness. "The Prophet said that water is the best scent. He meant that to be clean and pure is more important than using perfumes and luxuries. Water is the purest scent that shows real cleanliness. He said that cleanliness is half of faith; it completes faith."

Four weeks later, sitting in the courtyard of the Great Omayyad Mosque in Damascus, I was reminded of Heba's words as I watched men and women by the ablution fountain, the *mayda'a*. It was an octagonal water basin decorated with inlaid marble patterns and covered by a square roof. Small marble stools surrounded the fountain, allowing people to perform *wudu'*, washing their face, hands, arms, and feet before entering the prayer hall. This is not only a physical purification, it is also a spiritual cleansing as the ninth-century "Book of Purification" explains: "When a…believer washes his face,…every sin he contemplated with his eyes, will be washed away from his face along with the water…; when he washes his hands…, every sin they wrought will be effaced…; and when he washes his feet, every sin towards which his feet have walked will be washed away…, with the result that he comes out pure from all sins."

I watched as mothers veiled in wide black chadors helped their children through the ritual. A soldier rolled up his khaki trousers and vigorously rubbed his feet and ankles, carefully cleaning between his toes and scrubbing the soles of his feet. Old men kneeled down carefully and closed their eyes in concentration as they prepared for prayer through this cleansing. In Islam, purification is part of the act of worship and if it is not carried out ritually, prayer becomes invalid. This is the spiritual aspect of ablution: while the body is cleansed by washing away physical impurity with water, the mind must be completely focused on God through the expression of *niyyat*, intention. Carrying out *wudu'* or *ghusl* simply for refreshment in hot weather for instance, makes them invalid. The fact that there is both a physical and spiritual component to the purification ritual is related to the Islamic belief in the unity of body and mind in the performance of religious duties. Islam means "surrendering to God" and Muslims, "those who have surrendered to God," do so with body and mind. Most Muslim rituals such as prayer, fasting during Ramadan and the pilgrimage to Mecca, have both a spiritual and physical component. When praying, Muslims face Mecca and perform a series of movements. The fast requires both physical and spiritual commitment, for not only do believers abstain from food, drink, and sexual intercourse, they are also encouraged to avoid arguments and sinful thoughts. To attain a state of ritual purity believers must be physically and spiritually pure.

In Judaism, the water rituals have a much stronger spiritual aspect. The *mayim chayim* or "living waters"—the water of rain, rivers, seas and springs—do not remove dirt or physical impurity, they prepare the individual for change and repentance.

The ritual of *Nitilat Yada'im* (literally "the lifting/washing of the hands"), that is today mainly carried out by Orthodox Jews, consists of pouring water over each hand from a two-handled cup. It is performed before meals and prayer, when waking up and after having been near death—returning from a funeral for instance. Water is also associated with death in a medieval custom that is still practiced by some today, in which mourners pour out the water that is stored in their homes, sending news of the loss flowing through the streets. Water was

thought to act as a barrier against the spiritual forces that accompanied death and prevented them from causing any more harm. At death, the body is also purified through the ritual of *tahara*, in which a number of attendants pour water over the body in a continuous flow while reciting prayers. The ability of water to bring spiritual purity and change is most clearly represented in the ritual immersion in the living waters, which is most often performed in a ritual bath known as a mikvah.

## Mikvah, a Collection of Water

Ramat Shlomo is a modern suburb of Jerusalem, with neat limestone houses built up against a steep hill. The streets were deserted, and except for an Orthodox man with a large hat, a beard, and a long black coat walking down the hill, I saw no one, which was fine: dressed in jeans and a T-shirt, I felt a little out of place in this Orthodox neighborhood. I had come here to meet Elisheva Shushan, an Orthodox woman who worked as a "mikvah lady" and who had offered to explain the significance of the ritual to me. Initially, I had hoped to visit a mikvah myself, not to perform the ritual, but to see what the bath looked like, but this proved impossible: as many of the women who practice the ritual see it as a private affair, it would have been awkward.

In the staircase of the apartment block where Shushan lived, I realized I couldn't read any of the names on the doorbells. I wandered down the corridor and saw someone opening a front door. The man, again dressed in strict Orthodox fashion, looked rather startled at my apparition and silently pointed me to the end of the corridor as he hurried off. Now I had a choice between two front doors and I chose the one with a wood-carved flowery name board on it. A lady in a long morning coat and a hairnet opened the door. She looked at me searchingly and then exclaimed: "Oh goodness! I had completely forgotten you were coming! And the apartment is a mess.... But please come in." Mrs. Shushan explained that she and her family had been at a wedding until late the previous night.

Over a cup of coffee in the living room, she told me about her work at the mikvah and her role as an advisor to women who observe the Jewish laws of family purity, the *taharat ha'mishpachah*. According to these laws, a woman is considered impure during the period of her menstruation and for seven days after. During this time, she is *niddah*, separated, and must not have any physical contact with her husband; she may not touch him or sleep in the same bed with him. After seven "clean days," she can return to a state of purity after visiting the ritual bath and immersing herself in the waters of the mikvah. The mikvah ritual and the observance of the rules of family purity are today often seen as derogatory to women, but Shushan says that recently many women—also non-Orthodox women—have again embraced it. "I see it as a wonderful present, a moment of spirituality, when body and soul are fused. For many women it is something to look forward to, a sort of physical and spiritual retreat."

The use of the mikvah goes back to Second Temple times in Jerusalem. As it was dedicated entirely to the worship of God, entrance to this holy sanctuary was only permitted to the ritually pure. Scribes also had to immerse themselves in the waters of the mikvah before writing God's name, and on Yom Kippur the High Priest even immersed himself five times before entering the Holy of Holies where the Stone Tabernacles were kept. After the destruction of the Temple in 70 CE, many of the laws of purity were no longer applicable as the purity of the Temple sanctuary no longer needed to be protected. Instead, the rabbis who replaced the priests of the Temple increasingly used the concepts of purity and impurity metaphorically, and associated them with sin, such as sexual misdeeds, idolatry, or unethical behavior.

Today, the various rituals of purification recall the Temple, but are at the same time seen as spiritual acts in which the water changes the status of the believer, cleansing the mind and the soul, thus bringing him closer to God.

At first sight the mikvah—literally a "collection of water"—appears to be a plain bathing house, similar to those found elsewhere in the Middle East such as the Greek and Roman baths and the Islamic hammam. But unlike its regional counterparts and despite the fact that the mikvah ritual involves immersion in water, it has nothing to do with physical purification. It is part of the 613 commandments that God gave to man. It is one of the *chukkim*, commandments that cannot be understood, over which the human mind can form no judgement. Observing the *chukkim* shows real devotion, the obeying of God's word without questioning. This is also reflected in the following comment from the twelfth-century Jewish philosopher Maimonides: "Impurity is not mud or dirt that can be removed with water, it is a question of scriptural commandment and is related to the intentions of the heart." The immersion ritual is thus not about physical purification; it is a spiritual rebirth, a transformation through which the believer achieves an elevated spiritual status. And it is the nature of the water of the mikvah that elevates the immersion ritual far above the simple bath, and gives it a deeper spiritual meaning.

Mrs. Shushan explained that the believer must in fact be scrupulously clean before entering the mikvah. "Women have to carefully prepare themselves for it, and cleanse themselves entirely," she says. "They have to remove all barriers: any dirt, jewellery or make-up, makes the ritual invalid. After washing her body, the woman immerses in the mikvah—Jewish law states she must immerse herself fully once for the ritual to be valid. During the immersion she pronounces special blessings. It is a very sacred moment." Shushan explained that the Talmud says that the gates of heaven open when a believer performs the mikvah ritual and that it is a moment of prayer. Shushan's job as the "mikvah lady," is to observe the immersion and declare it kosher. "Even one hair sticking out of the water can make it invalid, so I have to ensure the immersion is complete," she says.

On a practical level, the mikvah is filled with living water: rainwater, water from rivers, or, occasionally, melted ice, that is collected in a reservoir called a *bor*. As it is often impossible to use only rainwater to fill the mikvah entirely—especially in urban contexts—the law prescribes that it should be filled to a capacity of forty *se'ah* or around 900 liters with water from the *bor*. The rest of the water can be supplemented by water from the tap which is also regularly drained to ensure cleanliness.

While many consider the synagogue to be more important, Jewish law states that the mikvah takes precedence. Indeed, private or communal prayer can take place anywhere, so that the synagogue is not essential to the religion's survival. The absence of a mikvah however, makes the perpetration of the Jewish family according to Jewish law impossible. This is also why Jewish law does not recognize a community as a village or a town until it has a mikvah. The Talmud says that the mikvah is more valuable than a Torah scroll or a synagogue; in fact, it states that both can be sold in order to raise funds for the construction of a mikvah.

While the mikvah is today mainly used by Orthodox women and Chassidic men who visit the bath before holidays and Shabbat, the ritual immersion is also practiced by members of the Jewish Reform movement. Here women have in the last twenty years been encouraged to "reclaim" the ritual as a moment of spirituality, and as a ritual that can also be practiced outside of the context of *niddah*, for example after an unsuccessful relationship, a miscarriage, or an illness. Several mikvahs in the United States have also started introducing new immersion rituals for men. Finally, the mikvah ritual forms the last step towards conversion, transforming a non-believer into a Jew.

## The Laws of Purity and the Inquisition

Heba explained how the Muslim laws of cleanliness led to tense situations during the Inquisition in sixteenth-century Spain when Muslims and Jews underwent forced baptisms. "Many Muslims quietly resisted the forced conversion. In public, they adopted the Catholic rituals and went to church, but at home and at heart they remained true to their faith, performing the prayer ritual in secret. When the Catholics learnt of this deceit, they started monitoring water usage per household: where more water was being used, they knew Muslims were still performing the ablution ritual in secret," she said.

After the Spanish *reconquista*, thousands of Muslims rejected forced baptism. Their resistance was endorsed by an edict that was issued by the *mufti* of the North African town of Orán. This gave Muslims living in Spain, the Moriscos, special dispensation from religious duties and allowed them to denounce their belief and its rituals in public. They were allowed to eat pork, drink wine, even insult the Prophet Mohammed and acknowledge Christ as the Son of God, as long as in their heart they remembered and constantly reaffirmed their true faith. Thus Islam went underground and became a secret religion. But there were tell-tale signs that the "New Christians" were practising the Muslim faith. Through dress, speech, customs, and food, they betrayed their true allegiance: the Catholics saw the ritual slaughter of meat, the avoidance of pork, and insistence on using olive oil instead of lard for cooking, as sure signs that conversion had failed. And there was another giveaway: the "New Christians" were too clean.

Spain's Catholic clergy condemned cleanliness, not only because it was a clear sign of Islamic belief, but also because they disapproved of bathing in principle. Excessive care to personal cleanliness was seen as vanity in medieval

Europe. Inspired by Plato's philosophy of duality, which describes a rational, controllable mind and a body governed by blind necessity, medieval Christian ascetics believed that physical suffering and deprivation would purify the spirit and bring them closer to Christ. Sixteenth-century Spanish mendicant monks even went so far as to consider physical dirt a test of moral purity and true faith. Thus one of their highest ambitions was to wear the same woolen cloak for years and thus attain "the odor of sanctity." Meanwhile lice, the "pearls of God," were considered a mark of saintliness and some saints boasted that water had never touched their feet—well, only when they had to wade across streams and rivers. The Reyes Catolicos, Ferdinand and Isabella, also disapproved of bathing and washing. During the *reconquista* and the eight-month siege of Granada, Queen Isabella famously declared she would not change her robe until the city fell.

The clergy condemned the Moorish bathing houses as "dens of carnal sin" where bathers indulged in "animal pleasures." A secretary to the Catholic monarchs clearly stated the royal view: baths were "the cause of certain softness of their [the Moriscos] bodies, and of excessive pleasure, from which there proceeded idleness and other deceits and evil dealings." In 1576, Philip II banned the public baths once and for all. From then on, bathing in any form was deemed suspicious, particularly on Thursday nights and on Fridays, the Muslim holy day. The Inquisition ordered for the doors of Morisco houses to be left open on Fridays so that ablution could not take place in secret—even wearing clean clothes on those days became suspect. As a response to this relentless persecution, the Moriscos resorted to performing ablutions in fields or swimming in rivers to replace *ghusl*.

The Jews living in Spain were known as *conversos* and many of them also continued to observe their religious rituals in secret. These New Christians who practiced the Jewish faith in secret were known as crypto-Jews. But unlike their Morisco counterparts, Jews were not in the first place recognizable by their bathing habit. Their observance of Jewish holy days such as Shabbat and Yom Kippur, and the preparation and blessing of kosher food and wine, was more conspicuous and gave them away to the Inquisition.

The Moriscos and Jews for their part saw the Catholics as filthy people with depraved morals. Muslim and Jewish texts from this period describe the unbearable stench that always seemed to surround Christians. A twelfth-century Morisco from Seville warned: "Muslim women must be prevented from entering disgusting churches, for the priests are fornicators, adulterers and pederasts." And in a tenth-century description of the Spanish, another Muslim observer stated: "The inhabitants are a treacherous people of depraved morals, who do not keep themselves clean and only wash once or twice a year in cold water. They do not wash their clothes once they have put them on until they fall into pieces on them, and assert that the filth that covers them thanks to their sweat is good for their bodies and keeps them healthy." Ferdinand and Isabella forbade not only the Christians, but also the Moriscos from using anything but holy water.

The symbolic nature of Christian holy water and the values ascribed to it differ from the water used in Jewish and Islamic rituals. In Islam, all water is treasured and sent as a gift from God; the Koran repeatedly affirms: "We provided you with sweet water." All water, as long as it is free from impurities and is not mixed with other liquids, can be used for ablution. In Judaism, water is also by nature a treasured resource. The holy water used in Christian rituals is different; it acquires a special status only after it has been consecrated by a member of the clergy and blessed in the name of Christ. Thus Christian holy water only attains its holy quality after human intervention, while in Judaism and Islam water is by nature a treasured resource.

In Islam and Judaism, baptism does not exist, revealing another fundamental difference with Christianity. The latter teaches that every child is born in original sin, a sin inherited by all men from Adam. Baptism washes away this sin and allows entry to heaven. Muslims on the other hand believe that Adam was expelled from the Garden of Eden for his sin and that God accepted his repentance; this means that each child is born sinless and innocent. Judaism also rejects the idea of original sin and teaches that man, whether he is a sinner by nature or not, can only come to repentance and reconciliation with God through the Torah.

However, the Christian ritual of baptism is partly inspired by Jewish immersion rituals. Early medieval sources assumed that the first Christian baptisms took place through immersion or the sprinkling of water over the person's head. Based on archaeological evidence and rabbinic teachings, it seems that immersion was most common though. The baptisms of St. John took place in the Jordan River and the New Testament states that it required the use of "living" or flowing waters, a prescription of rabbinic law. These first Christian baptisms were at the same time purifications according to Jewish law. Of course Christian baptism cannot be entirely equated to the Jewish mikvah ritual, as the latter is a purification ritual that has to be repeated at regular intervals. Christian baptism takes place once, as an initiation rite and, in the Catholic Church, as a necessity for salvation and entry to heaven. As Christianity evolved, the baptism ritual no longer required full immersion and it became common practice to drink holy water or sprinkle it over the head. Certain Christian sects however still perform baptism through complete immersion.

## The Hammam: Between Purity and Impurity

A waiter came to clear away our trays and brought us small cups of sweet Egyptian tea. The more we talked, the more ideas, stories and anecdotes came bubbling up in Heba's mind—she talked of the water metaphors in Egyptian folk songs, the importance of the Nile to Egyptian cultural identity, and how water had also become an inseparable part of the Islamic city in the form of the water fountains and public bathhouses, hammams. Already in the Middle Ages, it was unimaginable for a town not to have a hammam: in tenth-century Baghdad, chroniclers boasted there were between 27,500 and 200,000 baths,

Depending on the prosperity of the inhabitants, even the smallest village would have a bathhouse. Middle Eastern bathing culture long predates Islam, going back to pre-Christian times. The tradition was handed down through ancient Egyptian and Mesopotamian cultures via the Greeks and Romans to the Arabs. Islamic tradition has however attributed the creation of the bathhouse to King Solomon: the eleventh-century *Stories of the Prophets*, a book about the Prophet Mohammed's predecessors, describes how he built the first hammam for Bilqís—known in Hebrew tradition as Balquis—the Queen of Sheba.

In the Muslim story, Solomon invites Bilqís to come and visit him after he hears that she and her people are sun worshippers possessed by the devil. As the palace demons do not want their king to be seduced by the beautiful queen, they tell Solomon that she has mule's feet and hairy legs and that her mother was a djinn. Solomon gets a bit worried and orders the demons to build a transparent palace with glass floors under which water flows. When Bilqís arrives at the palace she is invited to enter and, thinking the place is made of water, she lifts her robes to wade to the king's throne, showing "a beautiful pair of legs and feet, covered in thick hair." The king is duly shocked and has to avert his gaze. Luckily though, Bilqís falls in love with the wise king and converts to Islam. Solomon decides to marry her, but not before her legs are smooth. The djinns and demons promise they will find a way of making her legs "white as silver" and it is for this purpose that they create the first hammam.

The biblical version of this story only tells that the Queen of Sheba is awed by the king's wisdom, power and knowledge and that she gives him a vast array of gifts before returning to her country with her servants. The Islamic interpretation of the legend of the Queen of Sheba and King Solomon emphasizes the polarity between the two sovereigns and shows good winning over evil: the powerful but impure and unbelieving queen, half-woman, half-demon, is converted and tamed by the wise and pious King Solomon who makes a smooth, Muslim wife of her. While the story of Solomon and Bilqís is also recorded in the Koran, the hammam itself is not mentioned and scholars generally agree that the Prophet never visited one.

The hammam remained an ambiguous space in the eyes of many theologians and Islamic scholars. While Arab medical experts from the Middle Ages praised the medicinal value of the steam and hot water of the hammam, many early Islamic scholars saw it as a space on the edge between heaven and hell. The word hammam is related to the boiling waters of hell that are known as *hamiem*, thus emphasizing a demonic element. The Arabic expression "the whole world is a mosque, except the graveyard and the hammam" further illustrates the duality: the whole world is pure enough for prayer except the bathhouse and the burial place. The eleventh-century theologian Al-Ghazali also wrote about the paradoxical nature of the hammam: thus Ibn Omar, the son of the second caliph, was once seen standing blindfolded and facing the wall of a

bathhouse, so shocked was he by the shameless display of flesh there. Yet later he was quoted as saying that the bathhouse was a "heavenly blessing created by man." Water is strongly associated with spirits and genies in Islamic culture. Springs and caves, but also hammams, are home to djinns and demons. They like to dwell in impure places—toilets, garbage dumps—and places that mark a transition: the edge of the desert, burial grounds, spaces between light and dark and the hammam, which marks the limit between ritual purity and impurity. In normal circumstances, one can shield oneself from demons or other evil forces by invoking the protection of God. But in the bathhouse one is neither pure nor impure, so that it is forbidden to pray or recite passages from the Koran. A Koranic tradition records a conversation between God and the devil, in which the devil tells God: "My Lord, you have let me descend upon the earth and cursed me. Now give me a house!" God answers: "The bathhouse."

The ambiguous position of the bathhouse in Islamic belief is all the more surprising given that ablution is compulsory. But even though these cleansing rituals are obligatory and purity is of key importance in Islam, the Hadiths—texts written by the Prophet's companions recording his life and sayings—also urge moderation and thriftiness in the use of water. Thus the ninth-century Islamic theologian, al-Bukhari, records that the Prophet warned that wudu' should not be performed more than three times in a row before each prayer. The Prophet himself washed each part only two or three times without ever going beyond the number of three, even if water supplies were abundant. Al-Bukhari adds: "The men of science disapprove of exaggeration and also of exceeding the number of ablutions of the Prophet." Another Hadith reinforces this: "Allah's apostle happened to pass by Sa'd as he was performing ablution. Whereupon he said: 'Sa'd what is this extravagance?' He said: 'Can there be any idea of extravagance in ablution?' Whereupon the Prophet said: 'Yes even if you are by the side of a flowing river.'"

Al-Bukhari also tells of times of scarcity and the ritual of "dry *wudu*" or *tayammum*, which was revealed to the Prophet Mohammed during one of his journeys. One day when the Prophet was traveling through the desert with his companions, his wife Aisha lost her necklace. They searched for it, and the delay this brought meant that when prayer time came the company was nowhere near a water source. It was then that God revealed the ritual of *tayammum* to the Prophet, saying: "O you who believe,…if you are sick or on a journey,…and if you can find no water, then have recourse to clean dust and wipe your faces and your hands with it." This principle of dry ablution is also mentioned in the Talmud where a rabbi who moved from Israel to Babylon is quoted: "If someone does not have water with which to wash, he should clean his hands with dust, a rock or a piece of wood." Even in biblical times, Israel was an arid land with a harsh climate and in the months of drought, people commonly used sand or earth to cleanse themselves, both in everyday life and in the context of religious ritual.

## The Deluge, Water that Punishes and Cleanses

The ambivalent nature of water in the hammam ritual is illustrated in a more abstract manner in the flood myth, a universal catastrophe recorded in the Bible, the Koran and, in its earliest version, in the Babylonian Epic of Athrakhasis. Here again water's power has a twofold significance. Its destructive forces wipe away mankind but at the same time purify the earth and wash away sin, allowing for the rebirth of humanity.

In Jewish, Christian, and Islamic tradition, the flood is seen as God's punishment for the wickedness and corruption of man. The flood story in the Bible's Genesis says that when God sees that the world is full of violence of man's making, he regrets his creation and decides to rid the earth's face of man. The only man who finds favor with God is Noah, a pious man who "walked with the Lord."

God instructs Noah to build a great ark with three decks and hundreds of cabins so that he can house all animals, birds and creeping things, as well as his family. Then the Deluge comes, shaking the earth, making her foundations tremble and casting a dark shadow over the sun. Accounts in the Midrash[1] say that a deafening voice, the like of which has never been heard before, rolls across mountain and plain. It rains for forty days and forty nights, and the floods spread rapidly over the earth. Desperately seeking refuge from the rising waters, 700,000 evil-doers crowd around the ark, pleading to Noah to let them in. But Noah tells them it is too late to repent. The waters steadily rise until the ark floats high above the highest peaks. Some say God even heated the Deluge, punishing man's fiery lusts with scalding water and raining fire on the evil-doers. All life on earth—"everything with the breath of life in its nostrils"—dies, destroyed by the furious power of the waters.

After forty days God takes pity on Noah and his companions in the ark. The Deluge slowly subsides, but it is months before they can emerge from the ark onto dry land. As soon as Noah disembarks, he builds an altar of stone and burns incense. God smells the sweet aroma and promises that he will never again use water to destroy mankind. "Henceforth, so long as Earth lasts, let seed-time follow harvest; and harvest, seed-time—as summer follows winter; and day, night."

The Koranic account of the flood is not as detailed as the biblical tale, but several suras relate the story of Noah, the building of the ark and the ensuing flood. According to the Koran, when the waters subsided, the ark was perched on Mount al-Judi, a mountain that lies on the eastern banks of the Tigris in what is today northeastern Iraq. The biblical and Koranic accounts of the great flood can be traced to much earlier Mesopotamian flood myths. Dating back to the second millennium BC, the oldest record of the Babylonian flood myth is preserved in the Epic of Atrakhasis, a series of stories about the primeval history of mankind.

The epic opens with the rebellion of a group of lesser gods, who are tired of the hard work that the God Enlil has given them. The gods decide that to alleviate the junior gods' workload, they will create a new race from clay, blood and spit. Thus mankind is born. But Enlil soon finds that his creation is getting out of control. The seven couples he created rapidly multiplied and now their noisy behavior is keeping him from sleep. He tries to limit their numbers by sending all sorts of plagues, famine, and drought down to earth—all to no avail. Indeed, his rival, the god Enki, is all the while instructing his devotee Atrakhasis, the "exceedingly wise," on how to appease the other gods. Enraged, Enlil decides to annihilate the human race completely by sending a devastating flood down. Once again, Enki warns Atrakhasis, who builds a multi-story boat with many chambers and launches it before the coming of the flood. It is laden with precious metals, "the seeds of life of all kinds," animals of every kind, his kith and kin, and artisans.

The flood that then descends upon the earth is terrible. "Everything light turned to darkness/.../No man could see his fellow/Nor could people be distinguished from the sky/Even the gods were afraid of the flood-weapon/ They withdrew; they went to the heaven of Anu/The gods cowered like dogs." After seven days, when "all of man had returned to clay," the flood subsides. Atrakhasis releases all the animals and people and carries out a sacrifice to the gods, lighting incense sticks and pouring seven libations of wine. When Enlil discovers Enki's treachery and sees the survivors of the flood, he is initially furious but then repents and proceeds to bless Atrakhasis and grant him and his wife eternal life.

The motive for the flood in both the Israelite and the Mesopotamian stories is not just human sin, but also mankind's desire to attain a divine status and gain independence from the divine realm. Thus a passage in Genesis tells of the cohabitation of the "daughters of men" with "the sons of God," while the "noise" that disturbs the Mesopotamian god Enlil in his sleep has also been interpreted to signify humanity's quest for technological advancement and growth, or god-like power.

## The Gap between Scripture and Everyday Life

Water's symbolism in Islamic images of paradise, the Jewish prayers for rain and dew, Christian baptism in holy water, the rituals of *wudu'* and *ghusl* in Islam and the spiritual value of mikvah in Judaism, all point towards the important role of water in the religious cultures of the Middle East. And yet, in everyday life—the street scenes from Marrakesh to Cairo, the conversations held from Khartoum to Tel Aviv and the attitudes observed all along the route—I had seen nothing of this reverence.

As we drove back through the dusty streets of Cairo towards the Nile and Downtown, images floated back into my mind: little incidents, passing comments and careless gestures that spoke of a complete indifference—or was it lack of awareness—towards an invaluable and undervalued liquid. Sudanese taxi drivers washing their cars with a large hose in the scorching midday sun; leaking and burst pipes flooding a street in downtown Cairo for days; the taps at the ablution fountains of an Aleppo mosque dripping, creating a pool of mud around the mosque entrance—not to mention the enormous amounts of water that are wasted in agriculture throughout the region.

In many Arab countries, I had sensed indifference but also resignation, a certain acceptance of situations and events. Thus in the dying Ghuta Oasis near Damascus, a disillusioned farmer explained the continuing drought as God's will; at the site of the Hassan Addakhil Dam in southern Morocco, the director of the dam smiled happily as he looked down into the nearly empty reservoir and commented: "It will rain soon, *Insha'allah*. Last year we had rains, heavy rains, but they fell further south, washing away roads and some houses. But we had no rain in the reservoir. God willing, this year we will have rain in the right place." He seemed completely carefree: it was out of his hands. *Allah katib*—God decreed it. When God was not held accountable for the sad state of the environment and the dwindling water resources, the blame was shoved on the government. Thus unhappy farmers in the Egyptian Nile Delta had told me that the government should "give" them more water, never pausing to think that perhaps there simply *wasn't* any more water.

In Israel, the lack of awareness about water scarcity is reinforced by Zionist ideology which has shaped Israeli water and agricultural policy for the past fifty years. The young state has harnessed the country's water resources so as to transform the landscapes of the Promised Land and "make the desert bloom."

Israel's technological advancements have made it a world leader in many areas of water management and engineering, but it has also created an illusion of plenty among the general public.

Such attitudes stand in stark contrast to the Jewish and Islamic views of the environment in which man is designated as the steward of the Earth's resources and in which believers are encouraged to use these resources with consideration. Respect for nature as God's creation is deeply rooted in Judaic tradition. The most important rabbinic law that is derived from this principle is *ba'al taschit*, "do not destroy," which admonishes man not to damage any natural resource that may be useful to others. In a description of the principal Jewish laws and observances, Rabbi Samson Raphael Hirsch, one of the founders of modern Orthodoxy, explains the principle. "God's call proclaims to you: 'If you destroy, if you ruin—at that moment you are not human, you are an animal, and you have no right to the things around you. I lent them to you. As soon as you use them unwisely, be it the greatest or the smallest, you commit treachery against my world, you commit murder and robbery against my property, you sin against me.'"

As its Jewish counterpart, Islamic environmental philosophy is first of all holistic, acknowledging a fundamental interdependency between all natural elements. If man abuses or exhausts one element, the natural world as a whole will suffer the direct consequences. This belief is nowhere formulated in one concise phrase; it is rather an underlying principle of the Islamic view of nature. The Prophet Mohammed said that God is in everything. Therefore abusing one of his creations, whether it is a living being or a natural resource, is a sin. The Koran repeatedly warns believers that they are no better than other creatures. "Surely the creation of the heavens and the earth is greater than the creation of man; but most people know not."

Traditionally, both Jewish and Islamic cultures show a deep reverence for water, a resource that is central to many rituals and that plays an important role in religious scripture. However, this reverence seems all too often to be limited to the abstract and the spiritual, while in everyday life it is forgotten.

## Note

1.    The term Midrash, which literally means "exposition" or "investigation," refers to a mode of biblical interpretation used in Talmudic literature and also to a separate body of commentaries on the scriptures using this interpretative mode.

# 3

# Fading Traditions

*"We want to preserve the khettara, even if it is no longer in use. You see, this is not just a piece of agricultural equipment; this is part of a cultural heritage, something which tells us about our history and our traditions. We can't just let it collapse and be forgotten."—Ahmed Bourrim, water expert, Rhmate, Morocco*

## Mining Invisible Sources

The Institut français d'études arabes lies in the modern part of Damascus, in a quiet side street lined with stately villas and large overgrown gardens. The heavy stone building exudes a stern air of French studiousness and academic rigor. Inside, there is strict order. From behind a neat desk, the Parisian secretary looks over her half glasses and tells me in clipped tones that I may not enter the library without special permission. She promptly adds that once I have obtained this permission and a temporary library pass, I may not apply for more than five books in each reading day, and that I may not photocopy more than 10 percent of any book I read. I imagine she takes great pleasure in upholding and enforcing the archaic bureaucracy of rules and regulations that governs the movement of people and books in this little empire of French learning.

It was now the end of June and temperatures reached 40 °C in the afternoons. The asphalt on the roads grew soft under my feet and the otherwise bustling streets of old Damascus were deserted. The best place to be at this time was the shade of a Damascene teahouse, or, as in my case, the library. The thick stone walls kept out the heat and a sense of calm reigned among the books. I had spent five days here now, reveling in the cool serenity of the space, the smell of dry old paper and dust around me. The silence was broken only by the rustle of turning pages and the scribble of pen on paper as studious figures sat hunched over sixteenth-century works of poetry and classical Arabic syntax. I had also started learning the Arabic alphabet several months ago but had stalled at the letter *'ayn,* an impossible sound that was produced, according to my Arabic teacher, by pretending you were being strangled and then saying "ayn" deep in the throat. Now I was rapidly forgetting the other letters too: the curves and angles of *thaa, jiim,* and *siin* were once again becoming meaningless shapes.

As the summer heat reached its climax, I was still immersed in water, still obsessed with its history, seeking out new stories, observing everything through a mirror of water. Here in Damascus I had gone back to the library, taking a step back from the journey to dig through dusty archives, finding books on Ottoman water law, Roman water taxes in the oasis town of Palmyra and the history of Damascus' water supply system.

There were far more obscure titles too, like the French translation of an eleventh-century Arab text on "invisible waters." Written by the Arab mathematician Mohammad Al Karagi, *La Civilisation des Eaux Cachées* (The Civilization of Hidden Waters) contained an elaborate description of the "mining of subterranean waters" and the construction of the Persian qanat, an ancient system of interconnected wells and tunnels that taps the groundwater and directs it to villages, towns and crops. The ingenious technique was developed more than 3,000 years ago in the Kingdom of Urartu, in the region that now lies between northwestern Persia, eastern Turkey, and Armenia, and is believed to be derived from ancient Akkadian mining techniques. The long tunnels that today bring the water to users were originally drainage channels that eliminated excess water from copper and bronze mines. Over the centuries, the value of the water that flowed from the depths was recognized and the men who had started by mining precious metals became "water miners." The word qanat itself is derived from the Akkadian word for reed, *qanu*, and came via Hebrew and Aramaic to the Persian language; it is also related to the Greek *kanna* and the Latin *canna* from which the term *cannalis* or canal was in turn derived.

As an irrigation technique, it is first mentioned in the accounts of the Assyrian king Sargon II who led a military campaign against the Kingdom of Urartu in 714 BC. Written in Akkadian on a clay tablet that is today housed in Paris' Louvre Museum, the text describes how the Urartian king Ursa "revealed the water outlets" to his people and caused the water to flow in abundance "like the Euphrates." Sargon admired Ursa's ability to exploit the hidden sources and adopted the technique which was subsequently diffused over the whole Iranian plateau: Sargon's son Sennacherib used it to build an irrigation system around the capital of the Assyrian empire Nineveh, while the capital of the powerful Achaemenid Empire, Persepolis, was also watered by qanats.

In the following centuries, the qanat technique spread from Urartu and the Persian Empire to India and China in the east, the Arabian Peninsula in the south and across North Africa and Southern Europe to Morocco, Spain and beyond. In Egypt, the qanat was introduced by the Persian armies of Darius I in the fifth century BC, where they were used away from the Nile in the oases of the arid Western Desert. Known as foggaras here, the water tunnels stretched over impressive distances: one of the surviving structures in Kharga Oasis is said to be made up of more than 700 vertical shafts. On the Arabian Peninsula, the rise of powerful Islamic empires was responsible for the spread of the tunneling technique. As the Umayyad Caliphate expanded across the region, it took the karez and falaj—as the underground watercourses were known there—with it. Already under the reign of the Umayyad Caliph Hisham in the eighth century, extensive qanat networks were being built between Damascus and Mecca.

As Islam spread westward in the following centuries, the conquering Arab armies brought qanats to North Africa and Spain. In Morocco the new water supply systems were known as khettaras and thousands were built throughout the Saharan oases, the valleys of the Atlas Mountains and in the plains around Marrakech. Their Spanish counterparts, the madjiras, continued to play an important role in the Spanish water distribution system until 1860. They also gave their name to the Spanish capital, Madrid, which was for centuries watered by these invisible rivers. Ancient legends describe Madrid as the city "built over the water," a direct allusion to the numerous qanats that fed the convents, monasteries, palaces and fountains. The qanat's journey did not end there however and from the Iberian Peninsula the technique was taken across the Atlantic to the Canary Islands, Mexico, Chile and North America where fourteenth-century Spanish conquistadors used the Persian technique to bring water to the newly founded city of Los Angeles.

Sitting in the cool reading room of the Damascene library, I was spellbound by Al-Karagi's treatise and the wondrous tunnels he described. In my mind's eye, hovering over the land and looking down at the vast deserts, I visualized a dotted string of well-heads stretching across the Arabian Peninsula, through the Sahara and to Africa's western edge, hinting at the invisible trail of water that flows across continents through narrow and carefully constructed channels, covering thousands of kilometers and more than three millennia of history.

Al-Karagi describes the principles behind the construction of the underground aqueduct in great detail, explaining how to ensure the qanat channel slopes down at the correct angle, detailing a list of instruments used for topographical survey—including "some instruments invented by me." The process of qanat construction is an art in itself that requires expert knowledge of soil types, groundwater, and construction principles.

The first step in the construction process is the identification of a subterranean source. This was traditionally the work of the water diviner who used experience and intuition to study the soil, the plants and the slope of the land. Al-Karagi describes the types and the color of "Mountains and Rocks that reveal the Presence of Water," and lists the plants and grasses that indicate the hidden presence of water. He also records that the "Ancients," the Persians, used a piece of wool coated in wax to ascertain the presence of water in the soil. Placing the wool in a hole in the ground overnight, they would cover it with a small bowl. If the wool was damp in the morning, it was a sign of water's presence.

Once the water diviner had identified a spot, the surveyors were called to sink a trial shaft to a depth of 100 meters or until water was found. If they were successful, the team of qanat builders was assembled. Given the specialized nature of the work, qanat builders were usually close-knit communities, who jealously guarded the secrets of their trade and handed the art down from father to son. Called *moqannis* in Iran and *khatariya* in Morocco, the qanat builders often came from a specific region in the country, as in Morocco where the first builders came from the southern valleys of the Atlas Mountains, the Tafilalet, the Draa, and the Todra. When they moved to Marrakech, they went to live in their own neighborhood, "Djher Todra," or the Todra quarter. The Spanish qanat builders, the *qanawiyn*, were often Jewish and, like their Iranian and Moroccan counterparts, they formed exclusive corporations around their profession. Even today, the construction of the Omani falaj is a craft reserved to the select few in the know, in this case the 'Awamir, a partly settled, partly nomadic tribe who travel throughout the country to practice their trade.

The first task of the qanat builders is to dig the mother well. From there the course of the qanat tunnel is set out and a series of "guiding wells" is sunk at 100-meter intervals as reference points for the tunnel diggers. As the continuous flow of water from the mother well would make work there impossible, digging starts at the mouth of the qanat. Extra shafts are sunk between the guiding wells, providing much-needed ventilation for the workers and allowing for the removal of excavated dirt and rocks. Lifted from the depths in small baskets, in medieval times the excavated rubble used to be weighed to determine the workmen's salary.

Working their way gently uphill to the mother well, the qanat builders keep a close eye on the flames of their oil lamps, for the continued burning of these small lights also indicates sufficient levels of oxygen and thus indirectly guards them from suffocation. The length of the tunnel depends on the distance from the source to the village, covering just a few 100 meters, but sometimes also snaking its way over more than 100 kilometers. Qanats can even cross whole continents, if we are to believe the Omani legend that tells of a camel stick that was dropped into the Euphrates by the Caliph of Baghdad, only to surface several hundreds of miles further in an Omani well.

The work of the qanat builders is extremely strenuous and risky. Besides the danger of falling rocks and collapsing tunnels, they also risk drowning in sudden surging floodwaters and suffocating in the narrow spaces—no wonder that in Iran the qanat has been nicknamed "the murderer" and that the Persian qanat builders were strongly superstitious: a bad dream or someone in the family sneezing was enough to keep the *moqannis* at home, and the qanat-owner had no way of forcing him to go down or even to withhold his wages.

The final stage of the digging is also the most dangerous, as breaking through to the mother well can cause a sudden surge of water to wash through the tunnel and drown the workers. To prevent such disaster, the water from the mother well was often drained before the final hand was laid to the qanat.

Despite all these difficulties and dangers, the art of qanat-building was Al-Karagi's passion and he affirms that there is "no subject more beautiful, no art more useful or more profitable than the exploitation of the subterranean waters." Al-Karagi even throws in a dash of cosmology as, in a flowery prose, he affirms

**Section and plan of a qanat**

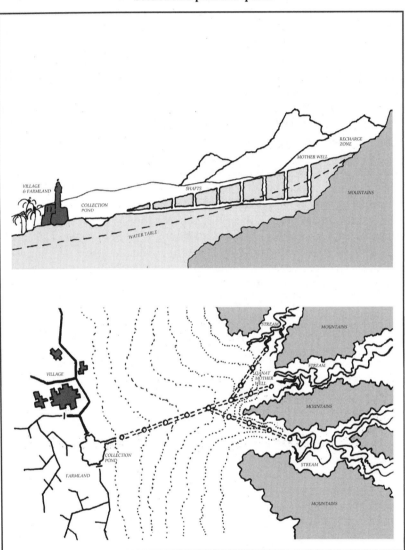

that the earth has "the shape of a polo ball that Allah placed in the center of the Universe" and that hidden "in the entrails" of this earth lies the water that Allah created. Al-Karagi conceives of the earth and the water in it like elements of a living body: to him "the water in the entrails of the earth dwells there just as the blood lives in the body of an animal…. This primeval water fills all the pores of the earth and binds them together. And this water runs through the veins of the earth."

Al-Karagi's treatise is more than a construction manual; through the descriptions of land, water and the ways in which the latter can be harnessed for the benefit of mankind, he reveals an essential difference between East and West, and the way in which water is perceived in arid and wet climates. This is also confirmed by Aly Mazaheri, who translated Al-Karagi's treatise into French. He describes a polarity between East and West, a fundamental difference in the value of water and land. "If one were to draw up a cultural map of the history of economic systems, two poles would emerge: a land and its agriculture in the West; a water and its hydroculture in the region of Isphahan," he writes.

Mazaheri continues by saying that the architects of the East are hydrographers, men who design the waterways and invent ingenious methods of collecting and distributing water, enabling the creation of villages. In eastern Iran, the hydronomer is given the prestigious title *paydâ-gar*, the discoverer and founder of the village. He is seen as its architect, as his work, the creation of an underground aqueduct that brings water to the village, is prerequisite to its very existence. This is why the Persian term *âpâdy*, "irrigation," evolved to mean village, culture, city and civilization; and why the suffix *-âbâd*, "irrigated by," preceded by the name of the founder, designates many towns in the Persian civilization: Ahmedabad, Hyderabad, Hosseinabad....

It struck me that Mazaheri was utterly right: I had spent the last few months in cultures where the common values of land and water had traditionally been inverted. Where in the West it was land that traditionally brought wealth and power, in the East it was water that brought these things, for without water, the land was dead, worthless. In the East, land ownership was insignificant, and often meaningless without water. This is why land was often sold with its water, and it was said that the land was "married to the water." Farmers who endeavored to bring life to so-called "dead" land, to irrigate the desert, subsequently acquired ownership of the land: by bringing water to the worthless land, it acquired real value. The more I thought and read of these inverted values, the more they confused me; I felt as though I was reversing an order and value that I had unconsciously always ascribed to such fundamental concepts as land and water.

In Holland water is so ubiquitous that one never really thinks about it—except when one is trying to get rid of it. Mirroring the Islamic principles of land and water ownership, the Dutch have always tried to "divorce" the land from the advancing waters, distilling firm ground from the salty marshlands. In medieval times, farmers who were prepared to settle on the low, waterlogged coastal lands were exonerated from tax and other obligations; here, keeping the encroaching waters out, gave the land value.

In the rocky deserts of the Middle East, in the sand dunes of the Sahara and the arid mountain lands of Asia, everything is inverted. The endless undulating plains of sand are like vast oceans; and the wells, water points and oases are their ports, havens from the ceaseless beat of the sun.

The *noria's* or waterwheels in the Syrian town of Hama were in the past used to direct the water of the Orontes River to nearby agricultural fields

The French desert explorer, Théodore Monod, compares desert with ocean, evoking the lonely emptiness of both spaces with the comment that they are "spaces that every day drive unceasing motion, navigation, nomadism, eternal flight across the ever-repeating and never-crossed borders of a horizon that moves ahead of you, that seems to be waiting for you at times, mockingly, but is never attained." The fight here is against a desert encroaching upon fertile land, its dryness creeping surreptitiously into the green; the quest is for water—from melting glaciers, from underground reservoirs, or from the great rivers that snake their way through the deserts. As Mazaheri explained, the biblical phrase "Seek, and you will find," stems from the Persian original "Dig and you will reach the water."

Besides the qanats and khettaras that were built across the Middle East and North Africa, there were many other techniques to collect and store the scarce resource and distribute it to users and their crops. The world's first irrigation systems were developed in the region, in the alluvial plain between the Tigris and the Euphrates. The Sumerians, known as the "men of dikes and canals" in ancient Mesopotamian myths, managed to control the unruly waters of the Twin Rivers from the fifth millennium BC onwards, diverting water into canals and leading it to the fields where they cultivated a mixture of grain, forage and date palms. From the third millennium BC onwards, the Ancient Egyptians also harnessed the water of the Nile, constructing irrigation channels and watering the surrounding desert land.

In other areas of the Middle East, in what is now Jordan, Syria and Israel, there are no large rivers. More than 90 percent of the land here is arid or semi-arid, and throughout history man was forced to develop special techniques to collect and preserve water. In Jordan, the ruins of the ancient city of Petra still testify to the ingenious methods of water collection that were developed by the Nabataean civilization from the sixth to the second centuries BC. The water channels, wells, cisterns and reservoirs that are today still scattered around the site show the crucial role of water for survival in this harsh desert climate.

## When the Springs Run Dry

I saw my first qanat in the Iranian Desert, the Dasht-é-Kavír: traveling east through Iran towards Pakistan, I had come to the ancient town of Yazd, which lies in the vast emptiness of the Asian plains at the foot of the Zágros Mountains. In this rugged desolation, water can only be found underground for there are no rivers, springs, or oases and the land is ostensibly barren. Yet it is a deceptive absence, for the foothills of the Zágros harbor large reserves. To tap into this invisible resource and lead it to the desert town, the "water miners" of Yazd spared no pains, digging wells up to 240 meters deep and excavating tunnels that were sometimes 120 kilometers long. I visited one of the town's qanats by climbing down a long, narrow stairwell beneath the courtyard of the main mosque to a small channel where, until ten years ago, women came every day to fill their jars and bowls.

Today the water that flows through the qanat is a mere trickle, no longer fit for use, and a new, more modern system of domestic water supply has replaced the web of tunnels. As elsewhere in the Middle East, the qanat is being relegated to the past, the technology washed into history. The knowledge of the soils and the hidden waters that Al-Karagi describes so meticulously, is no longer handed down to younger generations who now rely on more modern though less sustainable technologies.

For not only are wells and motor pumps taking over the role of the qanat; the water that used to gently seep through the rock face into the tunnel is being sucked away by the power of the pumps, leaving a growing number of qanats dry. Where the qanat tapped the groundwater only up to and never beyond the limits of natural replenishment—and therefore didn't destabilize the hydrological and ecological equilibrium of the region—pumping can quickly go beyond that natural limit and deplete groundwater reserves lastingly. And yet the qanat has today largely been replaced by wells with motor pumps: in the 1950s more than 70 percent of Iran's water supply for both domestic and agricultural use still came from qanats; today this figure has dropped below 10 percent.

It is the same in many of the countries that used to rely on the ancient Persian water mining technique to secure their water supply. In the Moroccan Haouz plain south of Marrakech, a combination of drought and neglect has left many of the local khettaras dry in recent years. Of the 500 khettaras that were still in use in the Haouz in 1970, today more than half have fallen into disuse. Many others are poorly maintained so that their flow has diminished considerably. Alarmed villagers in the town of Rhmate at the foot of the Atlas Mountains now want to restore their khettara, even if the water never flows through it again.

Ahmed Bourrim, one of the villagers, explained the situation to me. It was late in the afternoon and the light of the sun was turning golden over the pink houses, as we sat down at a makeshift teashop with two of Bourrim's friends. Though it was only mid-January, it felt like a lovely summer's afternoon, far too warm for the time of year. "See that bee?" said Bourrim. "It's another sign of the drought. It wouldn't be coming so close to us if there wasn't such a bad drought; it would be going to the flowers. Now there are no flowers, so it wants the sugary tea we drink."

Bourrim was born in Rhmate; he grew up playing in the fields and orchards that surrounded the village and now works as a water engineer in the region. I listened to the animated conversation, which took place in Berber with French interjections. After a while Bourrim turned to me and explained that they were discussing the work of a new association that wants to restore the nearly 1,000-year-old village khettara.

Brought to Morocco from Moorish Spain by the Almoravids, the khettara technique was first used in the region of Marrakech. The twelfth-century Arab geographer al-Idrisi records that the first khettara here was built in 1107, by an Andalusian engineer of Jewish descent, Obeïd-allah Ben Younes al-Muhandes, who built a khettara that fed the only garden that existed in Marrakech at the time. Once the inhabitants of Marrakech saw the results of the new tunnel system, they "hastened to dig into the ground and bring the water to the gardens," transforming the town into a wealthy city and giving it an "aspect of sparkling brilliance" with its many palaces, public squares and fountains. More than fifty khettaras were dug around Marrakech in the next thirty years, and many more tunnels were built in the nearby Haouz plain, bringing water to villages and crops.

The khettara in the village of Rhmate was built before those of Marrakech and has been in permanent use ever since. In his travel journal Al Idrisi wrote that the town was "covered in greenery and has many streams" filled with "excellent waters." He added that there were "no richer people than the inhabitants of Rhmate." Today, things are different—both the great wealth and the abundant water have disappeared. Even worse, for the first time in living memory, the village khettara has run dry.

Climbing over thick shrubbery and making our way between dense hedges of cactus plants, we walked to the khettara. The well-heads form a neat line across the land, like a series of man-sized mole hills that indicate the course of the subterranean river. Standing over one of the well-heads, Bourrim pointed to the stonework that lined the wall of the well-shaft. "You see, this is good workmanship: using local stones and no mortar; just professional work. But it also needs maintenance and upkeep," he said, as he pointed to the underground channels that were slowly silting up: "We want to preserve the khettara, even if it is no longer in use. This is not just a piece of agricultural equipment; it is part of our cultural heritage, something which tells us about our history and our traditions. We can't just let it collapse and be forgotten."

The fact that this khettara has dried out is part of a wider, more worrying scenario: droughts are becoming more and more frequent in the Haouz region and the local government now allows farmers to tap into the non-renewable groundwater resources. Abdelaziz El Hebil, the director of regional water board, had told me that the inhabitants of the Haouz were suffering terribly. "Luckily there are large subterranean water reserves which we have allowed the farmers to use to make up for the deficit," he said. "Until today we have been managing that water [from underground aquifers] economically, so that we never tapped into reserves, only into the renewable sources. In 2001, we authorized farmers to tap into the non-renewable sources for the first time. Given the conditions, we were forced to do this; it is a big step to take. *C'est une gestion dans l'espérance* [It is a policy of hope]."

Since 1970, the Haouz region has suffered a succession of serious droughts. El Hebil says it is hard to know whether these droughts are an effect of global climate change or whether this is only a fluctuation. "In my view the hydraulic crisis is inevitable. By 2025, 2030 Morocco will be suffering a hydrological crisis. Already today, some regions suffer from scarcity and it will only get worse. This crisis can't be avoided, but its impact can be lessened or postponed by ensuring better water management and also by developing research into the water types we are not using yet, like brackish groundwater and seawater."

El Hebil believes that Arab countries as a whole are not making the effort they should in the domain of sustainable water management. "There is no real aware- ness among decision makers and governments of Arab countries. In Morocco, you only have to look at the population figures to see where the problem stems from: in 1956 there were 8 million inhabitants, today there are 31 million and the predictions say that there will be 46 million of us by the year 2050—it's not hard to figure out what this means for the water resources," he says.

It is not just the drought that is having an impact on the flow of the khettaras in the Haouz plain. As I had observed in Iran and Syria, the introduction of modern technology like motor pumps has led to the over-pumping of ground- water, which has had a negative impact on the flow of khettaras. The ancient *khatariyas* were already aware of the danger of depleting the groundwater and customary law throughout the Middle East stipulated that khettaras, qanats and wells should never be built too close to each other. This rule was also incorporated into Islamic water legislation, where the area around the course of a qanat became known as the *harîm* or forbidden area. As soon as a well is equipped with a motor pump however, the traditional *harîm* area—which was usually between 100 and 300 meters—has to be significantly increased to take the power of the pumps into account.

The negative effect of modern technology on khettaras is poignantly illustrated in the Moroccan Tafilalet Valley, 500 kilometers southeast of the Haouz plain on the edge of the Sahara Desert. Until the construction of the Hassan Addakhil Dam at the head of the valley, nearby villages drew their water from eighty khettaras, some of which dated back to the late fourteenth century. Since the construction of the dam though, the flow of the khettaras has dropped considerably and most of them have today been abandoned. For not only is the surface water impounded in the dam reservoir, the water that is carried further south for irrigation flows in concrete-lined canals which prevent any groundwater recharge.

Yet the underground aqueduct has not been completely forgotten: in Oman and Yemen the falaj (plural: aflaj) still supplies most of the water used for the irrigation of crops in the isolated valleys and on the edge of the desert. In Oman, where some of the aflaj have been in use for more than 1,000 years, the Ministry of Water Resources even launched a large-scale restoration project in the 1980s and continues to invest significant amounts in the repair and upgrading of the country's aflaj. Thus in 1999 authorities spent $1.75 million on the restoration of sixty-eight aflaj and yearly maintenance work is carried out on aflaj around the country. Of the 4,112 existing aflaj in Oman, 3,017 are in use, forming the main source of irrigation water after wells. Special measures have been introduced to protect these remaining antiquities from pollution and drying out, such as the creation of well-field protection zones that increase the width of the *harîm* area to 3.5 kilometers.

The falaj is part of life in Oman and has become inseparable from Omani culture. Thus when an Omani farmer greets his neighbors, he not only enquires after the health of the family, but also asks about that of the falaj. This is just one reflection of the central role of the falaj in Oman. But its significance goes further: the word denotes not only the underground water channels, but also the irrigation network that relies on them and the social system that divides the water between the users. The aflaj have had an important influence on Oman's history, determining social structures and settlement patterns. Thus the resource flowing from the hidden sources and the rules that determine its division in the community is more than just water; it is the element that binds communities together.

# 4

# *Chafa* and *Chirb*, the Laws of Water

*"The old laws have been tried and tested, they have worked for centuries. We should reflect on this before discarding their wisdom."—Abdelaziz El Hebil, regional director of the Tensift water board, Marrakech, Morocco*

The precious nature of water in the Middle East makes the regulation of its distribution all the more important. In the rocky deserts of the Levant, in the sand dunes of the Sahara and the arid mountain lands of Asia, water laws are much more detailed and precise than in cultures where water has always been plentiful. The less water there is, the more intricate and complex the laws and rituals. In all the countries I traveled through, a string of traditions, customs and unwritten rules still form the basis of water's distribution in rural communities. In many places the later colonial, post-independence and international legislation have little impact on the daily practice of water allocation.

With the rise of Islam many of these customary laws—some dating back to Byzantine, Roman, and even pre-Roman times—were adopted by the shariah, the body of Islamic law. Covering all aspects of human life, the shariah is derived from the Koran and an ancient collection of narrations about the Prophet's life, the Sunnah, and the Hadiths. The shariah devotes extensive passages to water, categorizing the facets of water use and distribution in a series of books: *The Book of Water Distribution, The Book of Purification, The Book of the Hammam, The Book of Rain....*

The word shariah itself is closely related to water: the fourteenth-century lexicographer Ibn Manzur recorded that shariah is the place from which one descends to water, but also the law of water, and the *shur'at al-ma'*—literally the laws of water—were originally a series of rules that regulated water use in pre-Islamic Arabia. The term later evolved to include the body of laws and rules given by God; an eighteenth-century lexicographer explained that the divine law had been called shariah "by comparison with the shariah of water in that the one who legislates...quenches his thirst and purifies himself, and I mean by quenching what some wise men have said: 'I used to drink and remained thirsty, but when I knew God I quenched my thirst without drinking,'" once again emphasizing the pivotal role of water in Islam, in both symbolic and economic sense.

The close relationship between justice and religion in the Islamic world—Islamic law is directly derived from the word of God as revealed in the Koran—gives added force to the shariah: breaking it is not just crossing a forbidden boundary, it is sinning against God, breaking His Law. Only a handful of Islamic countries—Saudi Arabia, Iran and Sudan among others—fully observe the shariah, yet true secularism is practically nonexistent. Even in the more Westernized countries like Morocco and Tunisia, the influence of Islam in state and civil affairs can be clearly identified. So for example a Western government would probably not quote the Bible to incite citizens to save water, yet the Egyptian, Jordanian, and Syrian governments use quotes from the Koran to promote water conservation and increase environmental awareness.

As a religion born in a harsh desert climate, Islam ascribes the most sacred qualities to water as a purifying and life-giving resource. It is the basis of all life as the Holy Koran emphasizes: "We made from water every living thing." Together with grass as pasture for animals, and fire, water is one of the three things to which every Muslim has an inalienable right. It is a gift from God and should be freely available to all; any Muslim who withholds unneeded supplies sins against Allah: "No one can refuse surplus water without sinning against Allah and against man." The Hadiths also stipulate that among the three people whom Allah will ignore on the day of resurrection there will be "the man who, having water in excess of his needs, refuses it to a traveler." Two fundamental precepts guide the right to water in traditional legislation. *Chafa*, the right of thirst, establishes the universal right for humans to quench their thirst and that of their animals; *chirb*, the right of irrigation, gives all users the right to water their crops.

## Valencia's Water Tribunal

Already on the fourth day of my journey I was confronted with the fading legacy of these customary laws in the Spanish town of Valencia. Locals had told me about the 1,000-year-old Tribunal de las Aguas, a public water tribunal held every Thursday in front of the cathedral and presided by eight elected judges. Dressed in traditional black tunics and sitting in high-backed leather armchairs in the cathedral's portico, they resolve water disputes between inhabitants of Valencia's *huerta*.

The tribunal's origins lie in Islamic Spain, where Berber and Arab invaders settled in the eighth century. The region was initially a province of the Umayyad Caliphate of Damascus, which ruled the Muslim world from Baghdad to the Atlantic coasts until 929 AD. Later the Iberian province gained independence and was ruled from Cordoba, which rapidly became a cultural, scientific and political center. The new inhabitants developed the *huerta*, expanding upon a network of seven canals that had been created by the Romans. Using ceramic pipes, water was diverted from its natural course and led to fields and orchards around the town. The canals led the water from the river to an intricate network

4 January 2001
Valencia Cathedral

of secondary canals and side streams—thus irrigating and fertilizing 1,000 hectares of land.

The water tribunal was established around 960 AD under Abderramán III, the first Caliph of Cordoba. Within the *huerta*, water users are grouped into seven "communities," one for each canal and each with its elected representative. Each canal has its own system of rules, determining rights of water use and the share of water allocated, while the tribunal ensures all rules are obeyed and fraud is punished. Even after Islamic rule had been banished from Spain, and the Catholic kings were doing everything they could to destroy any Muslim legacy, the Tribunal de las Aguas was preserved. King Jaime I of Aragon, El Conquistador, openly acknowledged the value of the system set up in Valencia's *huerta*, donating the waters of the River Turia to the towns' citizens in 1239, and declaring that what had been "created and established by the Saracens" should be preserved and perpetrated.

An ornate fountain on the cathedral square still bears testimony to the importance of Valencia's seven canals: a colossal reclining Neptune is surrounded by seven muse-like women holding tilted amphorae that spout water. Together they represent the River Turia with its seven channels. Cooing pigeons and snowy doves flutter around the spray, settling on Neptune's head or shoulder, and pecking at the pools of water that lie at the muses' feet, oblivious to the water allegory that is represented here.

By ten to twelve a considerable crowd had gathered by the cathedral entrance, waiting expectantly. Old men smoking little cigarillos stood around in groups, mothers waited with their immaculately dressed children, and a handful of tourists held their cameras ready to capture the events for posterity. As the bells rang midday there was still no sign of the judges. A murmur started moving through the crowd: the tribunal would not take place today. An old man told a group of ladies in fur coats that the event was canceled. "Last week they didn't turn up either," he explained in a grave tone to a thickset Dutch lady. Her husband sat down dejectedly and started packing away his video camera, as she sauntered off to order coffee at the nearest café. The Spaniards had not given up yet: a small crowd gathered around a policeman. "Not today, not today, it will not take place this week," he said authoritatively. "But," clamored a small lady in green, "at the town hall they told us it was on." The policeman remained stoic: "No. The Tribunal de las Aguas will not take place. Perhaps next week." The importance of Valencia's *huerta* with its tribunal was apparently not what it had once been. With the modernization of irrigation techniques and the diversion of the Turia through a new channel that runs outside the city, the *huerta* has changed and the tribunal no longer carries the weight it once did.

### The Water Sheikh of Ourika

Traveling through Morocco's Atlas Mountains three weeks later, I saw how an oral heritage of water distribution that is many centuries old is still in use despite colonial, and more recently, governmental efforts to reform the system and rationalize rules. Authorities in the capital, Rabat, would like to see the country's water use conform to international standards to reflect the progressive nature of their policies and governance. But 400 kilometers to the south in the Atlas Mountains and beyond, rural populations feel little need to reform a system that has worked efficiently for centuries. Rabat's Loi 10-95 aims to rationalize water use by introducing a pricing system that punishes squanderers and polluters. While it was passed more than ten years ago, it has had little impact on life in these isolated rural environments.

In the Haouz plain south of Marrakech, local authorities are faced with this clash between customary traditions and modern legislation on a daily basis. Abdelaziz El Hebil, the director of the local water board, finds himself constantly having to bridge the gap between the rational, modern rules from Rabat and traditional ways. Looking at the messy piles of paperwork strewn across his desk, the portly middle-aged director told me: "The new water law is good in that it still involves the user in water management. It also sanctions wasteful use and pollution. Still, the government—us in this case—will have to work with the traditions of local inhabitants: we will be forced to listen to the committees of wise men, we will be obliged to adapt. The old laws will continue to be influential in everyday life. Our only role will be to support these traditions, to improve their performance and to ensure the sustainability of the systems. We have to try to apply the new law so that we comply with international standards, and at the same time respect tradition. The main thing we have to beware of is that politics and administrative clutter stays out of this; it should not alter these traditions. The old laws have been tried and tested, they have worked for centuries. We should reflect on this before discarding their wisdom."

As we talked El Hebil grew more and more passionate about a value system that was now threatened by modernization and forgetfulness. He suggested I accompany one of his water experts to the Ourika Valley south of Marrakech the following day. Ahmed Bourrim, a Berber from the mouth of the valley, knew all the locals and could introduce me to an old man who would tell me about the ancient laws.

Early the next day we headed off in Bourrim's battered Toyota pick-up along the winding road to the Ourika Valley. Bourrim, a small man with a beard and a shy smile, said little. "*Il ne parlait pas pour ne rien dire,*" as they say in French—until I asked about water in the Ourika Valley and he told me extensively about this secluded valley, its inhabitants and the unpredictable water that played such an important role in their lives. Life in the Ourika Valley has always been hard, but the last twenty years have been particularly punishing. Droughts have been followed by destructive flash floods that wiped entire sections of the valley away. The signs of destruction can still be seen where the road was washed away, houses ripped up and bridges destroyed by powerful floods that hit the valley in 1995. "It was one day after the Setti Fatma *moussem*, a local festival that takes place once a year," Bourrim said. "Luckily. But people were still in the valley finishing off celebrations. The water came within the space of two hours, it just washed straight through the valley. Several people were killed and there was a lot of damage." As we drive along the road, Bourrim points to ruins of houses that stand as reminders of the destruction. "Since then we have had no rain though."

Situated in the northern foothills of the Atlas range, the Ourika Valley is only an hour's drive from Marrakech across the Haouz plain, yet it feels like it is several centuries removed. The valley still lives to the rhythm of the evermore unpredictable Ourika River[1] that runs through it, its inhabitants sticking to the ancient laws that define the distribution of water. With rainfall in the region so sporadic and unreliable, the crops depend on irrigation from the river to survive.

We entered the valley, leaving the flat plains south of Marrakech behind us. The landscape became richer, with extensive olive groves and orchards crowding around the dry, rocky riverbed. We pulled up in front of a tall house surrounded by high white walls. There were no windows, just a door in the wall, where an elderly man in a long woollen *burnous*, the traditional cloak worn by Moroccan

**Map 3**
**Marrakech and the Ourika Valley, Morocco**

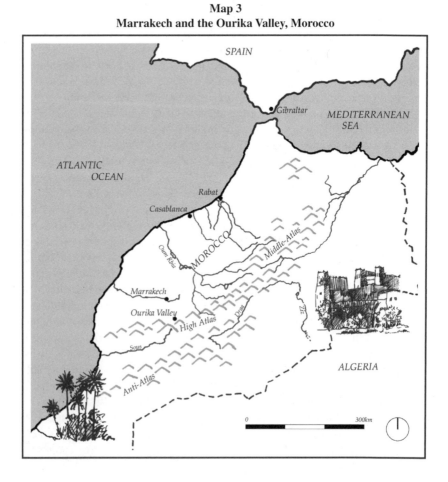

men, greeted us. His white moustache twitched as he smiled and shook our hands warmly, gesturing for us to come inside. Monsieur le Hajj Aït Aaddi was a man of power. Everything about him said it. His title, Hajj, indicating the respect he enjoyed within the community; his large house, with a tiled inner courtyard and a terrace on the first floor that looked out over the endless olive groves that he owned; the dignified demeanor that inspired respect of all that met him; and, of course, his thorough knowledge of the waters of the Ourika Valley.

As we sipped sweet mint tea on the large flowery sofa in his reception room, Monsieur Aït Aaddi told me about the laws of the Ourika Valley and how the water is distributed to the inhabitants. A combination of local customary law, pre-Islamic law and shariah, they are based upon the fundamental principle that every member of the *jama'a*, the community, should have a right to water.

"The water is taken from the river and led into four main canals[2] which in turn flow through many secondary channels to the individual plots of land and the crops," explained Aït Aaddi. "The users of each canal are grouped into a user association, each with its own rules and system of allocation. They elect an *amazzal*, a caretaker who has a thorough knowledge of the canal network and the water rights of each side channel, village, and individual member of the community. He makes sure the water goes to the right places at the right times." The Berber word *amazzal* literally means "the man who runs in front of the water," a very graphic description of the role, as the *amazzal* has to check the course of the water as it passes the successive junctions and branches, ensuring distribution takes place efficiently and that farmers do not abuse their rights.

As he talked, Aït Aaddi had taken off his slippers and tucked his feet underneath him, making himself comfortable amidst velvet cushions. His granddaughter came in and offered us more tea on a silver tray, then cakes and home-made sweetmeats. Bourrim sat timidly next to Aït Aaddi, who was explaining the flow of the seven canals and their side branches with great gestures. They spoke in Berber dialect and Bourrim translated to French, always respectfully addressing the old man as "Monsieur le Hajj." The old man was like a local water almanac, going into great detail about the intricacies of the law, the differences between the channels, how much water flowed through each of them, and what this meant for water allocation.

Water in the Ourika Valley is allocated in time units, not in fixed volumes, so that each user is allowed to take water from the canal to his fields for a set amount of time. Large stones or bricks are used to block up a channel when the time is up and the *amazzal* is there to check that there are no leaks and that no one tries to "steal" more time or more water by opening up his channel without entitlement. Depending on how much land he owns, and his status within the community, the user owns a number of "water shares."

Time-based water allocation is common throughout the Middle East and I would encounter it again in other parts of Morocco, Syria, and Iran. Traditionally, before clocks were in common use, time was measured in a variety of ways: in eastern Iran, in the villages around Yazd and Kerman, a bowl with a small hole would be set afloat in a container of water. The time it took for the container to fill up would become the unit for the allocation of water from the qanats; pierced containers such as these are still in use today and lie at the origin of Arabic water clocks. In North Africa, where the pierced bowl system was also sometimes used, it was more common for time to be measured by the shortening and lengthening of shadows, by watching the stretching out of the shadow of a tree or the encroaching movement of a mountain's shadow across a valley.

In the Draa Valley, on the edge of the Moroccan Sahara, and in Libya's Western Desert, such measurement of time and the parceling out of water shares became the task of a specialist "water decoder" or *ferray lma*, who calculated the basic unit of time by determining the length of a man's shadow at a given point in the day in terms of the length of that same man's feet. In the afternoon, the right to water might start, for instance, when the man's shadow was seven feet long and end when it was ten feet long.

Asking for a piece of paper, Aït Aaddi began to explain the rotating system of time allocation by drawing a circle and subdividing it into the different segments that make up the water cycle. Crouched on the floor before him, Bourrim translated as the water story unfolded. "There are fourteen water days per cycle," Aït Aaddi commenced. "Their length varies depending on the amount of water available, the time of year, and the number of users. The water days are divided into two parts that represent night and day. He blackened one half of the circle. "Each day and night is split into sixteen units, which are allocated on a rotating basis among the users."

In practice this means that the length of the basic time unit changes as the seasons evolve. In winter and summer, at the equinox and the solstice, the basic value of one unit changes as days shorten or lengthen. Thus in the long days of summer, daytime units will always be longer than night-time units. To ensure that all users receive comparable amounts, the distribution system also rotates through the day, and the user who received his water in daytime during one cycle, will receive his next share during the night. While the length of the water cycle varies per region, the principles of the water distribution system are the same everywhere.

The *ferray lma* has the onerous task of determining the value of the units and establishing how much water each user will get and at what point in the water cycle he will get it. At night, time used to be calculated by observing the position of the stars, but this practice has long been abandoned. Today, watches are used to calculate the length of the night-time units.

Just how important the *amazzal* and the *ferray lma* are to their communities is emphasized by the fact that none of these rules or details of the system are recorded in writing. Traditionally, the order of allocation was sometimes described in a poem that was memorized by the local storyteller. In theory each user knows how much water he is entitled to, and when it is his turn to use the

**The traditional system of water distribution based on time units**

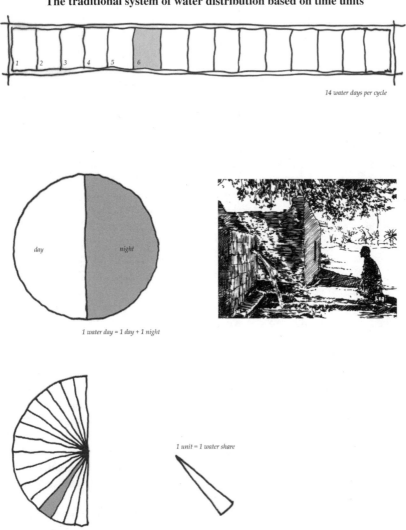

*14 water days per cycle*

*1 water day = 1 day + 1 night*

*1 unit = 1 water share*

*days and nights are divided into 16 units*

of entitlements, particularly on the rare cloudy days, when there are heated discussions about the exact time of sunrise and sunset, and the consequent length of the water shares. This is when the *amazzal* is called upon to resolve disputes.

When I asked how the quantity of water per person was determined, and whether all portions were equal or whether some users were more equal than others, the Hajj took a new sheet of paper and started drawing again. This time it was a schematic map of the valley with the rivers and the canals that led away from it.

It looked like a tree with long branches. When he had finished he looked up. "There are many rules to determine the rights of each user," he said. "First of all, upstream users have priority over those living further down in the valley. When there is little water in the river, it does not reach the bottom of the valley or the lower canals—it evaporates or is absorbed by the riverbed. This is why the upstream users have priority, and why it is more advantageous to own lands high in the valley. When there is enough water, the upstream users still have priority, but they can only take a limited amount of water. The water they lead into their *seguia* is not allowed to reach over the ankle—this is to make sure they don't abuse their right."

I liked this rule: it seemed so simple and self-evident. No need for complicated measuring devices, for archives-full of books and papers listing the clauses and their exceptions. An ankle was all one needed. The amount of water measured was approximate, but it was a deeply physical and intuitive law, showing the close bond between man and water in the Ourika Valley. As systems and societies develop, as agriculture is modernized and people are urbanized, they lose their connection to water. As soon as water reliably flows from a tap, or is collected in a dam reservoir, that direct relationship between man and the water he uses disappears; the tactile association disappears and water very rapidly loses its value. Here in the Ourika Valley were there was no dam, this connection still existed and people lived in harmony with the water.

Later I learnt that the ankle rule, along with that of upstream priority, was neither exclusive to Ourika nor even to North Africa, for both date back many centuries. They are also both incorporated in the Hadiths, where it is recorded that the Prophet Mohammed intervened in a dispute between two water users in the Valley of Harra in the Arabian Desert. He told the upstream farmer, Abdallah-ben-Ez-Zubayr: "Water your crops and then let the water flow to your neighbor." The downstream user, Ansar, rudely accused the Prophet of favoritism but the latter remained calm and repeated: "Water your crops and stop as soon as the water reaches the height of the trunk." The two men then took the Prophet's words to heart and calculated that the "height of the trunk," equalled the height of the ankle. The law's strength and survival lies in its simplicity: no one is likely to forget or dispute any part of it, and these rules will survive so long as the canal system does.

"Secondly," Hajj Aït Aaddi continued, "although everyone has a right to water, some are entitled to more water than others, depending on how much they or their fathers contributed to the digging of the channel and how much maintenance work they do for the community." He looked up and smiled: "It is a good system. Very just—as long as the *amazzal* is honest and does not accept bribes, or favor certain families."

Did this ever happen, I asked. Bourrim smiled deferentially and, looking at the old man out of the corner of his eye, said: "Not when Monsieur le Hajj was the *amazzal*—he is a very just and correct man." Hajj Aït Aaddi suddenly understood French and smiled. "But elsewhere it happens a lot," Bourrim continued. "Important people, the old families and tribes, the rich—they often get more water because they can pay for it; also because they feel they have a right over others. There is a saying: *'L'eau, l'ami du puissant,'* (Water, the friend of the powerful)—it is still true today. The water rights you have show your place in society." Traditional Moroccan society is divided into strata: the *chorfa* and *m'rabtine,* the religious classes, the *hrar,* the Arabs and Berbers, and, lowest of all, the *haratine,* descendants of the Sudanese slaves transported across the Sahara for centuries. While the importance of the class system is decreasing, there is still a clear hierarchy in the structure of water allocation in the remote valleys. Thus the privileged upper class owns most of the land and the water shares, while the *haratine* are often landless and waterless.

We left Monsieur le Hajj at the end of the morning. He stood in the doorway surrounded by his large family as we got into the car and drove away. Bourrim was quiet for a while. At length he said: "You see, it is not easy to bring in new laws when the old ones are so strong and work so well for the people here."

## Rationalizing the Laws

Much as Rabat seeks change today, so, seventy years ago, the colonizing French ran up against the strength of Moroccan customary law. They tried to replace traditional laws with French law that would give them full control of this vital development resource. But instead of the straightforward law reform they had implemented in their other North African colonies, in Morocco the French were confronted with a scenario where each region and each tribe, right to each secluded valley, had its own laws, and where exclusive agreements governed water allocation between neighboring tribes. The French law, which effectively made all water a state-owned resource, was strongly resisted, despite the fact that the French claimed it followed the principles of Islamic water law in which water was a public good. In the end, the only way that the French *Code des Eaux* could be implemented in 1935 was by including many exceptions to the new rules, thus acknowledging the validity of local and customary laws.

The problems the French encountered in Morocco were partly due to the fact that it was the only French colony in North Africa not to have been part of the Ottoman Empire. As such, its population had never been subjected to lasting unified rule and was a patchwork of tribal groups, whose shifting alliances and successive bids for power constantly redefined the nature and center of government. France's other North African colonies, Tunisia and Algeria, had fallen under Ottoman rule from the seventeenth century. Further east in the Levant, Syria, and Lebanon had been under the Sultan's rule from the early sixteenth century.

As an Islamic power, the Ottoman Empire based its civil law code, *Al Majalla Othmaniyah,* on the shariah, attaching great importance to water and its use within the community. Eighty-two articles of the *Majalla* are dedicated to water law. When the French colonized Algeria and Tunisia (in 1830 and 1881 respectively) and later received the mandate over Syria and Lebanon in 1916, they rationalized the existing legislation in the form of the *Code des Eaux*, which combined basic principles of local customary law and shariah with French law, establishing a legal code which is still influential across North Africa and the Levant. In Tunisia and Algeria, the *Majalla's* water laws were kept in place until the late 1970s and in Syria, the *Majalla* and later French law still govern the system of water distribution in the canals of Damascus.

In many ways, the Damascene water system is remarkably similar to that of Valencia: seven canals run through the capital, leading the waters of the Barada to the surrounding gardens and orchards of the Ghuta Oasis. In the library of the French Institute in Damascus I found an article from 1929, "L'Irrigation dans la Ghouta de Damas," that explained how water was distributed in Damascus. Just as in Valencia and Morocco, the water from the canals was divided into time units and each village and farm had a right to its share. It was all just as Hajj Aït Aaddi had explained to me in the Ourika Valley.

Today, the Barada has virtually dried out and its remaining waters are diverted through pipelines to be used as drinking water. The little water that does still run through the channels falls under a unique legislation that combines customary and Islamic law with the Ottoman Majalla and the French Code des Eaux. The Syrian government is drawing up new national water legislation to replace French and Ottoman laws but for the waters of the Barada it will make little difference; the ancient canal system is today rapidly falling into disuse. As in Spain, where the Tribunal de las Aguas has become a tourist attraction and ancient water distribution systems have been largely superseded by modern technologies, the traditions surrounding water allocation in the Damascene Ghuta Oasis are dying, along with the orchard and gardens which they watered.

## Notes

1.  The Ourika is an oued, a seasonal river that only flows in the rainy season, comparable to the Levantine and Egyptian wadi.
2.  These earthen canals that are derived from the oued are known as seguias. The seguia system exists across the Middle East and North Africa.

# 5

# The Value of Water

*"Governments don't give water the attention it deserves. This is valid for all countries. It is a core issue from which other issues evolve. Tough decisions have to be taken: farming activities must be curtailed, political decisions need to be made in function of the water scarcity, not just with economics in mind. The right time will come for this. You see, water is politics and these policy decisions have technical consequences."—Professor Mohamed Al-Eryani, water resources specialist, United Nations Economic and Social Commission for Western Asia, Beirut, Lebanon*

With the development of new technologies, the intensification of agricultural techniques and urbanization, people are losing their connection to water. As soon as water flows reliably from a tap, or is collected in a dam reservoir, the direct relationship between man and the water he uses disappears. Traditions and customs are forgotten, and water quickly loses its value.

## Myth and Reality

The Romans said of Egypt *"aut Nilus, aut nihil"*—the Nile or nothing. The country's life and livelihood have since time immemorial been determined by the Nile's rhythm, by high years and low years and the flood that yearly washed the fertile mud from Ethiopia onto the arid land. The movement of the Nile was like a slow breathing across the sands of the Egyptian desert. The rising waters in the first weeks of June were awaited with trepidation and anxiety by a whole country that knew that high floods could wreak destruction on crops and villages, while low floods meant famine and death. As the water rose through the summer months, all the lands along the Nile were submerged. Writing in the fifth century BC, the Greek historian Herodotus recorded that the "whole country is converted into a sea and the towns, which alone remain above water, look like the islands of the Aegean." From October onwards, the waters gradually subsided until in February the Nile was again a tame river flowing through the vast desert.

The world of the Ancient Egyptians revolved around the Nile in an ambivalent manner. As the country's only source of water, the river was so central to life that its presence went almost unnoticed. Thus the Ancient Egyptians did not even have a name for the Nile; it was simply known as "the river." In their eyes the Nile's presence and the yearly flood were a natural state of affairs and the rain that fell in other countries was designated as an "inundation in the sky." Similarly, their world was oriented upside down from our point of view as they situated north at the sources of the Nile and south on the Mediterranean Coast. The three seasons were also defined by the river: "Emergence" from November to March was followed by "Heat"—the time of low waters and harvests—and "Inundation." But while the Ancient Egyptians took the river and its cycle largely for granted, the origins of the flood and the river that brought it were shrouded in mystery.

Herodotus said that no one he spoke to, whether Egyptian, Libyan, or Greek, knew where the source was, but that a scribe in the city of Saïs told him that the Nile sprang from fathomless depths near two mountains called Crophi and Mophi. The fact that these springs were bottomless, he said, was proven by the Egyptian king Psammetichus who had a rope made many thousands of fathoms long, which he let down into the water without finding the bottom. One of the first maps of the Nile Basin was drawn in the second century AD by a scholar from the Library of Alexandria, Claudius Ptolemy, who situated the sources of the Nile far beyond the southern borders of Egypt at the "Mountains of the Moon."

As long as the sources remained unknown, the flood itself was also an incomprehensible occurrence and the subject of numerous myths and rituals. In ancient Egypt, the yearly flood was associated with the god Hapi, a fat figure who symbolized abundance and prosperity, and in honor of whom sacrificial ceremonies were held at the beginning of every flood season. As a representative of the gods on earth, the pharaoh also participated in these rituals by throwing a written order into the Nile, commanding it to rise.

Perhaps the best-known myth associated with the Nile was that of Osiris and Isis. Recorded on the walls in the pyramids of Saqqara around 2500 BC, the myth weaves a colorful picture of Osiris as the god of the underworld and death, but also as the god of corn and vegetation, and the personification of the returning flood and the rebirth of life in the desert. His sister and wife, Isis, represents fertility and motherhood. The myth says that Osiris and Isis brought Order to Egypt, introducing law and civilization, and teaching the Egyptians to worship the gods and cultivate wheat and barley. But Osiris' reign was brought to an abrupt end by his brother Set, who represents confusion and disorder. His arrival marks "the beginning of conflict" as he murders Osiris and dismembers the body, spreading the different parts across the country. Hearing of the cruel murder, Isis is distraught and sets out to find her husband's body. Her desperate lamentations are at length heard by the sun god Ra who takes pity on the faithful wife and helps her find most of the pieces of the body, which she revives.

As this myth evolved through the centuries, the Ancient Egyptians came to associate Osiris' death and resurrection with the yearly death and revival of corn and vegetation. Osiris himself was seen as the personification of the recurring Nile flood and the rebirth of human and plant life. The arrival of the floodwaters was also associated with the myth of Osiris and Isis; the Ancient Egyptians celebrated the festival of Isis at this time, as they believed that the tears she wept for her dead husband made the river swell. In ancient inscriptions, Isis is spoken of as she "who maketh the Nile swell and overflow." This tradition was for a long time perpetuated by Egypt's Copts who celebrate St. Michael's Day on 17 June. According to an ancient Coptic tradition, it is on this night—Leylet al Nuktah or the Night of the Drop—that the archangel lets a miraculous drop fall into the Nile to make its waters rise.

As the flood rose, its height was carefully monitored. Measurements were regularly taken at the so-called "Nilometers" that were built along the Nile's course at Aswan, Karnak and Roda Island in Cairo. The levels and daily fluctuations were proclaimed in the streets of Cairo by *Al-Munadee El Nil*, the Nile crier. As soon as the river reached a level of sixteen cubits[1]—the ideal level for inundation—feeder canals were opened and the fields were inundated. In Graeco-Roman times a true cult of the Nile developed. The flood and the number sixteen became universal symbols of life and prosperity throughout the Mediterranean as the Roman historian Pliny explained: "With a use of twelve cubits it [the Province of Memphis] senses the onset of starvation and even with thirteen it is still hungry. But fourteen brings joyfulness, fifteen freedom from care and sixteen sheer delight." Under the Emperor Trajan in the first century AD, medals were coined depicting the Nile as a male god together with an angel who pointed to a large numeral XVI. An allegorical statue of the Nile from this period also survives in the Vatican Museum. The central male figure, the Nile, reclines beside a sphinx and a crocodile. A cornucopia in his right hand symbolizes abundance, while sixteen cherub-like, cubit-high boys climb over and around him to represent the ideal flood.

Until the beginning of the twentieth century, the admission of water to canals and fields was marked by yearly ceremonies that celebrated the plenitude of the Nile or *wafa'a*. In Cairo, a large earthen dam was constructed before or soon after the Nile started rising and as soon as the river reached "plenitude," the dam was cut. A truncated cone of earth called *'aroosa* or the bride was also built in front of the dam, and grain was sown on top of it. Within a week, the bride would have been washed down by the rising flood, a symbolic ceremony which married the male river to the virgin land, and ensured a good harvest. This "washing of the bride," which was practiced until the early twentieth century, is believed to have replaced an ancient ritual in which a young virgin dressed in fine garments was sacrificed to the river to ensure a plentiful inundation.

The other agricultural festival that was closely associated with Osiris was the sowing of the seed in the autumn after the retreat of the floodwaters. During solemn funerary ceremonies, an effigy of Osiris moulded from earth and corn was buried in the ground. The farmers of Ancient Egypt believed that the charm would ensure the growth of their crops and that by dying in the soil, the corn god would be reborn in the form of new sprouts. In the temple of Isis at Philae, a series of bas-reliefs depict Osiris' dead body with stalks of corn growing from it, while a priest stands by and waters them. A hieroglyphic inscription above the bas-reliefs reads: "This is the form of whom one may not name, Osiris of the mysteries, who springs from the returning waters." Osiris thus became the embodiment of the corn which springs from the earth after the inundation: the grain growing from the effigies was seen as an omen but also as the cause of the growth of crops throughout the land. The corn god had brought forth the corn, relinquishing his body to feed the people. He had died so that they might live.

Besides his role as god of corn and his yearly rebirth, Osiris was also associated with human death and his resurrection was a symbol of eternal life. Not only did the god make seed spring from the ground, he also resurrected the dead from dust and embodied the hope of immortality. Corn-stuffed effigies of Osiris were therefore commonly placed in tombs as symbolic emblems and instruments of resurrection. The yearly ceremonies to commemorate Osiris' death may also have marked the commemoration of all the dead. One of the central events of the celebrations was the lighting of oil lamps in front of all houses on the night of the celebrations. Scholars believe this nocturnal illumination on one night of the year was part of a general mourning of the dead and may be related to the Christian All Souls' Day. Indeed, it was a widespread belief that the souls of the deceased revisited their homes on one night in the year; on this occasion people set out food to welcome the spirits and prepared oil lamps along their path to guide them from their graves.

Today these rituals have disappeared together with the Nile flood. The Egyptians have forgotten the yearly cycle of rising and falling waters and their seasons have disappeared. The extremes have been evened out, blunted, and replaced by a uniform, constant flow of water. Since the completion of the High Dam on the southern border with Sudan in 1971, the water that flows from Aswan to the Mediterranean has been contained, reined in, and shaped to serve the people. This constancy creates a dependability, which has given Egypt the opportunity to intensify and develop its agriculture, but which has also dulled people's awareness of water's value. Six hundred kilometers south of Aswan in Sudan's capital, Khartoum, the Nile is still a wild, unruly river that spills across the country—now in floods, now as a tame river—touching the lives and the lands through which it flows both physically and psychologically.

"North of Aswan the Nile no longer exists," Dr Sugheiroun el Zain Sugheiroun, a former Minister for Water Resources in Sudan, told me. We were sitting in the library of the UNESCO Chair for Water Resources in Khartoum, the ex-minister surrounded by documents and notes, his long, thin hands slowly leafing through loose sheets of paper in his briefcase. He was an old man with dark wrinkles and a calm gaze.

He said nothing for a time, then barely audible, with slow words: "The Nile waters used to flow freely through the valley. They came from Ethiopia, from Uganda, went through Sudan, north to Aswan, then through Egypt and into the Mediterranean." His eyes looked past me, to the map of Sudan that was on the wall behind, tracing the flow of the Blue and the White Nile, their meeting point at The Mugran in Khartoum, where they flowed together and continued their course northward as one. "In Egypt, there used to be periods of high water and low water. During the four months of the rainy season, the water flooded the land. Some years there was too much water; other years, the waters were low. Now it is different: the water goes north but is collected at the Aswan High Dam into a huge lake that covers thousands of kilometers. So now, for Egyptians, there is no difference anymore between the high years and the low years." His voice trailed off and he talked about the parable in the Bible and the Koran that tells of the pharaoh's dream of seven fat cows and seven lean cows, which Joseph interpreted to mean that there would be seven years of plenty, followed by seven years of famine. All this, he said, was now lost to the Egyptians.

Dr Sugheiroun's words came back to me several weeks later in Aswan, in southern Egypt. Sitting by the reception, the owner of Hotel Noorhan was smoking and chatting with friends. An open bottle of water stood on a side table and as I walked past, I knocked it over. When I apologized, the owner just laughed and, with a grand gesture, said: "Don't worry, it's only water! We have plenty of it, just look at the Nile!" This is when I saw: most Egyptians have no perception or memory of water scarcity. They live in one of the harshest deserts, but also along the longest river, which is controlled by one of the largest dams in the world, and therefore there is no sense of uncertainty about water. People count on the steady flow of the Nile and do not need to think beyond the southern borders or beyond that massive wall of concrete that holds Egypt's sense of security behind it. You can't blame them: when you see the Nile flowing by—that huge, gray, languid mass—you have no reason to think water is precious or scarce. The farmers who do experience scarcity blame the government for not "giving" them more water and, without ever wondering where their water comes from, expect the authorities in Cairo to solve the problem. And while the 165 billion cubic meters of water that lie in Lake Nasser have protected Egypt against the devastating famines that hit Ethiopia and Sudan in the 1980s, the Aswan High Dam has also created a deceptive sense of invulnerability.

In this case it is however not just about an over-reliance on technology, it is also about the exploding population, which is rapidly growing beyond the capacity of the Nile waters. Politicians still argue that there is no scarcity, that water distribution is in fact very efficient as supplies are reused three to four times. What they avoid saying is that while Egypt's yearly water supply remains a constant 55.5 billion cubic meters per year, according to the agreement signed with Sudan in 1959, the population of more than 74 million is growing by more than 100,000 a month. If growth continues at the current rate, the population will reach 126 million by 2050. And despite concerted efforts to curb the huge population growth, on average, women still have three to four children.

Mohammed Nasr Allam, a professor of irrigation engineering at Cairo University, predicts a bleak future. "It is not difficult to diagnose: there is less than

750 cubic meters of water per capita per year, a situation of water stress that is only going to get worse," he says. The constraints imposed by the limited water supply in Egypt are exacerbated by the fact that the Nile is Egypt's only source of water: 98 percent of the country's water supply comes from the river, and 96 percent of the population lives in the Nile Valley which constitutes less than 5.5 percent of the total area of the country.

## Exploding Populations

Sharply rising population figures combined with dwindling water supplies are common in many countries in the region. In the water-rich countries of Northern Europe and North America, the average per capita water availability varies between 1,500 and 20,000 cubic meters per year. In the Middle East, many countries have an average per capita water availability far below 500 cubic meters per year.[2] In 2002 the annual amount of freshwater per capita available in Jordan, Tunisia and Yemen was 179, 482, and 223 cubic meters respectively. At the same time, the Middle East and North Africa region[3] has one of the highest population growth rates in the world. Since 1975 the population has exploded, leaping from 172 million to 405 million in 2005, a figure that is expected to rise to 695 million by 2050. Improvements in the standards of living and better healthcare and nutrition have all contributed to this sharp rise. Life expectancy has also risen dramatically from forty-one years in the 1950s to sixty-eight years in 2005, while infant mortality has been drastically reduced. Thirty-eight percent of the population in Arab countries is under the age of fourteen and birth rates remain high.

In these conditions, water scarcity forms an obvious threat, for while other regions may have less water, none combines such high population growth rates with such scarce water resources. With 6 percent of the world's population living in the Middle East and North Africa, the region has less than 0.5 percent of the world's freshwater resources. An alarming report from the UN Environmental Programme in 2003 predicted that 95 percent of the Middle East will be suffering severe water shortages by 2032. In the past, the limited availability of water always set natural limits to the exploitation of the land and population growth. The amount of water determined how much food could be produced and thus the population that could live off the land. "There have always been droughts and scarcity in this region," Professor Elias Salameh of the University of Jordan in Amman explains. "The population was accordingly controlled and kept in check by the amount that the land could produce. In the last 100 years though, the picture has changed: since we started importing food, the population has grown at a much higher rate, stretching water reserves to the limit."

While the region has always had to cope with a degree of scarcity, today the quality of the water is also increasingly affected by pollution from industrial, agricultural and human sources. Dr David Brooks of Friends of the Earth

Canada, an expert on water in the Middle East, says that while the problem of water quality is more recent, it is rapidly becoming more pressing. "It is almost as important to conserve the quality of water as to conserve its quantity. Once degraded, it is expensive to restore surface water to its original quality, and all but impossible to restore the quality of underground water," he comments. He explains that most problems of water quality stem from three principal factors: the overpumping of aquifers, pollution by agricultural pesticides and fertilizers, and inadequate sewage collection and treatment.

The overpumping of groundwater causes water tables to decline, which leads to a lowering of pressure in the aquifer and the intrusion of other, often lower quality water. Many Mediterranean countries have overpumped their coastal aquifers to such an extent that seawater can be found three kilometers inland. Some have even been so badly affected that the water is no longer fit for use, even in agriculture.

Pollution by agricultural pesticides and fertilizers such as phosphorous and nitrogen further contributes to declining water quality in the region. Brooks comments: "Per hectare use of pesticides and fertilizer in the region rates among the highest in the world, and run-off is correspondingly high." As an example he cites the Coastal Aquifer in Gaza and Israel, where nitrate concentrations have doubled over the past twenty years. The damage caused by this type of pollution can easily be prevented by various agricultural methods, but authorities are reluctant to impose any regulations that may affect the price of export crops grown on these lands.

As urbanization rates continue to grow throughout the region, the water supply and sewage systems of many Middle Eastern cities can no longer cope with the growing demand. Losses through leakage are a common occurrence in water delivery systems around the world and losses of around 20 percent are considered normal in many European countries. However, in the cities of the Middle East and North Africa the figures are startling: in large cities like Amman more than 50 percent of water is classified as UFW, "unaccounted-for water." While much of this water is lost in the system, some of it is also tapped through illegal connections, a frequent occurrence in Gaza City among others. In Cairo, 40 percent of water that is delivered to municipal users is wasted through faulty water networks, leakage and illegal tapping. Worn-out water delivery systems, burst pipes and leaking taps all contribute to this situation and while authorities are committed to the restoration and renewal of the networks, work is slow. Wastewater is also often not adequately captured so that sewage frequently flows into the surrounding environment or seeps into the groundwater.

Brooks also points to the loss of natural habitat and the role it plays in degrading water quality in the region. The drainage of swamps, the canalization of rivers and the expansion of urban or agricultural land can seriously affect water quality. He cites the example of Bahrain where the reclamation of land to expand urban space not only destroyed the commercial fishing grounds, but also prevented the drainage of agricultural land and increased salinity of groundwater. "Water in place has value," he explains. "Some of these values, as with fisheries and hydro-power, can be measured in conventional economic terms. Other values are partially calculable, as with recreation and tourism.... Finally, water in place supports values that are all difficult to capture in economic terms…as with regulation of river flows, ecological balance, habitat protection, and the sheer beauty of natural sites." An example of this is the Lower Jordan River which is heavily polluted but which is still used by Christian pilgrims who immerse themselves in the water that they see as holy.

## The Encroaching Desert

The water situation in the Middle East is further complicated by the extreme climatic conditions and the effects of climate change. Decreasing rainfall levels, long periods of drought and desertification are all part of this phenomenon. The regions and countries suffering most from this growing aridity are those that depend primarily on rainfall for their water supplies such as Morocco, Sudan, Syria, and Jordan. The rain that does fall in many regions, comes in violent downpours that cause devastating flash floods. "[The Middle East and North Africa region] is one of the few areas in the world to suffer from floods as well as droughts. It is as important to design structures that can withstand high peak flows as to develop livelihood patterns that can survive extended low flows," says Brooks. He adds that average rainfall levels for Middle Eastern countries can be highly misleading, with certain hyper-arid areas receiving as little as

five millimeters a year, which most often corresponds to a single torrential downpour every ten years.

Sudan is one such country where averages can be misleading. If one looks just at the figures, it would appear that the Sudanese have ample supplies with more than 3,000 cubic meters of water per capita per year. The reality however is that this water is very unevenly distributed, with ample resources in the Nile Valley and the subtropical south and extreme aridity in the other areas. The underdeveloped economy and years of conflict in the south and west, mean that infrastructure is minimally developed. Dr Osman Alton of the Ministry of Water Resources in Khartoum says that in the area of Khartoum and to the north, rainfall levels are dropping below the already low yearly average of 200 millimeters. "Around the Nile we do not suffer so much, but the provinces of Kordofan and Darfur in the west have suffered a lot from the lack of rain. Rainfall is their main source of water."

Alton says that desertification is also a growing problem in the north of the country. "Sand encroachment and desertification are a real menace to Sudan: as rainfall patterns become more erratic, the sand threatens fertile land. In some places the sand even moves right up to the banks of the Nile and into the Nile itself forming islands of sand in the river. Date palms are buried up to two-thirds of their height in sand, houses are covered by sand and deserted.... In other places, people build new floors on top of the old houses to be able to get inside. It is terrifying. The sand encroachment happens very quickly as well; the sand particles are fine and uniform and move very quickly across the land." Sheltering belts of drought-resistant plants and trees are now being planted to protect the fertile land, but because of the scale of the problem, it is hard to fight the rapidly spreading desert.

While climate change is part of the cause of the spreading sands in Sudan, deforestation and the disruption of the traditional nomadic routes across the land also play an important role. Dr Mauwwia Sheddad, the president of the Sudanese Environment Conservation Society, says that the last fifty years have been a "disaster of deforestation." "There are people who still remember villages outside the Nile Valley when they were surrounded by forests," he says. "They remember hunting for deer and gazelles. Now their huts are being buried in the sand and there is no life there." In the 1950s 38 percent of the land here was covered in woodlands and acacia trees. Today that figure has fallen to 8 percent. The wood of the acacia has over the years been harvested and used as fuel, leaving the bare land to turn into desert.

Professor Driss El Niel of the University of Omdurman near Khartoum explains that deforestation is however not the only culprit. "The problem also stems from the interference in the traditional nomadic system. Nomads know where to take their cattle, they know the soil types and the capacity of the land. They plan their routes across the desert based on this knowledge. They know how to live in this way and how to use the land well.

"Now, since the government has made efforts to create a more rational grouping of the tribes by organizing the territory and building villages to settle the nomads, the traditional routes have been disrupted. Instead of running north to south, the routes have been displaced and now run east to west, crossing lands that were already ecologically fragile and that cannot sustain the nomadic movements. For instance, the Kennara and Rafaha tribes have been driven off the land between the White and Blue Niles: they used to cross the Blue Nile to spend the summer along the White Nile. The construction of a sugar plant on the Blue Nile has meant they can no longer use the land on the White Nile. Instead they stay in the east, where they are using land that is slowly turning to desert through over-grazing."

Sheddad is sombre about the future, predicting a huge flux of environmental refugees from the desert lands towards the Nile Valley: "If people do not work seriously on the problem of desertification, it will have an enormous impact on Sudan: there will be environmental refugees, there will be conflict and there will be overcrowding in the Nile Valley." In other parts of the Middle East such as Syria, Israel, Jordan and Lebanon, the effects of climate change are less noticeable, as rainy years still appear to alternate with years of drought.

## Agriculture, the Water-Guzzler

In the midst of all these fluctuating variables—soaring population figures, dropping rainfall levels and decreasing water availability per person—there is one constant: agriculture. In most countries in the region, it is the main consumer of water, sucking up between 60 and 90 percent of the supply. Yet governments still subsidize farmers and continue to expand irrigation schemes. This stems partly from a concern over food security. For while these countries can never be self-sufficient, they seek to attain "relative food security," ensuring basic food needs are met. This does not necessarily mean producing those foods that are most consumed, but those that a country can produce with a "comparative advantage"—better and cheaper than other countries. Theib Oweis, a water specialist at the International Center for Agricultural Research in Dry Areas (ICARDA) in Aleppo, explains: "The United States has a comparative advantage to produce wheat; in Jordan it would be ridiculous to try to produce wheat, but there is a comparative advantage to produce strawberries in winter. Egypt has a comparative advantage to produce cotton, in Yemen it is coffee and in the Gulf States it is oil. Everyone has their own comparative advantage, and this means they can exchange goods and ensure food security."

The other reason for supporting agriculture is purely social though, as it effectively limits further urbanization, and supports small-scale subsistence farming in the region. "It is not just economics that affects the use of water in these countries; there is also a strong social dimension," says Oweis. "Most people here live in the countryside and have a rural lifestyle. They depend on the countryside. So water has a very special status in their life. This is why many countries in the region aim to maintain an agricultural society: to ensure stable societies. That is also why there are subsidies; people depend on these. It's not just the money. You also need to evaluate the other aspects that come into the equation such as environment, society and politics. It's fine to say: 'Farmers should not produce rice or wheat because it is costly and uneconomic.' But this means throwing them straight into the dark streets of the cities. And then the cost is higher. The cost of doing nothing is higher than the cost of setting up a system of subsidies and trying to maintain the rural life."

The continued support for agriculture as it exists now is unsustainable. At the same time, as Oweis explained, any kind of reform is fraught with difficulties as this agriculture also represents a way of life that has existed for thousands of years in the Middle East. It is thus easier for governments to maintain the status quo, subsidize agriculture and turn a blind eye to the lowering groundwater levels, the depleting aquifers and the huge wastage that takes place everywhere.

Daniel Hillel, an environmental scientist who has studied water resources in the Middle East and North Africa for years, believes that current water policies in the Middle East have engendered a culture of waste. Despite the growing scarcity, water remains a free good in many Middle Eastern countries, while in others it is heavily under-priced. This means that farmers often undervalue the precious resource, which in turn leads to the production of water-intensive crops and over-irrigation. In Egypt, 30 percent of the irrigated land is dedicated to the cultivation of water-intensive crops like rice and sugar cane; Libyan farmers are still encouraged to grow wheat even in the areas with poor soils and erratic rainfall patterns, while bananas—a tropical and thirsty plant—are grown in Jordan, Lebanon and Israel. The under-pricing of water also leads to widespread over-irrigation. As Hillel comments, "it is a universal fallacy of humans to assume that if a little of something is good, then more must be better." In fact, in irrigation, excessive use of water can have very harmful consequences as it impedes aeration of the soil, induces greater evaporation, which raises the water table and causes salinization, ultimately killing the soil.

Furthermore, traditional methods of irrigation are extremely inefficient. They use earthen canals to convey water to the land, which leads to high levels of seepage and evaporation. The land itself is irrigated by simply letting the water flood the land, entailing losses of 50 to 70 percent. In Syria 93 percent of the land is irrigated by traditional methods and efficiency throughout the country is less than 60 percent.

The main reason for water's undervaluing is its under-pricing, or even, as in Egypt, the absence of pricing of agricultural water. The reasons behind this reluctance to price water at its true value are a complex combination of religious and political factors. In the Muslim world in particular, religion plays an important role in the debate surrounding water pricing. According to Muslim teaching, water is a gift from God that should be freely available to all and the Prophet Mohammed discouraged the selling of water. In several Muslim countries government policy is still influenced by this injunction, despite the fact that other Islamic sources show that water was bought and sold in the time of the Prophet. In the context of water trade and ownership of water, Islam distinguishes between three types of water resources: private, restricted public, and public. The water of a well, for example, is private and can be sold. The water of rivers and springs that run through private land does not belong to the owner in the strict sense of the word: while he has special rights and privileges, other users can use the water for drinking and basic needs. The water of lakes, rivers, underground sources and rain is a public good. It can be used by anybody for drinking and for irrigation.

In practice, many countries nevertheless charge far too little for water. As a consequence, the cost of operating, maintaining and expanding the water supply and wastewater systems is not recovered and network systems are often worn out and leaky. As the quality of services declines, users become more reluctant to pay for the water supply, engendering an unsustainable use of water. In Syria the domestic user only pays a nominal price for water, and Syrian farmers have only recently started paying a fee for water diverted from government irrigation networks. Rates are calculated between $40 and $120 per hectare and are designed to recover part of the cost of operation and maintenance of the network. However out of the total irrigated area, 59 percent of the land is irrigated with water from private—and often illegal—wells. The absence of any control over the water that is pumped from these wells has led to a severe decrease in groundwater levels throughout the country.

In Egypt neither municipal users nor farmers pay the full price for the water they use and monthly water bills in Cairo can be as low as $1. Pricing in agriculture remains a taboo, as I realized during numerous interviews at the Ministry of Water Resources in Cairo, where I received shocked responses from many. "Pricing is a very sensitive issue," engineer Gamil Mahmoud of the Water Policy Advisory Unit explained to me. "Culturally, socially and economically, it is very delicate. And it would actually be quite complicated to introduce a pricing system in Egypt; our irrigation system does not really allow for this."

Among the Arab countries in the region, Morocco and Tunisia were the first to introduce water pricing policies for both domestic users and farmers in the 1960s. They circumnavigated the tricky religious question by saying that the user pays not for the water, but for the service of having it brought to his field or house. "In the past, water was a free good, to which everyone had a right," Abdelslam Zouggar at the Moroccan Ministry of Water Resources in Rabat commented. "But with droughts, increasing population and higher standards of living we have had to rethink this premise. We now work with the management of demand rather than that of supply. This policy will prevent losses and will ensure a more economic management of supplies."

In Morocco the new water policy is being enforced in towns and along the coastal plain where modern farms occupy large parcels of land. But in the secluded valleys in the south, many villages are not even connected to the water system yet and farmers get their water where they can from seasonal rivers or shallow wells, making it hard for the government to charge a fee. In addition, water use efficiency is very low in Morocco with 85 percent of the land being irrigated by traditional methods that have an efficiency of less than 50 percent.

On average urban water rates in the Middle East and North Africa region are one-sixth of the full cost of water provision. Israel forms the only notable exception in this respect, as it is the only country that charges water at its full cost or higher in urban areas, between $0.61 and $1.27 per cubic meter depending on the quantity consumed. But even in Israel where all users pay for water, there is an ongoing debate about the price farmers pay for water.

## Addressing Water Scarcity

There is not one single solution to the growing problem of water scarcity and wastage. The answer lies in a combination of measures that can restore water to its real value. Such measures are increasingly being introduced throughout the region, in some places more successfully than in others.

In the agricultural sector, a combination of appropriate pricing policies and more efficient irrigation systems could already provide huge savings. Modern irrigation techniques, by which water is delivered in closed conduits and applied in small volumes at high frequency to the root zone of crops, offer the greatest opportunities for water conservation. Israel has led the way in the development of this technology, which is known as drip irrigation. Developed in the 1950s, it is seen as the most important invention since the founding of the state and is now being increasingly applied throughout the Middle East and North Africa. While the installation of such drip irrigation devices is costly, in the long run it offers huge savings, not only in direct financial terms but also in terms of water wastage, land degradation due to over-irrigation and the securing of water reserves for future generations. In cities, the repair and modernization of the water supply and wastewater systems can also lead to huge savings.

Besides improving efficiency and thus saving existing supplies, there is a growing interest in alternative sources of water and the additional supplies they could offer. While some of these, such as rainwater harvesting from roofs and the construction of small dams in desert *wadis*, make use of traditional techniques, policy makers and researchers are also investing in the development of new techniques such as desalination and wastewater recycling. The latter can provide an important source of freshwater for irrigation of food and non-food crops, while at the same time preventing untreated sewage from flowing into the sea or seeping into the groundwater, as is today often the case. The use of treated wastewater for irrigation is widespread in Israel, Jordan, Tunisia, and Morocco.

Desalination of brackish and seawater is already widely used in the oil-rich countries of the Gulf such as Kuwait and Saudi Arabia. Despite being very energy intensive in production, desalinated water is likely to play a growing role in the Middle East. Technological advances mean that the price of desalinated water has come down drastically in the last twenty years, and today lies between $0.50 and $1 per cubic meter. Even then, it is unlikely that desalinated water will ever be used on a large scale in agriculture; it will rather be used in urban contexts.

As population figures in the region continue to rise and the movement from rural areas to the larger cities continues, there will also have to be a shift in water allocations, with less water being given to agriculture and more to domestic users. At the same time, birth rates in the Arab countries in the Middle East and North Africa have to be drastically brought down for any solution to be really sustainable.

If implemented rapidly and efficiently, these measures could attenuate the situation of water scarcity. Some water experts however believe that more radical steps should be taken; besides bringing down the birth rate and increasing efficiency and prices, they say that the arid countries of the Middle East should make a decisive move away from traditional agriculture and reorient their economies towards industry and services. Brooks: "The greater question about water and agriculture in [the region] is not whether water is used efficiently in irrigation but whether irrigation is an efficient use of water. In most cases national economies would be stronger and the total output greater if water were transferred from agriculture to industrial or municipal uses." Professor Mohamed Nasr Allam of Cairo University says that in Egypt drastic changes are needed. "The situation in Egypt is very serious," he says. "We have a huge food gap despite the fact that we use all the water we can. And there is no hope of reducing this gap—only of limiting it. Our only option is to move away from agriculture and expand into other sectors. At the moment we still export agricultural produce, even though we know we have to conserve water. We still plant rice and sugar cane, even though they consume great quantities of water. The whole strategy needs to change from the bottom up."

Professor Tony Allan of the School of Oriental and African Studies at the University of London believes that the solution to the Middle East water crisis lies in a shift away from agriculture and the import of food or "virtual water." As crops like wheat are very water-intensive, importing such goods effectively means importing water that is embedded in food. "To raise a tonne of wheat, you need 1,000 tonnes of water. Importing a million tonnes of wheat is the equivalent of importing a billion tonnes (cubic meters) of water," he explains, adding that already today the food imported into the region contains a volume of water that is equivalent to the annual flow of the Nile into Egypt. Today, the percentage of food imports into the region is constantly rising as population figures continue to increase and the available water resources for agriculture decrease. On average, food imports represent 15 to 20 percent of total imports to countries in the Middle East and North Africa. In Egypt this figure rises to 30 percent, while oil-rich Kuwait imports all its food.

But large-scale food importation would have far-reaching consequences for rural societies that are based on traditional agriculture. Making the transition to an economy based on industry and services would almost inevitably entail uprooting this traditional structure. The concept of virtual water focuses mainly on the value of water as a resource for agricultural irrigation, and ignores the values of water in social contexts. The fact that food imports into the region are increasing as a result of growing population and a decrease in water for agriculture is undeniable. But a continuation of this trend doesn't solve the problem of water scarcity and the related problems of population growth, urbanization, climate change and wastage of the resource.

Besides such radical shifts, there is also a growing recognition in the region that policies should focus on reducing demand instead of constantly seeking to increase supply. Measures to curb water use and encourage efficiency include information, education and demonstrations, but also economic incentives. Governments traditionally focused on the provision of new sources of supply, constantly seeking to increase availability and meet the growing demand. Since the 1990s, the focus has shifted to managing the demand of water by seeking

to increase efficiency and change patterns of use. Brooks is a strong advocate of a shift from increasing supply to a reduction and reallocation of demand. "Except for those few nations with enough energy to run desalination plants, greater efficiency in water use and wastewater reuse, or shifts of water from one sector to another, are the only big options left," he says.

One of the most striking elements in this intricate web of factors that contribute to the water crisis in the Middle East is the lack of awareness among the general public. It is like a huge blindfold that is wrapped around the collective consciousness and shields off reality. There are several causes for this blindness, and the causes also vary throughout the region. In countries like Syria, Egypt and Lebanon under-pricing is an important cause of wastage on urban and agricultural levels. A lack of political transparency and a lack of education also play an important role in masking the realities. Nasr Allam says that in Egypt there is a serious lack of awareness among the general public. "I have given lectures and when I tell people what the situation is, they don't believe me: they ask how Egypt can be reclaiming all this land [in the desert] if there is so little water," he says. "Only the specialists are aware of the gravity of the situation.

And I am not just talking about the man in the street; this is also true for educated people." Allam blames the government for this situation: "The government is not transparent and not honest. It will not tell people the truth."

In many Arab countries this lack of awareness surrounding issues of water scarcity is compounded by a lack of education on the subject. "Most people—and I am not just talking about the uneducated classes here—most people have no idea what they are going to face," says Professor Nadhir Al Ansari of Al Al-Bayt University in Jordan. He says that in the Arab world, poverty also contributes to the misuse of the resource: "Those who have low standards of living have no interest in what happens around them, they just take what they can and try to survive." In this context he gives the example of a water pipeline that runs between Azraq and Amman in Jordan, which was riddled with bullet holes a few years ago: farmers had shot holes in the pipe to provide water for their herds, not thinking of the consequences.

Technology and the twenty-four-hour availability of water from a tap further contribute to the regional blindness towards water scarcity. In his research into perceptions of and attitudes to water in the Arava Valley, the Israeli environmental scientist Clive Lipchin revealed this with startling clarity. The Arava Valley runs through southern Israel and Jordan. It is an extremely arid environment with almost no rainfall and the only sources of water are two aquifers that lie deep below the ground. Lipchin conducted a survey among the inhabitants of the Arava Valley, on both sides of the border. In Jordan, he went to Rahmeh, a small Bedouin village with no electricity, no phones and no sewerage system. A single well supplies the water used by the entire village, but fuel shortages and generator breakdowns mean the water can often not be extracted from the well. The villagers here are strongly aware of the water scarcity and do everything to conserve the resource.

On the other side of the border, the Israeli kibbutzim use exactly the same water as their Bedouin neighbors, but here Lipchin received quite different responses. He explains that while people were aware that water scarcity was a problem in the region, they didn't think the problem affected their kibbutz. The fact that they do not feel the scarcity directly at the tap makes them confident that supply will always meet demand. Water consumption levels are therefore much higher and users are less concerned about saving water. Lipchin says there is a false sense of security over water in Israel. "People are disconnected from reality," he says. "The [water distribution] system is so efficient that one never feels the scarcity."

This is the most tragic part of the whole "Middle East water question"—that until it is too late and scarcity becomes physically tangible on a day-to-day basis, people will continue to waste water. In many places scarcity is already a reality: Yemen, the Gaza Strip, Jordan, parts of Syria, Morocco, and Sudan are facing serious water shortages that will only become more severe with time. Professor Mohamed Al-Eryani, a water resources specialist at the United Nations Western

Asia offices in Beirut says the issue is pressing: "The shortage is a reality: in the cities and in the farms, there is real suffering. This is not theoretical. It is happening *now*."

Echoing the words of Nasr Allam in Egypt, Al-Eryani says the issue of water scarcity is being ignored, not just by the general public but also by governments. "Governments don't give water the attention it deserves. This is valid for all countries; it is a core issue from which other issues evolve." In Al-Eryani's eyes the solution can only lie in radical measures. "Tough decisions have to be made: farming activities must be curtailed, political decisions need to be made in function of the water scarcity, not just with economics in mind. The right time will come for this. You see, water is politics and these policy decisions have technical consequences. The political price is not yet right, but politicians will eventually have to confront the issues," he says. "It is sad, because the damage that is being done now could be avoided. By making changes now, disasters could be prevented, even from an economic point of view."

## Notes

1.  A cubit is an ancient unit of length; 1 cubit = 0.524 meters. Originally, a cubit meant the distance from the elbow to the tip of the pharaoh's middle finger, and was thus a measure that varied from pharaoh to pharaoh.
2.  The internationally recognized minimum water supply per person, per year is 1,000 cubic meters. This includes water for the irrigation of crops. If one considers the requirement for domestic use and some modest industry and services, the figure drops to 125 cubic meters per person, per year.
3.  Algeria, Egypt, Iraq, Israel, Jordan, Kuwait, Lebanon, Libya, Morocco, the Palestinian Territories, Oman, Saudi Arabia, Sudan, Syria, Tunisia, Turkey, United Arab Emirates, Yemen.

# 6

# Myths of Concrete and Steel

*"They say dreamers live forever. And I believe we have to let ourselves dream more. That's the problem: we don't dream enough. We have to look at all the options and see that this project deserves consideration. Some say it is fiction, but I believe it can work. It could make the desert bloom in the true sense of the word and solve poverty in Africa once and for all."—Saad Alghariani, professor of water science and engineering, Al Fateh University, Tripoli, Libya*

## Monuments to Water

The Sanctuaire des Eaux of Zaghouan lies nestled on the slopes of Mount Zaghouan near Tunis. Surrounded by dense forests, the crumbling temple marks the ancient source that for centuries fed the city of Carthage. Though the structure today lies in ruins, one can still guess at the ornamented grandeur that this monument to water must have exuded when it was built in the second century AD. Two broad staircases curve their way up to the shrine, a semi-circular structure with alcoves, which used to contain statues of nymphs and deities. In the middle, a water basin now lies dry, but in the times of the Emperor Hadrian, it was the starting point of a waterway that stretched from Mount Zaghouan across the Oued Miliane to Carthage and the imperial Antonine Baths.

The aqueduct of Zaghouan was one of the longest aqueducts in the empire, a gray serpent of stone and mortar that traced an aquatic lifeline over 132 kilometers. Built in 120 AD, the aqueduct brought 32 million liters of water a day to the splendid Antonine Baths. Looking down over the plain today, one can distinguish the sprawling capital of Tunisia, Tunis, which lies on the site of ancient Carthage. Parts of the aqueduct can also still be traced through the landscape, the petrified legacy of the water lines that the Romans drew over the land. From the hilltop, the artificial river runs underground and descends into the plain, where elevated arches carry the water—sometimes up to a height of thirty-four meters—to the coast.

Of all the natural resources, water has, without a doubt, the greatest power over man. There is the obvious and very tangible physical power of water—its purifying, life-sustaining and life-giving properties—and its destructive ability. These are indisputable and real. But then there is the more complicated and abstract issue of the symbolic value man has attributed to water, making it today a potent tool for politicians and whole nations to express their power. More than any other natural resource, water seems to trigger a desire for control in man. The fluid and uncontrolled liquid meandering aimlessly through the landscape seems to be asking to be contained, reined in and disciplined in a nice straight canal, or behind a large dam.

The sanctuary built at the spring on Mount Zaghouan was a monument to water, but also an homage the Romans paid to their own prowess and skill. They were proud of their ability to tame the fickle waters that ran through their empire. Around Rome, more than a dozen aqueducts were built over the centuries, crossing valleys on high colonnades like the highways of today. East of the city, there was even a real spaghetti junction as five aqueducts intersected and twisted around each other on their journey to the imperial capital.

Practical and sophisticated, the grand aqueducts were seen as the essence of Roman civilization, and they went wherever Rome went, leaving an indelible mark on landscapes from France to Syria and from Germany to the Tunisian coast. Today awe-inspiring structures like the Pont du Gard in France, the aqueduct of Caesarea in Israel and the aqueduct of Segovia in Spain still survive as a legacy to the Roman genius.

Writing in a first-century AD treatise on aqueducts, the Roman senator and water commissioner, Sextus Julius Frontinus, proudly declared: "With such an array of indispensable structures carrying so many aqueducts, compare, if you please, the Pyramids, or the famous but useless works of the Greeks." The Roman structures were also long admired by Arab writers who described them as one of the wonders of Africa, and compared them to the pyramids of Egypt.

But were the aqueducts really as indispensable as Frontinus claimed? Trevor Hodge, a Canadian professor of classics, says that while we are often led to believe that the aqueducts were built to supply clean drinking water and ensure public hygiene in the cities of the Roman Empire, in fact they were usually built to supply the large and luxurious bathhouses. Most Roman cities developed without aqueducts, depending on the water of wells and cisterns, and the aqueduct was only built later too supply extra water, mainly to the baths. Thus, says Hodge, the aqueducts were not built to fulfill a basic human need; they were a luxury, a mark of prestige and prosperity.

Indeed, the construction of these waterways was ruinously expensive: the Roman historian Pliny writes that the town of Nicomedia nearly went bankrupt over the construction of a relatively small aqueduct. Frontinus recorded that the Aqua Marcia aqueduct near Rome cost 180 million sesterces, while the nearby Aqua Claudia aqueduct came at nearly double the price of 350 million sesterces. A public bathhouse was a bargain in comparison at 400,000 sesterces, while you could have yourself a triumphal arch built for a mere 77,000 sesterces.

And yet the Romans felt it was worth it. For with the aqueduct, they brought to town an uninterrupted and abundant flow of water that was not only used in baths, but in public fountains, cascades and water channels. They were monuments to water, celebrations of abundance adorned with nymphs and columns. Hodge comments: "Extravagances such as this surely reflect more than just a pride in the water system. They reflect the particular form that took: an ostentatious insistence on abundance, or, as we would now call it, conspicuous consumption."

Before the Romans, the Greeks and the Etruscans had also built aqueducts, but compared to their Roman counterparts, the Greek waterways were more modest. Not only were they shorter in length, they also formed a less obtrusive feature in the landscape. Where the Romans rigidly mapped their aqueducts along straight lines, the Greeks were more willing to adapt themselves to the curves and contour lines, integrating the structure in the surroundings and using any natural elements that could support or strengthen the construction. The Romans on the other hand, boldly superimposed their monuments on the landscape as artificial blocks, like physical statements of their dominance over nature.

In his book on dams, *Dammed*, the British environmental journalist, Fred Pearce, says that this Roman vision of nature had considerable influence on the engineers of the Renaissance and the modern era who always admired the Roman structures: "The Romans imparted from the ancient to the modern world a vision of nature tamed, remade in the image of engineering, of the land separated from the water. It was a world in which water flowing to the sea was wasted, in which marshes were for draining and floods for controlling."

Hodge also draws a parallel between modern dams and the Roman aqueducts. For just as aqueducts were admired and treasured in Roman times, today the dam is looked upon as not just a functional structure but as a monument. Dams are not just pieces of infrastructure; they are tourist attractions, with car parks, visitor centers and gift shops. The transformation of a functional water engineering work into a monument to water and engineering is undoubtedly best represented in the Marathon Dam, which was built in the 1920s in Greece, and which is entirely covered with panels of Pentelic marble like a temple.

But even these ancient and more recent monuments of self-admiration appear modest compared to some of the projects and "visionary" dreams alive today. As the threat of large-scale water scarcity in the Middle East and North Africa grows, politicians, engineers and even amateurs let their imagination run wild—it seems there is no limit to the possibilities. As Saad Alghariani, a Libyan professor of water science and engineering, commented: "These days, anything goes and anyone can propose solutions: Western experts, consultants, academics, politicians, local teams.... Water is big business; it's an open market for technology." His words came back to me as I listed the range of fantastic and ambitious schemes I had heard about. A Jesuit priest living in the desert east of Damascus believes the course of Syria's rivers should be reversed to provide water to the dry south; a professor at Cairo's American University told me about the idea of building a pipeline from the Congo River Basin to Egypt, while Israel has in the past raised the idea of bringing the water of the Nile to Israel by the construction of a canal through the Sinai Desert; in the meantime, Libya has tentative plans to build pipelines under the Mediterranean to import water from Spain and Italy—countries which are themselves struggling with water scarcity.

Those are the fantasies; on the ground, the projects are often even more extravagant in scale and ambition. Thus Egypt's Western Desert, with its summer temperatures of 50 °C, is to be turned into a second Nile valley, a "New Egypt" that will prosper alongside the old one. In Libya, water that has been conserved beneath the searing sands of the Sahara for more than 10,000 years, is today being pumped through a 3,500-kilometer network of pipelines and consumed at such a rate that reserves will probably be drained by the end of the century. And Turkey is building a series of twenty-two dams and nineteen hydroelectric power plants on the Tigris and Euphrates as part of a project that—if we believe the politicians—will transform the arid, underdeveloped southeastern corner of the country into the breadbasket of Europe and the Middle East.

## A Source of Everlasting Prosperity

The head of the Aswan State Information Center, Mohammed Hossein, was a fat little man with a limp and a tendency to sweatiness. Smiling like a clammy Cheshire cat, he was waiting for me at Aswan's train station and led me to the "special taxi" that was waiting outside. He told me it belonged to his "special friend" who would take us straight to the Aswan High Dam, where I was to get "special VIP treatment."

As we drove along the Nile Corniche past the large cruise ships that sat placidly waiting for tourists, the driver switched on the tape recorder. Suddenly Marlène Dietrich was with us, singing about Berlin in the autumn—a rather incongruous combination given the blinding summer heat and the desert landscape. Hossein quickly switched the tape off and started giving a little speech about the Aswan High Dam. It was, he told me with well-rehearsed gravity, the most important structure since the pyramids, a symbol of Egypt's sovereignty and power. He reeled off a list of impressively large figures: the dam is 111 meters high and nearly four kilometers long. Its reservoir, Lake Nasser, has a capacity of 140.5 billion cubic meters and covers 6,000 square kilometers. "It is our savior," he concluded solemnly. "It has allowed us to plant more crops and it has saved us from hunger." He was quiet for a moment, and sighed painfully. Then he turned to me and with a meek voice explained that he was very ill and had many children, thus, I rightly assumed, laying the groundwork for a groveling request of "more baksheesh" at the end of the day.

We had left Aswan by now and were driving along a desert road. In the distance a forest of electricity pylons and generators announced the High Dam, one of the largest dams in the world. Built of solid granite block, the dam is the work of 55,000 men. They spent eleven years from 1960 to 1971 erecting this structure that has altered Egypt's relation to the Nile so fundamentally. Hossein, continuing his marketing pitch for the dam, announced that the granite in the dam would allow the construction of seventeen Great Pyramids of Giza. "It is the greatest thing we have ever built," he said proudly.

The first Aswan Dam, which still stands at the foot of its larger sibling, today looks like a quaint Victorian attempt at taming the Nile waters. Built in 1902 by the British engineer William Willcocks, it allowed for the storage of floodwaters during the dry summer months. Its capacity was limited, but this was a conscious move as British hydrologists did not want to expand the storage of water in an area with such a harsh climate; instead they had drawn up a scheme to secure Egypt's water at the head of the White Nile in the Equatorial Lakes. The climate here was milder and the lakes deeper, so that there would be less evaporation. But Egypt did not trust upstream Sudan, Kenya, and Uganda with its water and after the revolution of 1952, the Free Officers declared their determination to control the waters of the Nile. Under the leadership of the then-still Lieutenant-Colonel and later President of Egypt, Gamal Abdel Nasser, they announced the plans for a grand project that would, in Nasser's words, create the "largest lake ever shaped by human hand" and be a "source of everlasting prosperity."

Nasser grew lyrical when talking of the dam. In his later public speeches he proclaimed that it would transform the motherland from "a semi-colony, help-less and governed by the British Ambassador, to a Great State." It soon became more than just a dam: it was a layered and symbolic structure that would al-low not only the expansion of agriculture and the generation of electricity, but also liberate Egypt from the clutches of colonialism, imperialism and a whole range of other evils including tyranny, occupation, despotism and domination. As the first stone of the dam was laid in 1960, Nasser painted the image not of a dam but of a living being that would deliver not only the Egyptians, but all Arabs: "[T]he High Dam is more than a mere mute monument of solid rock on which one may put wreaths of flowers; it is a live creative monument; it is a new rejuvenating life, an existing developing power as well as a support, a bulwark and a storehouse for battles that dot the long way to the attainment of the great Arab objectives."

Unfortunately for Nasser, the dam could not be built on grand rhetoric and lofty hopes alone, and financing for the great scheme was hard to find. The World Bank and U.S. aid agencies had refused to finance the project on the basis that there should first be a water-sharing agreement with Sudan. Immediately, a furious and defiant Nasser announced the nationalization of the Suez Canal, an important international trade route between Europe and the Persian Gulf and Asia. Nasser declared that the tolls collected in the canal would "pay for the dam" within five years. The move immediately triggered an international crisis with Britain, France, Israel, and later also the Soviet Union, the United States and the United Nations getting involved. Nasser emerged from the crisis as the hero of Arab nationalism and the still-unbuilt dam paraded as the symbol of Arab

**Map 4**
**The Egyptian Nile Valley and the High Aswan Dam,**
**Lake Nasser and the Toshka project**

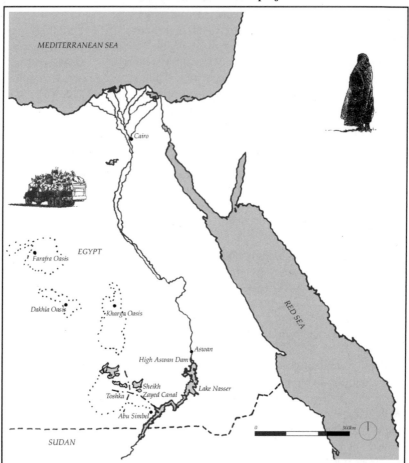

determination and opposition to the "imperialist stooges." Later it also became a monument of the Cold War and of Arab socialism, when Nasser turned to the Soviet Union and gained support for the financing and construction of the project from President Nikita Khrushchev.

A Soviet "Friendship Monument" still stands at the site of the dam today as a legacy to the collaboration. The tall circular monument in the shape of a stylized lotus flower is engraved with an elaborate allegory: the valiant Soviet worker gives water to the poor Egyptian peasant who in turn harvests perfectly shaped bushels of wheat; Russian and Egyptian engineers are depicted working shoulder to shoulder as the dam rises up before them, while quotes from the Koran entwined with the Soviet hammer and sickle surround all the scenes.

Hossein smiled sweatily and gave an extensive commentary on the meaning of the relief. Later, at the nearby visitor center, I was shown to the "VIP lounge" and he damply whispered to me: "The president himself comes here," as he gave me a significant look that again implied more baksheesh.

I managed to escape from the VIP tour and made my way onto the dam over a wide asphalted road. For being one of the largest dams in the world, it was strangely unimposing. Other dams had left me with a sense of awe at their overwhelming size, fascination with the grand folly behind them, or filled with admiration for the human genius. Here, I felt indifference. Looking south over the boundless expanse of Lake Nasser, I felt nothing—perhaps because it was too large and therefore impossible to gage its size when standing on it. And yet, the dam has had a huge impact, not just on its immediate environment, but also on the whole country.

Displacing more than 50,000 Nubians in Sudan and Egypt and flooding dozens of pharaonic monuments—and those are seen as the minor effects—the Aswan High Dam is still a controversial project. Some say it is Egypt's savior and an engineering wonder, while others flatly condemn it as a complete disaster. The advantages of the dam are clearly identifiable: not only has it protected Egypt from the droughts and famines that plagued Ethiopia and Sudan in the 1980s, the steady water flow has also allowed Egypt to step up its agricultural production to two or three crops a year, thus boosting the production of cash crops for export such as cotton, rice, and sugar cane—all, incidentally, large consumers of water.

The disadvantages are perhaps less easily discernible, yet in the long term they are at least as important. For while the dam has transformed the unpredictable Nile into a constant and dependable source, it has severely affected the quality of the water that now flows north from Aswan. The waters of the Nile were legendary for their power to bring life to the desert. In fact, it was not the water itself that fertilized the banks of the Nile, but the rich silt that the water carried along with it from the Ethiopian Highlands and Sudan. Since the construction of the High Dam, this silt remains trapped at the bottom of Lake Nasser and the water that flows north towards the Mediterranean today needs to be mixed with chemical fertilizers in order to make the soil productive. Staunch critics of the dam in Sudan delighted in telling me that all the electricity generated by the High Dam goes to powering a fertilizer plant, so that the net electricity gained thanks to the dam is nil. While this is probably not quite accurate, the construction of the dam and the subsequent trapping of the silt have made Egypt one of the largest consumers of fertilizer in the world. The water quality is further affected by the high level of evaporation in Lake Nasser. The torrid desert climate at Aswan causes the evaporation of nearly half a million liters of water per second or a fifth of the river's annual flow. And while Egyptian engineers claim the dam's life span is several hundreds of years, the question still remains what will happen when the reservoir has filled up with silt.

However, the dam's most invisible but most far-reaching effect lies not in its physical presence, but in its image as a "source of everlasting prosperity." Mohamed Sid Ahmed, a political journalist and commentator in Cairo, believes that the High Dam has given Egyptians an illusory sense of safety over water. "Much has changed with the High Dam: it saved us from disaster during the droughts in Ethiopia and Sudan, but it also means that people are less aware of the value of the water they use. They take it for granted in a way and don't see it as a precious resource. They think they can just press a button and that the water will come. This could lead to bad surprises."

## A Playground for Engineers

This sense of invulnerability has also made the Egyptians doggedly over-ambitious. From the moment of its conception it was clear that the dam was not only being built to secure water for the irrigation of existing farmland, it would also fulfil the Egyptian dream of "blooming the desert." It was not enough that the Nile Valley would be transformed, the scale of the project meant the whole country had to be transformed. In a speech he gave in 1960, Nasser regally spoke of "opening new horizons," announcing the reclamation of two million acres of desert land. "We only exploit four percent of the Egyptian territory; we must exploit it all. Today, my dear brethren, we are exploring the possibility of creating a new valley in the Western Desert, parallel to the Nile Valley.… We have lived on the banks of the Nile for thousands of years, and gave up the desert. But the miracle that will happen is the blooming of this desert beside the Nile."

By focussing on this promise of new land, the government could quietly ignore the need to reorganize traditional agriculture. The desert was a clean slate, a new beginning for Egypt. Nasser believed that the new society in the desert could serve as a model for conversion of the old lands to modern, collective agriculture. From the beginning of the 1960s until 1972, Egypt attempted the reclamation of vast tracts of desert land west of the Nile and in the Delta region. But bad planning and even worse management of the projects led to total failure. Most farmers who had left the Nile Valley to seek their fortune in the new Egypt were forced to return to their villages empty-handed after a few years.

And yet, even after witnessing the failure of so many reclamation projects, Egypt has today embarked on its most ambitious reclamation project to date. Lost in the vast emptiness of the Western Desert near Lake Nasser, 7,000 men are working sixteen-hour shifts to complete the grand "South Valley Development Project." Trucks and tractors lie scattered among piles of building materials and heaps of sand: the place looks like a playground for giants, abandoned in mid-play by a colossal child who carelessly left his toys in the sandpit.

This is Egypt's largest and most ambitious project since the dam; what the government promises will be "a second Egypt," the "New Valley" that will soon thrive alongside the old one. By 2017 and at a cost of $66 billion, the South Valley Development Project will reclaim and irrigate 2,340 square kilometers of desert land using water from three sources: Lake Nasser, the *wadis* close to the Nile and subterranean wells. The government promises that as the largest of a series of "mega national projects," the South Valley Development Project will increase Egypt's arable land by 10 percent, creating 2.8 million new jobs and attracting a population of 16.2 million people to the new desert towns that will arise here.

With its giant Mubarak Pumping Station, the fifty-kilometer Sheikh Zayed Canal and its numerous branches that take water from Lake Nasser to new agricultural lands, the Toshka Project is undoubtedly the most impressive component of the project. Financed by the Egyptian government and large international investors including the Saudi Prince Al Waleed ibn Talal, this hi-tech agricultural project takes advantage of local climatic conditions. Seasonal crops like strawberries, asparagus and grapes are produced during the winter months, and exported to cold northern climates with large profit margins.

The project's primary aim however, is to draw populations from the overcrowded Nile Valley to these new lands. Dr Dia El Din El Qosy, a senior advisor to the Minister of Water Resources and Irrigation, says the project will bring new life and livelihood to an area that was until now barren and uninhabited. "The Toshka Project is motivated by social reasons: we want to relieve Egypt's overcrowded and overpopulated towns, cities and urban centers by creating this new space, and by creating new employment opportunities. This part of the country has been neglected both from a social and a political point of view. We now want to bring development to the region," he says. El Qosy explains that this development will take place in several stages: "First we will focus on agriculture, then on the agro-industry, then on industry, tourism, and so on, until we create a vibrant, full community."

But as I stood in the vast emptiness of the Western Desert amid trucks and piles of construction debris, I found it hard to picture the vibrant, full communities that El Qosy had talked about. And as the midday sun beat down on the toiling workers, it was also hard to imagine Egyptians would prefer the heat-stricken wasteland of Toshka to the green familiarity of the Nile Valley. As one official in Cairo explained: "People in Egypt have a very strong link with the Nile Valley. In our minds the desert is associated with death and cemeteries. It is not easy to convince people to move to the desert."

But higher salaries reflect the tough conditions here and authorities are confident this will form an incentive for people to move to Toshka. El Qosy explains there will be other advantages too like tax breaks and subsidies, high-quality services, schools, and hospitals. Hussein El Gibaaly from the Ministry of Housing sees many factors that will draw people from the overcrowded Nile Valley to this new Egypt: cheaper housing and land, higher salaries and, most importantly, thousands of new jobs. "And then of course there is an airport near Abu Simbel," he says. "This is very important. It will make people feel connected to the rest of the country. They will feel they are not totally isolated in a remote area, knowing that there are direct connections to Cairo and Aswan every day." Apparently Gibaaly believes that knowing one can get out of a place can form an incentive to move there.

Both internationally and within Egypt, Toshka is regarded with much skepticism. Egyptians are generally wary of the project and many see it merely as an expression of the president's power. One shopkeeper in Aswan said: "Toshka is bad. It is bad for Egypt, it is bad for the Egyptians. The only person it is good for, is Mubarak. It is his pyramid." Political commentator Mohammed Sid Ahmed also has doubts: "There has been too much secrecy around this project. It has never been seriously discussed. They say there are feasibility studies, but is this true? Or were they just made up in haste, to justify the immense scale of the project? I am not enthusiastic about this project."

Others doubt whether the project is economically and strategically viable. With a population of 74 million and a water quota of 55.5 billion cubic meters per year, Egyptians have about 750 cubic meters of water per person per year, bringing Egypt below the internationally acknowledged water poverty line of 1,000 cubic meters. Given Egypt's high birth rates this situation is only going to get worse. And despite government initiatives to rationalize water use and limit wastage, the hard fact remains that Egypt doesn't have much water, leading many to question whether reclaiming more land in the hottest part of the country is wise.

Critics also say that most of the income from the project will go to the international investors instead of being reinvested in the Egyptian economy. Dr Mohamed Nasr Allam, a professor of irrigation engineering at Cairo University, comments: "Economically this project is not wise: we are giving the income from our water and land to foreigners who are developing large, mechanized farms that require limited labor force."

As an engineer, Jan Bron, a Dutchman working on various projects in Egypt, recognizes the Toshka Project as a great engineering feat, but he predicts the project will fail from a social point of view: "From an engineering point of view it is a great project: the largest pumping station in the world, the irrigation of thousands of hectares of land. Basically it is a playground for engineers. For now it is still justifiable and when it does finally go wrong, others will be in power. This is the way it works here: short-term planning to keep the president happy. Mubarak needed his pyramid and this is it. But the idea of sending the overflow of people from the Delta and the Valley to Toshka is delusional. I think the project will fail disastrously."

In a heated parliamentary debate in April 2006, MPs criticized the project saying that what had been described to the Egyptian population as a dream, "the country's fourth pyramid" and a "beautiful vision" in 1997, had turned into a nightmare. They claimed that the project had until now failed to meet any of its objectives and that instead of the millions of jobs that were meant to be generated through it, only 750 had been created, while the project had exceeded the budget by many millions of Egyptian pounds. Minister of Water Resources Mahmoud Abu Zeid however denied the claims and said that the project was on schedule and that it was of critical importance if Egypt were to meet the pressure from population growth.

Down at Toshka, engineers working at the site admit life there is tough. Abdel Fateh, the general site manager, and Abdel Hafez, a design engineer, say heat, long hours and homesickness take their toll off the men. Fateh explains: "Life here is difficult. There are no women, no children, there is no entertainment. Work is our only entertainment. When we go back to Aswan, we are so happy to see people that we want to shake hands with everyone in the street. Life here is hard."

Meanwhile in Cairo, an urban myth about the Toshka Project is doing the rounds: the reason it was built in such a rush was that the region around the High Dam has become geologically unstable and water needed to be evacuated from Lake Nasser as quickly as possible. As it goes with urban myths, no one knows whether it is true or not, or where it comes from, but the skeptical Egyptians like to speculate about these things. Thus there is another rumor about a German book that describes the collapse of the Aswan High Dam and the devastating ten-meter wall of water that subsequently washes through the valley destroying all of Egypt. Unsurprisingly, this book—of which no one knows the title—is banned in Egypt.

## The World's Eighth Wonder

Wearing a small blue beret and a chequered blue and white jacket, Professor Saad comes striding into the lobby of the Beach Hotel Annex in Tripoli. It is 8:30 in the morning on Sunday, the beginning of the new working week in Libya, but the professor has taken the day off to talk to me about water. He pulls a pack of cigarettes from his pocket as he sits back in the flowery velvet sofa across from me. Professor Saad Alghariani is a water expert, a professor of water science and engineering at Al-Fateh University in Tripoli. With his straggly gray beard, his horn-rimmed spectacles and quirky beret, he certainly has the look of an absent-minded professor.

As he fumbles with his pack of cigarettes, he asks: "You don't mind if I smoke do you? Unfortunately, I am a heavy smoker." And immediately: "Do you want some coffee? I think I want some coffee." He signals to a young boy behind the reception desk and orders a small espresso with a dab of foamed milk. "*Macchiato*," he says in Arabized Italian, the legacy of thirty years of Italian rule in Libya in the early twentieth century. Alghariani knows everything about water in Libya, and, as I would soon see, he has opinions about nearly everything else as well. First he talked about water—its use in Roman times, the current crisis and its possible solutions— but the conversation soon trailed off and as Alghariani had his second and third *macchiatos*, he told me about nomadic Tuareg culture, his views on the future of immigration in Europe, and the role of pan-Arab ideology in current politics, flitting from one subject to another like a restless bird. But eventually he returned to his pet subject and Libya's engineering pride: the Great Manmade River (GMR).

Hailed by Libyan engineers as the World's Eighth Wonder, this is the largest engineering project in the world, a 3,500-kilometer network of pipelines with hundreds of pumping stations that bring water from subterranean sources in the southern Sahara to the densely populated coastal strip. These pure reserves of spring water took several 10,000 years to accumulate in the layers of sandstone that lie deep under the desert sand. Now they are being pumped up from a depth of 450 meters and, at the current rate of consumption, they will probably be used up in the space of 100 years. The pipes through which the water is then led are large enough to drive a truck through and every day 6.5 million cubic meters flows through them. The list of components for this project is suitably impressive: 5 million tons of cement, 2 million kilometers of pre-stressed wiring and 25 million square meters of steel cylinders were used to bring water to the people. Cost: $27 billion.

It is a project of mythical proportions, not only because of its superhuman scale, but also because of the symbolic power of the water that is transported through the pipes to "green the desert." This water is no longer simply a natural resource; together with the gargantuan infrastructure that surrounds it, it is a monument to human control over nature, and, more specifically, to Colonel Qadhafi's power to transform a lifeless expanse of desert into a green fertile land. To underline this, the pipes of the Manmade River are painted emerald green, the color of Islam, of Qadhafi's Green Book and, the Colonel hopes, the color of the Libyan Desert once his masterpiece is completed. Like the Roman fountains from which a profusion of water gushed and cascaded twenty-four hours a day, the Great Manmade River is the substantiation of Qadhafi's heroic attempt to "make water available wherever it is needed"—even in the middle of the Sahara Desert. Viability was secondary in this project and when told that the water had to be pumped over 100-meter dunes in places, Qadhafi said that with the will of Allah, water could be made to "rise above the Empire State Building."

The story of Libya's national project goes back to the 1960s when the character of the newly independent state changed for good with the finding of large oil reserves in the southern desert. Until then, the country had scraped by, earning money from the sale of scrap metal parts that had been left trailing in the desert after the war, and collecting rent from land that was used by the American and British military. Now, overnight, a country that had been one of the poorest in the world after the Second World War, was transformed into a wealthy oil state where annual per capita incomes rose from $25 in 1960 to an average of $1,750 in 1969.

Captain Mu'ammar al-Qadhafi's military takeover of the country in 1969 marked a further turning point for Libya. The twenty-eight-year-old captain ousted the Sanusi royal family and launched his "Everlasting People's Revolution," a regime that was heavily inspired by nationalist, pan-Arab and socialist ideologies. Thanks to the newly found oil reserves, the standards of living increased dramatically in the "Great Socialist People's Libyan Arab Jama-hiriya," as did population figures, a combination which proved disastrous for the country's water supplies. With 95 percent of the country covered by deserts, water reserves in Libya have always been limited. There is little rain and there are no major rivers so that the population had traditionally relied on the water from shallow wells along the green coastal strip. The system was maintained during the period of colonial rule under the Italians, but the rise in demand that occurred during the oil boom led to a rapid decrease in groundwater levels. This in turn led to the intrusion of seawater along the Mediterranean coast, making the water unsuitable for use.

By 1980 almost half of the country's food supplies were being imported and water scarcity had become a real problem. Various solutions were considered, including water imports and desalination, but the mining of plentiful subter-ranean sources in the southern deserts was found to be the cheapest option. The unexpected water reserves were found by engineers drilling for oil in the 1960s and the thousands of cubic meters of new-found water would now serve the revolution, for the young leader planned to not only provide water to the people, but also to the land and to his vision of a green Libya. Qadhafi first encouraged the population to move south where the new water resources had been found and where he planned to build giant desert farms, but by 1983 it was clear that the people were not moving anywhere, so the water was brought to the people through the Great Manmade River.

The project, which is being built in five stages over a period of twenty-five years, is comprised of two branches, which bring water from two underground sources in the south of the country to the two main towns in the north, Tripoli and Benghazi. Construction started in 1984 and by 2004 two phases had been completed and phase three was under construction. Today 70 percent of the water of the Great Manmade River is used for the irrigation of crops as wheat, barley and a variety of fruits and vegetables, which are planted on the 135,000 hectares of new farmland. The fact that most of this high-quality water goes to agriculture has received heavy criticism from foreign observers. They say it is unwise to plant such water-thirsty crops as wheat in a region where 40 to 60 percent of the water used for irrigation is lost through evaporation. But Libya is a country emerging from more than a decade of international sanctions, and food security is still an important issue for its inhabitants.

Still, the Saharan wells will not flow forever and while the Colonel has reassured his people that there are "several hundred years of potential produc-tion" from the wells, experts in Libya and elsewhere estimate it to be more in the region of fifty to 100 years. Alghariani explains that no one knows exactly how much water is hidden below that vast sand sea in the south, or how long the supply will last. "We are now drilling between 100 and 500 meters to reach water. As time passes we may have to go down to 1,000 meters. And then in 100 or 200 years there may be no water left at all." By then, he says, there will be other solutions, like desalination. Thinking like a real engineer and working under the presumption that with technology anything is possible, Alghariani muses that by then, the course of the Great Manmade River will perhaps be reversed so that treated water from the coast can be brought to populations in the south—who will of course have no water anymore as it will all have been used up by the northerners.

Over a lunch of pizzas and cheeseburgers in an American-style diner, Alghariani is sombre about the future of the Middle East: high birth rates, modern lifestyles, pollution and climate change all mean that demand has outgrown supply. The rich countries of the region—the oil-rich countries of the Gulf, the industrialized economy of Israel, and also oil-rich Libya—can face the coming scarcity by introducing new, costly technologies. But countries like Jordan, Yemen, Syria, and Tunisia do not have the means to invest in such modern technologies and are struggling to fill the gap between the demand of a growing population in a modern society and the dwindling supplies.

"This is the problem in North Africa: we never plan beyond the next ten years. Most decisions are taken with expediency in mind; social impacts and other ramifications are not considered." While there are still vast reserves to be drawn upon, Alghariani insists on the need for research into new methods of water resource development. "When using a non-renewable resource, the additional cost of research into new methods should always be taken into account," he explains. He calls this the "depletion cost": the hidden cost of using a non-renewable resource. "The budget of the GMR should include a sum for research into desalination and water imports." While the idea is of course very sensible, I doubt that planners and politicians will ever take such considerations into account. Alghariani agrees: "Sustainability is a term that has been used too much, and that no longer has any value, yet the issues behind it are important. It is up to us, the specialists, to raise awareness among planners of the need to provide for future generations. Not to the average man, he will not be aware of this, but planners should be made to understand the importance of sustainability."

As he lights another cigarette after the meal, Alghariani sits back and sighs. "You may wonder why I even bother—no one listens to us. You can repeat the message over and over and the politicians will keep on being short-sighted. So why do I still work eight hours a day? I will tell you: I work for my children and for my children's children and for their grandchildren. They are the future. Decision makers should be made to realize the importance of acting now for the future." And just as I start thinking that more people like Alghariani should be put in charge of water management instead of some of the politicians I have spoken to so far, he tells me about *his* Project—without a doubt the most extravagant personal folly on my little list of grand water visions.

## Star Trek and the Dreams of Libyan Engineers

After getting stuck in an hour-long traffic jam caused by Qadhafi's passing motorcade, we are now in Alghariani's office at the university. He is pacing about, shifting stacks of paper on his desk. "There is a general rule," he says full of exasperation, "when you look for something, you never find it." He is looking for a newspaper cutting, an article he wrote for *Al Arab* newspaper. "Ah!" he exclaims, "here we are." He unfolds the creased page-long article and smoothes it down on an empty lab table. I cannot read any of it, but there is a large map of Africa in the center of the page. "This is the Congo River Project," Alghariani announces solemnly. "It could make the desert bloom in the true sense of the word and solve poverty in Africa once and for all."

He explains that he was inspired by the ideas of Herman Sörgel, a German architect and engineer who lived in the first half of the twentieth century. Believing that there were no limits to modern engineering, he launched a series of futuristic schemes including the construction of a "super dam" across the Straits of Gibraltar. This scheme would not only allow the reclamation of new land in the Mediterranean Basin; it would also transform it into a huge power plant that could supply all of Europe, Africa and Western Asia with electricity.

Sörgel's plans for Africa were just as grandiose, though they were not necessarily designed for the benefit of the Africans themselves; instead he hoped to turn the "empty" continent—which in his eyes was void of culture or history—into a "territory actually useful to Europe." Developed in the 1930s, the Congo River Project was set on a backdrop of colonialism and the rise of Nazism in Germany. The European powers were dividing up the last remaining bits of Africa, and Germany was left to collect the scraps. But as Adolph Hitler's power grew, German Nazis started believing in a new world order, in which they would inherit all of the French and British colonies in Africa. With their great natural and mineral wealth, Central and Western Africa were of particular interest to the Germans; North Africa would be left in the hands of the Italians who already controlled Libya.

Sörgel immediately saw potential in the Congo River: as the continent's largest river in terms of annual discharge, its waters could green the desert. He conceived of a plan to dam the river and create a large lake in its river basin, a huge body of renewable freshwater in the center of the continent. Sörgel said that by blocking the course of the Congo, he was in fact restoring the area to its prehistoric state, when the Congo Basin had been a large lake surrounded by high mountains. It had all gone wrong many thousands of years ago, when the water had found its way between the mountains and started flowing out to sea, entirely upsetting the natural balance. Sörgel believed that by re-flooding the area, the original state would be restored. Of course millions of hectares of rainforest would be flooded and millions of people would be displaced, but that was secondary if one considered the benefits.

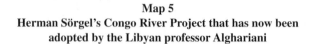

Map 5
Herman Sörgel's Congo River Project that has now been
adopted by the Libyan professor Alghariani

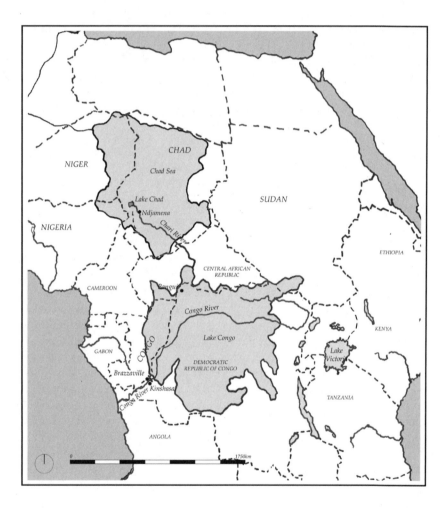

First of all the rising waters would eradicate the breeding ground of dangerous tropical diseases such as malaria, yellow fever and sleeping sickness. But the flooding of the Congo Basin would have impacts far beyond Western Africa: over time the new "Lake Congo" would be saturated and the water would start flowing northwards through the Chari River which would function as an overflow channel and bring the excess water to the severely depleted Lake Chad. Here again, the new water in Lake Chad would restore the situation of 10,000 years ago. Sörgel renamed this ur-Lake Chad the "Sea of Chad" and predicted that it too would overflow, forming a channel that would cross the Sahara and link Central Africa to the Mediterranean.

Sörgel's dream never made it beyond the drawing board. Eight years after his death in 1952, the Atlantropa Institute, which had been founded to study the technical, financial and political viability of his projects, was quietly dissolved, ostensibly condemning the grandiose vision to the realm of Star Trek enthusiasts—the Gibraltar super dam is featured in Gene Roddenberry's 1979 book version of *Star Trek: The Motion Picture*—and eccentric Libyan water professors. Indeed, seventy-five years after Sörgel came up with his master plan, Alghariani believes the time is ripe for this grand project. He points out that if one looks at the global water balance—that is the total amount of freshwater available globally—there is plenty for everyone. The problem is that the distribution is increasingly unequal, leaving some countries to cope with frequent floods and high rainfall levels, while countries like Libya go thirsty. Alghariani believes that it is up to the specialists in the field to develop water management in a more comprehensive, global way. "There is a total of 35 million cubic kilometers of fresh water on earth. Man uses 8 million of this; the rest is inaccessible or uneconomical to use. As demand increases we face the challenge of distributing water equally: this means transferring supply within countries, continents and even at a global level. Technically this is feasible."

Alghariani is passionate about the opportunity that lies unexploited at the center of the African continent. "The Congo River is immense. It has a discharge of 1,298 billion cubic meters per year, or 3.5 billion cubic meters a day—that's the equivalent of fifteen Nile Rivers! Most of this water just flows into the sea and is wasted," he says. Alghariani believes that by causing several nuclear explosions in the mountains on either side of the river and blocking its course with exploded rubble, one would in fact "restore the hydrological arrangement of the area 10,000 years ago" when the Sahara was a rich, green savannah teaming with wildlife and vegetation.

I can almost see the mirage of damp greenery shimmering in his eyes. Full of conviction he says: "More than 10,000 million hectares of Saharan wasteland could be irrigated from a sustainable, renewable source and turned into green fields. And the river that would be created between the Mediterranean and Central Africa could facilitate trade and communication, and create a 'second Nile' in Western Africa. All that is required is shutting off a hole in a rocky barrier, building a two-mile wide dam. That's not a serious obstacle in the face of advanced technology.

"Politically it is of course not feasible yet," he concedes. "It would require the unification of the continent. But this is also not unthinkable.... Losers would also have to be compensated by those who benefit, and the displaced would have to be relocated in a suitable environment. There are also environmental objections. Rain forests would be flooded and considerable amounts of mineral wealth would be lost." With a sweeping gesture, he says: "But all these disadvantages are largely outweighed by the environmental benefits of the project." He explains that the millions of Africans who would be displaced by the project are so poor anyway that they would not mind the resettlement. I am lost for words: does he really mean this project could be a viable solution to water scarcity in North Africa and poverty in Africa? "Some say this project is fiction but I believe it can work."

Indeed, while Alghariani muses over Sörgel's visions, the Lake Chad Basin Commission—made up of representatives from Chad, Niger, Cameroon, Nigeria and the Central African Republic—is drawing up plans to replenish the dying Lake Chad, pumping water uphill from the Congo and Chari Rivers. After years of fund raising, the commission had in 2006 collected the $6.4 million for a feasibility study. Next they will start looking for international donors and, who knows, make the dreams of Herman Sörgel and Professor Alghariani come true.

As he lights another cigarette, Alghariani continues casually: "The other option is to connect South America to Africa, to bring the water from the Amazon to the Sahara through pipelines under the sea. Technically this would be quite possible, and financially too perhaps." I must again be looking stunned, because Alghariani continues adamantly: "Well it is feasible if, for example, NASA would stop spending billions of dollars each year on space programs and technology we don't need. If they gave that money to better causes, we could solve world poverty completely. Look at the Channel Tunnel: that also took 300 years to happen—when they had the idea, people thought it was madness, but now there are trains passing through it every day. When Stanley discovered the sources of the Congo and the Nile, no one thought that the Aswan Dam and Lake Nasser could be built: just look now, there it is, protecting Egypt from disaster and famine....

"They say dreamers live forever. And I believe we have to let ourselves dream more. That is the problem: we don't dream enough. We have to look at all the options and see that this project deserves consideration. If we did, the Congo River Project could solve Africa's poverty at once."

# 7

# Making the Desert Bloom

*"In order to fully understand the decline in water resources in Israel, you have to look at the role ideology played in the development of water resources. Perceptions, attitudes and behavior, whether shaped by ideology or religion, have a strong influence on water policy in arid regions." –Clive Lipchin, environmental scientist, Arava Institute for Environmental Studies, Israel*

The illusion of plenty that still dominates among many in the Middle East and North Africa is rooted in the skewed relationship that has developed between man and his natural environment. In the course of the twentieth century, technological advances have made it possible for man to control nature more than ever before. Through its fluidity, water was seen as nature's most controllable resource, and thus became a symbol of human power over nature. By controlling its flow and its distribution, man could revive dead land and transform landscapes to create illusions of plenty. On a national level, the power of water to transform the land and bring prosperity became a potent symbol. Not only did it serve individual political leaders, it contributed to the development of political ideologies that continue to influence present-day policy making and political rhetoric. In Morocco, Egypt, Israel, and several other Middle Eastern countries, powerful ideological rhetoric was combined with ambitious engineering schemes to transform the landscape and create a belief in the limitless power of technology to resolve issues of water scarcity.

## A Moroccan Mirage

In Morocco, colonial and post-colonial water and land development policies have played an important role in shaping national perceptions of water availability. Current government policy is tinted by the colonial desire to transform the Moroccan landscape and its resources. Arriving in Morocco at the turn of the twentieth century, the French had little knowledge of the country and its geography beyond the coastline. Until the end of the nineteenth century, Morocco had been able to keep itself out of the hands of European colonizing powers. By playing them off against each other, the sultans managed to avoid any one power taking over. As the authority of the sultans weakened though, the Europeans—the French, British, Spanish, and Portuguese—closed in, jumping at every opportunity to gain control over Moroccan territory. The French—who had colonized and explored Algeria as early as 1848 and established a protectorate in Tunisia by 1881—occupied Casablanca in 1907, and in 1912 the Treaty of Fès was signed, creating a French and Spanish protectorate in Morocco. Spanish ideas about colonial rule were pretty basic: their presence in the south was largely military with no policies for settlement or economic development. The French on the other hand, had grand aspirations. They brought a whole colonial ideology with them and felt a *mission civilisatrice* towards their new subjects.

They were especially ambitious on an economic level and believed that they had found a new Eldorado in Morocco. Of their three North African colonies, Morocco was seen as the one with most potential for development. Since 1900 the French government had sent numerous research teams to assess the country's potentials. The many reports that were produced as a result painted idyllic images of Morocco as a rich and fertile land that remained largely undeveloped; some experts even claimed its sparsely populated coastal plains were the most fertile in the world.

The new settlers and the Protectorate's administrators were keen to embrace these images which were reinforced by powerful catchphrases and slogans designed to convince the public—both the *bourgeoisie* at home and the settlers on the ground—that Morocco was indeed the country of rich resources it was made out to be. Thus Morocco was first depicted as a former "granary of Rome"—cereals had been cultivated on Moroccan soil since Roman times—and therefore, experts said, the country had the potential to become the future "breadbasket of France." Later, when the wheat policy proved a failure, Morocco was the new California, or also a new Egypt, and could even become, according to one author, an "Egypt multiplied by a California." By the mid-1930s the French had fully embraced the Californian model, including its policy of large-scale dam construction and irrigation. The engineers employed to survey the potential of the country's rivers vowed that Morocco would not let "a drop of water flow to the sea" unused. By harnessing the country's water resources, experts believed they would be able to create "1 million hectares of irrigated land," just like in California.

These superlative slogans and colorful visions reveal just how ambitious the French were about the development of Moroccan resources, but also, in hindsight, the misplaced illusions they had about the country and its people. It was as though their lack of knowledge about Morocco led them to look elsewhere to see what the country might be like, instead of focusing more seriously on the economic, social and environmental situation on the ground. Morocco was effectively colonized and incorporated into the French empire before administrators and authorities had any clear idea of how to develop it.

## The Shiny Façade

It was my fourth day in Rabat when I went to meet the communications consultant of the Ministry of Equipment, Madame Bellioua, a small, elegant woman who spoke perfect French and English, and had worked for the UN in New York. It seemed her job now was to tell people like me how great Morocco was: how developed, forward-looking, liberal, Westernized, and safe. And the young king was wonderful too: dynamic, open-minded, and good-looking. But then the late king Hassan II was also a great man, a visionary: he had introduced *la politique des barrages* after independence in the 1960s. While it was in fact a continuation of colonial policy, Moroccans like to see it as an initiative of the late king. "He saw that Morocco had to be protected from water scarcity and that the construction of dams was the best way," she told me. "Thus today the population never lacks water, even in periods of drought, only a very small part of the population suffers from water scarcity."

Formulated towards the end of the 1960s, *la politique des barrages* was a major dam-building campaign to harness 11 billion cubic meters of water, or 55 percent of Morocco's water supply, for irrigation. An accelerated program of dam construction was to achieve the irrigation of a million hectares of land by the year 2000. This grand vision had two principal aims: assuring the country's nutritional needs and developing agricultural exports to earn foreign currency.

The million hectares were achieved by 1997. Since 1956, when there were twelve dams with a total capacity of 1.8 billion cubic meters, ninety-eight large dams have been built, boosting the storage capacity to 16 billion cubic meters. In addition, there are eighty-four smaller dams and manmade lakes. Current long-term policies aim at the construction of two to three dams a year until 2030, at an estimated cost of $344 million a year. Yet Morocco's development has been very unequal. The accelerated policy consciously neglected the development of the traditional agrarian sector, which was described as "an *ensemble* which resists the slightest innovation," so that there is today a great imbalance, a large gap separating traditional agriculture and the irrigated sector. In 2005, the irrigated land constituted only 16 percent of the total usable agricultural lands, but it yielded 75 percent of the export goods.

I spent an afternoon with Madame Bellioua, talking about water and then trailing off into a conversation about her children. She said she would arrange for me to meet Monsieur Zouggar, whom she talked about as a god, but who was actually the director of the hydraulic division of the Ministry of Equipment—the man who decides which dams are going to be built where. He was a tall, dark-skinned man with a small gray goatee and attentive eyes. He acknowledged that shortage and increasingly irregular rainfall patterns were now considered "structural" parts of Morocco's climate, but he assured me the government was fully equipped to deal with this. Their answer to climate change and frequent droughts: more dams.

"Without dams Morocco would be in a critical situation, in terms of drinking water and agriculture," he said. "The dams ensure our security on all levels:
food, flooding, and drinking water, also electricity production. Of course in
periods of drought, wheat and other products are imported." Zouggar seemed
very confident of Morocco's situation and capacity in the domain of water.
"Morocco has water security, we can meet all needs, even locally," he said.
"Our main priority in the next twenty-five years is to continue expanding
dam-building policies, and generally adopt sustainable, long-term policies
that fit into larger frameworks." Listening to Zouggar, it was easy to be convinced that Morocco has no problems of water scarcity, that there is no threat
of water shortage in the future, and that the more dams you build, the more
water there will be. Leafing through the piles of reports, glossy brochures and
diagrams I had picked up during my stay in Rabat, Morocco appeared to be a
highly organized and developed country.

But the image was shattered as soon as the train rolled out of Rabat's station
and we passed through the slum areas that sprawl down the coast between Rabat
and Casablanca. Large fields of rubbish lay rotting as children in dirty clothes
played in heaps of waste. Makeshift houses, built of mud bricks and sheets of
corrugated plastic, swarmed with small children, as women dressed in grubby
kaftans and headscarves stood by the doors of their houses chatting. Low standards of living in the rural areas and a succession of droughts since 1980 have
caused many people to come to the cities in the hope of finding work and prosperity. For many though, the move only results in further impoverishment.

The development of Morocco's rural areas is lagging behind the rest of the
country by decades. In 2003, literacy rates outside the urban areas were as low
as 33 percent, while only 16 percent of the rural population had electricity.
Only 56 percent of the rural population was connected to the drinking water
network, compared to 99 percent of the urban population and mechanization
of the farms remains low at less than 50 percent, a figure that is confirmed by
the sight of men arduously tilling the soil with donkeys. In addition, birth rates
are still high and Morocco's population is exploding, increasing from 9 million
in 1950 to 31.5 million today and with 32 percent of the population under the

age of fifteen. The current government is working to bridge the gap between the urban and rural environment, but before there are roads, let alone hospitals, schools, and clean running water, in all these places many more foreign loans will be spent. The campaign for the development of the rural areas is important though, as Morocco's cities are rapidly growing beyond their capacity. Since 1982 the urban population has practically doubled to reach 58 percent in 2003. As I looked out of the train window, I guessed much of this new urban population had ended up in these seaside slums.

Leaving the coast and turning southward to Marrakesh, the landscape is flat and green, with soft hills flowing into each other under a large sky. Riding slowly through this landscape where the green of the grass and the orchards reaches to the horizon, it is hard to imagine water is a scarce resource. But the scenery soon changes, becoming harsher and drier. The earth is more arid and barren; the fields are strewn with rocks and lie uncultivated in the winter months. The odd herd of sheep crosses over a hill, followed by their shepherd who ambles along seemingly without aim. Small villages glide past, nestling at the foot of a hill. Low reddish walls of mud enclose the houses. It is the slow train from Rabat to Marrakesh. Very slow, creeping gently around the edge of the hills and into the valleys. The light is changing, becoming more orange and golden as the train approaches Marrakech. The earth is a deep, dark brown.

When the first colonists saw this dark, rich color they thought it was a sign of the soil's exceptional fertility; they believed Morocco could become one of the most fertile grain-producing regions in the world. It was only later that they discovered the dark color was due to the high iron content of the soil, not the presence of organic matter. For twelve years the French strove to develop cereal culture, promoting the creation of large farms, paying out lavish subsidies and making tax concessions to farmers. Production was boosted from 1.9 million hectares to 3 million hectares between 1918 and 1929. But the miracle they had hoped for did not happen. Morocco was not the granary of Rome the French thought it might be; wheat prices remained high and productivity low, mainly because of the sporadic rains and the lack of organic matter in the soil.

The French increasingly realized that one of Morocco's main problems was the erratic and unpredictable rainfall patterns: the country had abundant sources of water but they were untamed and therefore largely unexploited. While one school of policy makers was dreaming its "granary of Rome" dream, another was developing the Egyptian dream. Several writers compared the Sebou and the Oum Rbia—comparatively small, local rivers—to the Nile, and believed Morocco was the ideal environment for the development of a cotton industry. By controlling Morocco's rivers, the country could be transformed into a "little Egypt." Further research ordered by the French Minister of Commerce soon revealed that the land was unsuitable for cotton cultivation—one should not imagine that Morocco was the Nile Valley, as the French Commissary-General to Morocco, Hubert Lyautey, sternly commented. The idea of controlling the flow of rivers and installing irrigation works remained though: Morocco would not let a single drop of water flow to the sea! This catchphrase, allegedly a memorable pronunciation of Napoleon as he stood on the banks of the Nile in 1798, was adopted by the French Protectorate and still reverberates in Moroccan policy today.

As the wheat crisis reached new depths in 1928, the French started looking for new models and dreams. This time they looked over the Atlantic: Morocco was to be the new California. Between 1929 and 1933, half a dozen study missions set out to the United States, all returning with the conviction that what the Americans had achieved in the Californian deserts, the French could achieve in Morocco. Morocco lay at the same latitude as California—on the west coast of a continent with a range of high mountains cutting through it—and it had roughly the same semi-arid climate and similar temperature and precipitation ranges. Monsieur Laguerre, the French commercial attaché in San Francisco, spoke of the "*grandes analogies*" between California and Morocco. He was convinced that Morocco could achieve the million hectares of irrigated land that California had: the granary would be converted into an orchard.

The secret lay in marketing. California was a model of agricultural development, but much more importantly, a model of marketing genius, with growers joining large cooperatives, establishing strict standards and packaging rules for each crop. And after consultation with marketing experts, they had created the Sunkist brand. According to Laguerre, Morocco should follow California's example "blindly." And indeed, by 1932, the *Office Chérifien de Contrôle et d'Exportation* had been established, setting the standards and ensuring top-quality of export goods, but also creating the still-familiar Maroc brand for citrus and other fruits.

The train was winding between rolling hills under a low winter sun as I caught the first glimpses of the snow-covered Atlas Mountains with the city of Marrakesh sprawling in the plain below. The light was pink and warm, casting long shadows over the dark earth. We arrived at Marrakesh station just as the sun was setting and the sound of the *muezzins* started ringing out over the town. Driving to the center in a *petit taxi* with my bags stacked on the roof rack, we headed for the central landmark of Marrakesh, the Koutoubia tower, the minaret of the central mosque. It is visible from everywhere in the city, a stern tower that looks down forbiddingly on the Djemaa el Fna Square.

Arriving in Marrakech from Rabat you are blinded, in my case literally as the sun was setting right in my eyes, but also metaphorically by the buzz of life, the explosion of color and sound that floods over you. It is like going from downtown Washington to the Rio de Janeiro carnival. Suddenly you feel alive, all senses are awakened. Smells waft towards you, carrying hints of grilled meats and spices. Over the noise of the traffic, cymbals and drums can be distinguished and voices can be heard chanting, laughing and shouting. Everywhere you look, there is something fascinating to watch. Performers coaxing a monkey along on a tricycle, dancers in colorful clothing moving to the rhythm of the drums, spinning the tassel on their fez hats to the beat of the cymbals.

Go out onto the Djemaa el Fna and it is like stepping into a Breughel painting. Here you find everything to satisfy your desires. A dense wall of oranges surrounds the square; they are heaped up on carts where vendors squeeze and pour all day for anyone who wants. Next to the orange carts are the vendors of dried fruit, poking their heads out between the piles of dates, figs and nuts. Further to the center of the square are the restaurant stalls that are set up each evening with large clouds of smoke billowing from them, carrying smells of grilled meats, spices and vegetables over the square. There are more than fifty of these stalls, each of them vying for your custom and shouting out to you as you walk past: "*Madame, regardez! Ici! Comme c'est bon: des brochettes, des poissons, c'est frais, ce n'est pas cher, venez!* [Madame! Look here! Doesn't it look good? Kebabs, fish, it's fresh, it's not expensive, come!]"

I knew that here I was seeing the other Morocco, quite different from the one I had seen in Rabat; not only was it grittier, it also seemed more true to reality. Half of the population lives in this Morocco, in isolated rural areas with basic facilities, where the grand transformation that parts of the country's landscape have witnessed in the twentieth century have little significance. Slogans that announce "1 million irrigated hectares by the year 2000" and the great drive to control the country's waters have little meaning for many of these people who still face the capricious rhythm of Morocco's climate with its droughts and floods. The difference between these two Morocco's—that of Rabat and that of the valleys—became even more clear to me during my trip to the Ourika Valley, where neither the dreams of the French colonists, nor the visionary wisdom of the late king Hassan II have had any impact. Here people's lives are still determined by the unpredictable water of the Ourika River that is not controlled by any technology.

The Morocco that had been described to me in Rabat and that exists in the narrow coastal strip around Rabat and Casablanca is different, a neat and ordered system. Created and elaborated through the course of the twentieth century, this landscape is built upon the myth of unlimited water resources and the power of human ingenuity and technology that can resolve any of nature's shortcomings. Instead of recognizing that the limits of the country's water resources had been reached, and that the erratic climate cannot be changed through the construction of more dams, authorities continued to seek further development.

It is only in the last few years that policy makers have started acknowledging the need for a new approach to water management. While they cannot quite let go of the image of abundance that dams bring with them, they now recognize that water demand also needs to be managed in a more sustainable manner. As the country's dams are increasingly suffering from siltation problems—7 percent of Morocco's dam capacity had been lost to silt by 2003 and large dams like the Barrage Mohamed V has lost over half of its storage capacity—the limits of technology are beginning to be recognized.

## The Zionist Dream: Redeeming the Land of Israel

More than anywhere in the Middle East, in Israel political ideology has played a central role in the development and management of the country's water resources. Indeed, even before the creation of the independent state of Israel, Zionist leaders in Europe made the quest for water in Palestine a priority. Developed in late nineteenth-century Europe, Zionism is the movement to establish a home for the Jewish people in Palestine. It is rooted in traditional Jewish beliefs and practices and emphasizes the strong connection that Jews around the world continue to feel to the Land of Israel. Historically, this enduring link to the Land of Israel meant that the Jews were considered by others—and considered themselves—a separate people with a distinct ethnic and national identity. During 2,000 years of exile, Jews in Europe and the Middle East prayed three times a day for the Return to Jerusalem and always considered Israel the homeland of their past and future. However, it was only at the end of the nineteenth century that this abstract spiritual longing for the homeland was translated into concrete political action in the form of the Zionist movement. The growth of nationalism in Europe had led to a sharp increase in anti-Semitic attitudes and actions, particularly in Russia where pogroms and anti-Semitic policies drove nearly 3 million Jews to emigrate between 1882 and 1914. At the same time, many parts of Europe were becoming more liberal and secular, which meant Jews were able to participate more freely in society. The assimilation that was taking place as a consequence posed problems to many European Jews, who struggled to find a balance between their Jewish identity and a new national identity.

Zionism developed under the influence of both these trends, giving way to a new Jewish nationalism in response to the growth of European nationalism. A combination of traditional religious beliefs and modern nationalist and socialist ideals, Zionism strove to create a homeland in which the Jews could put down their roots in the land of their ancestors and become once again an "indigenous people." Land and its settlement played a central role in this ideology, with an emphasis on agriculture and rural life. During the centuries of exile, Jews had rarely owned land or engaged in farming activities, yet many of the Jewish festivals continued to focus on agricultural and seasonal themes such as harvest and springtime in the Promised Land.

The Zionist settlers in Palestine vehemently rejected the Jewish condition in Diaspora. Not only had they felt a chronic physical vulnerability and political weakness, they were also pervaded by a sense of alienation. In addition, their persecution had often meant that they were prevented from owning land and practicing many professions, which led many of the Zionists to characterize life in exile as parasitic and non-productive. By returning to their homeland, they sought to create a new Jewish identity in which the land of Israel would play an important part. Following the biblical view that conceives of the Land of Israel as imbued with human characteristics, the Zionist settlers felt they were coming home to redeem the land and be redeemed. Through physical labor, and especially agricultural work, the Jewish people would cast off centuries of persecution. In the words of one of the most influential thinkers in pre-state Israel, Aharon Gordon: "The Land of Israel will not be Jewish, even if Jews settle in it and buy land, unless they work the land with their own hands."

The development of agriculture in pre-state Israel took place according to the socialist principles that turn-of-the-century immigrants brought with them from Eastern Europe and Russia. This led to the creation of the kibbutzim (singular: kibbutz), agricultural cooperatives based on principles of cooperation and communal ownership. In the 1920s they were complemented by another agricultural settlement, the *moshav*, in which the land was divided among the settlement families and not owned collectively as in the kibbutz. Although the total population of these collective settlements never exceeded 8 percent of the population of Jewish Palestine and today constitutes less than 4 percent, the utopian principles of communalism and egalitarianism that they represented have become an integral part of Zionist ideology. They have also had a significant impact on the shaping of agricultural policies.

Many of the early settlers came to the Promised Land with high expectations and romanticized ideas of the homeland. During the centuries of persecution and exile, they had always clung to the image of the Promised Land, an image that had taken on mythical dimensions. Often inspired by the scenery in their direct surroundings, these images bore little resemblance to the harsh realities of nineteenth-century Palestine. While the region has always had an arid climate, the land had suffered profound environmental changes since biblical times. Forests had been cleared for fuel or timber, the slopes of the hillsides had been overgrazed and many of the valleys had been clogged with sediment, creating swamps, which in turn bred malaria. Traveling to the Holy Land in 1867, the American author Mark Twain was deeply disappointed. Describing it as "desolate and unlovely," he wrote: "Of all the lands there are for dismal scenery, I think Palestine must be the prince. The hills are barren, they are dull of color.... The valleys are unsightly deserts fringed with a feeble vegetation." It was in this land that the first Zionist settlers arrived.

In his book, *Pollution in a Promised Land,* Alon Tal describes the diary entries of some of the early settlers: upon arrival, these pioneers were filled with a sense of euphoria, only to face great disillusionment as they confronted the harsh desert landscape, the relentless heat and a local population that was increasingly hostile. In addition, and more prosaically, many suffered from physical ills such as diarrhea from the unreliable water and food supply, and malaria. It was a paradoxical feeling of coming home to the cradle of Jewish history, and yet finding oneself in a totally alien and hostile environment.

In the end, many found the disparity between dream and reality too great. David Ben-Gurion, Israel's first Prime Minister, estimated that 90 percent of immigrants that came during the Second Aliyah between 1904 and 1914, left Israel after finding it impossible to adapt to the new lifestyle. Even those who did decide to stay, continued to feel nostalgic for their land of birth; the lush green landscapes of Eastern Europe with their forests and fertile fields formed a key element in this longing for the "other homeland." In this context, Tal tells an anecdote about former Prime Minister Levi Eshkol, who asks his fellow ministers: "*Nu*, when can we finish the job here already so we can go back home to Russia?"

The most obvious way to overcome these feelings of alienation and nostalgia was to transform the arid mountains of Palestine into a more familiar and friendly landscape. The early Zionists saw themselves as "a landless nation returning to a nationless land" and they believed that the local inhabitants had little regard for the land they lived on. The Zionists thus saw it as their task to revive this wasteland and transform it into the biblical "Land of Milk and Honey." To this end, the early romantic notions were soon replaced by a more aggressive development ethos, in which mastering the alien surroundings became a way to overcome feelings of anxiety and estrangement.

The pre-state phrase for agricultural settlement, "Conquering the Wilderness," implied a battle with nature, in which the Zionists not only worked to create new agricultural land, but also fought to transform the landscape to correspond to their ideals of natural beauty. The new pioneers suffered hardship and disease in order to achieve their goal: they dug wells to provide water for irrigation of the land; they planted forests that would transform the local climate; and drained swamps to open up new land to agriculture. Foreign species including conifers and eucalyptus were introduced, while the new rural settlements, the kibbutzim, were surrounded by European-style lawns and landscaped gardens. The settlers thought of themselves as liberating the Holy Land and restoring it

**Map 6**
**The limits of the Zionist State as envisaged in the beginning of the twentieth century by the pre-State Zionists.**

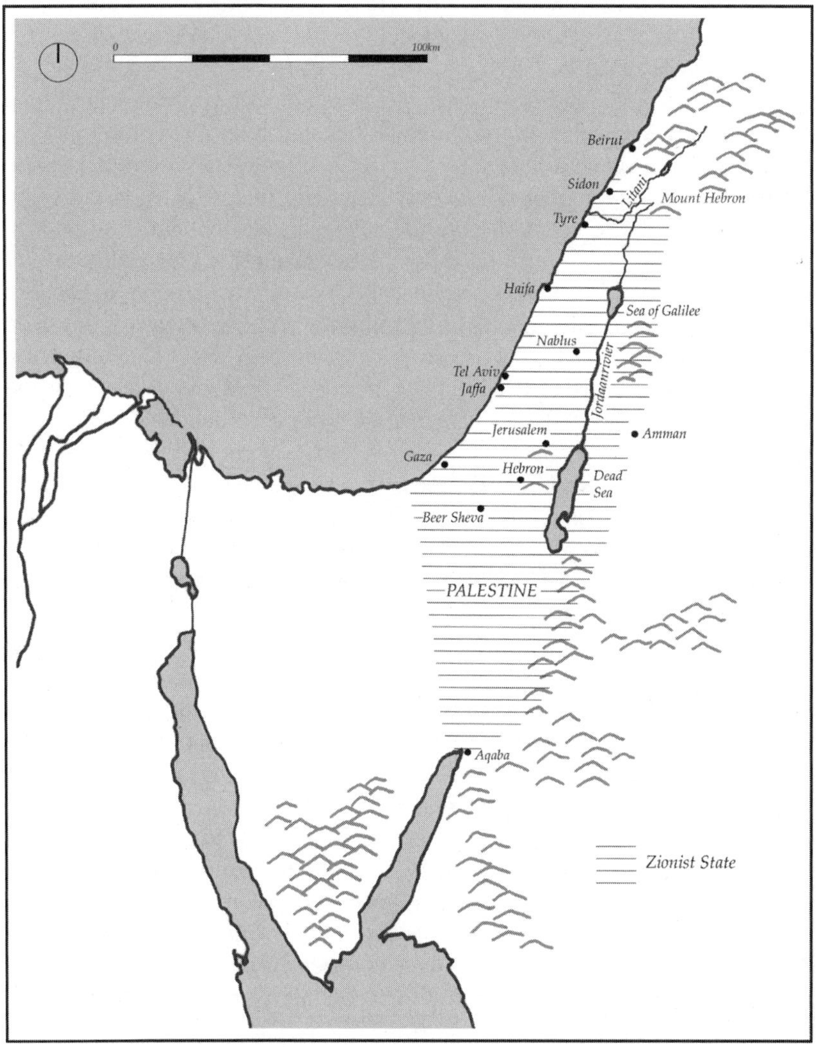

to its former glory, but the underlying attitude towards the environment would, over the years, place a growing and unsustainable demand on the country's water resources.

Indeed, for the Zionist dream to be fulfilled, water was needed. This meant that from the outset, the territorial aspirations of the Zionist movement included access to water resources. Without sufficient water, the existence and growth of a

Jewish state in Palestine was not viable. As the colonial powers, the French and British, discussed how they would divide the Middle East between themselves after the demise of the Ottoman Empire, Zionist leaders feared their interests would be overlooked. Attending the 1919 Paris Peace Conference, they lobbied for the creation of a Jewish state that would include not just the region's rivers, but also their headwaters.

This would place the Jewish state's northern border near the town of Sidon in present-day Lebanon and give the Jewish people control over the waters of the Litani Basin and all the sources of the Jordan River. The Zionist delegation argued that this claim reflected not only economic necessity, but also historic considerations. "The economic life of Palestine...depends on the available water supply. It is, therefore, of vital importance not only to secure all the water resources already feeding the country but also to be able to conserve and control them at their sources," they said. After months of wrangling between the French, the Lebanese, the British, and the Zionist representatives, the final boundary agreements were signed in 1923, leaving the control of Mount Hermon and the Litani Basin in Arab hands. The upper sources of the Jordan were split among four countries, leaving only the water of the Dan (which contributes 50 percent to the flow of the upper Jordan) to Palestine. The Zionist leaders were deeply disappointed by this arrangement and throughout the period of the British Mandate (1917-1948), the World Zionist Organization continued to seek out new water resources by purchasing land, promoting settlement and investing in water resource development.

## Conquering the Wilderness

The quest for the development and acquisition of water resources continued to play an important role in the definition of national policy after Israel's independence in 1948. Former Prime Minister Levi Eshkol described water as "the blood flowing through the arteries of the nation," and it came to be seen not just as a natural resource but as the instrument of Israel's transformation and prosperity. Water was more than an economic commodity; it was part of an ideology. And as technological capacities increased, water resource development became a symbol of the unlimited power of technology in transforming the land. The Israelis believed that with hard work and the development of sophisticated hydrological projects, there was no limit to the development of the land and its water. Thus ideology and geopolitics took precedence over economic and environmental realities.

Water was only valuable if it could be harnessed for agricultural expansion, giving water an added geopolitical importance: agricultural activity was no longer only a means of fulfilling the Zionist vision of "redeeming the land," but also a means of "conquering the unsettled." Farming thus came to serve important strategic and military purposes, enabling the defense of borders and distant areas with few inhabitants. The development of agriculture in peripheral areas was—and still is—encouraged by government policies that provide generous subsidies for agricultural water in the more remote areas.

Tal sees the passion for water that dominated during the early years of the Israeli state as almost a "Shakespearean tragic flaw." On the one hand, it led to the development of innovative water development projects on a scale hitherto unknown in the Middle East. Also, the new state was not hampered by traditional legislation and ancient land ownership structures; it was a clean slate. And while the new immigrants had less experience with the development of agriculture in arid climates, as pioneers they also had the freedom to innovate and improvise. On the other hand, it created an unrealistic appetite and blinded decision makers to the long-term implications of stress on a fragile resource. "The argument could be made that they almost loved Israel's water resources to death," says Tal.

The pressure on water resource development was especially high in the first years after independence: the large number of immigrants from Europe and the Middle East meant that jobs had to be created and food production had to be vastly increased. As less than 1 percent of the new immigrants were professionally trained and Israel's industry was insufficiently developed to absorb the huge influx, the agricultural sector was expanded. Between 1948 and 1958, the land cultivated by Jews increased from 160,000 to 390,000 hectares. During the 1950s, Israel's agricultural sector grew tremendously, showing a 500 percent growth in yields. Dozens of wells were drilled along the coast and the underlying aquifer, the Coastal Aquifer, soon began to suffer the effects of over-pumping, which in turn led to the intrusion of seawater and pollution. By the mid-1950s, the wells supplying Tel Aviv had become too salty for drinking.

A large number of the new arrivals were also settled in the under-populated areas of the Negev and the Galilee, making access to water even more crucial, particularly in the arid south where rainfall was sparse. Nisan Tzuri, one of the first settlers in Israel's Negev Desert in 1946, recalls the struggle for water and land that took place in the years preceding the foundation of the state. At the age of eighty-eight, Tzuri is like a living museum exhibit, the embodiment of the Zionist dream. He forms an almost integral part of the Water and Defense Museum that he has created at Kibbutz Nir Am near the Gaza Strip.

Located in a disused water reservoir that was built in the 1940s to supply water to the kibbutzim in the region, the museum documents the creation of the first Jewish settlements in the area. Faded black-and-white photographs and maps tell the story of the Jewish conquest of the Negev. Tzuri remembers how he arrived in the Negev from the fertile north where he had initially wanted to settle. "The leaders of the World Zionist Organization wanted us to come south. There in the north, there is water at fifteen or twenty meters depth and there is also rain. Here in the Negev we did twelve drillings up to a depth of 300 meters and we still found no water. But they still wanted us to come here and live on the land."

Ignoring the British ruling that prohibited Jews from settling in the Negev, the Zionist movement in Palestine moved in overnight, creating eleven new settlements by morning. Tzuri recalls: "The British were shocked, they had no idea this would happen. One morning they woke up to find the beginnings of settlements all over the Negev. There was a tower, a fence and tents at each location. We had transported everything on 300 trucks and by morning 1,100 people were living and farming in the desert. London was scandalized, asking where their soldiers and their intelligence had been for this to be possible in one night. The British vowed they would dismantle the settlements, but in the end they did nothing to stop them staying."

But the new settlers needed water. "When we came here there was nothing, only desert," says Tzuri. "Now you see how we have transformed it: there are trees twenty meters high. We came and we found water in the ground and we used it to make everything green." With the help of a geologist from Tel Aviv, the settlers identified a large aquifer beneath the area on which Nir Am is today built. They built the water reservoir and began to develop a system to transport water to other settlements in the area, first by tanker and later—in an epitome of the Zionist spirit of pioneering and inventiveness—through water hoses that had been used by British fire fighters in the London Blitz. "We bought 220 kilometers worth of fire extinguishing pipes and led them from the Nir Am reservoir to the settlements to the east and west in two branches." The reservoir and its local supply system remained in use until 1964 when the national water system was taken in use.

Tzuri's story is a testimony to the pioneering spirit of the early Zionists, who struggled to gain control over the Land of Israel and harness its resources to serve the needs of the Jewish people. With limited resources, they managed to transform the landscape and fulfill a powerful vision. In the words of David Ben-Gurion, the young state had managed to fulfill dreams which were "capable of transforming the natural order by the power of vision, science and pioneering capacity." And now that the state had acquired independence, the next goal, in Ben-Gurion's words, was to "make the desert bloom." In order to make this happen, there would have to be an integrated water network that allowed the transfer of the resource throughout the country, and that gave the government full control of it. Within the space of ten years, the necessary legal, institutional and technical measures to solve the problems of water accessibility were taken.

In 1959 the country's water resources were declared public property as part of the Water Law. The centralization of all water resources meant that it was strictly regulated and controlled by a system of quotas and rigid pricing policies. Over the decades, different ministries were charged with water policy making, including the Ministry of Health and, after 1972, the Ministry of the Environment. However, the Ministry of Agriculture was the most important policy making authority and was in practice responsible for the entire water system in the country. It appointed the water company, Mekorot, to the status of national water utility. Through the Water Law, the young Israeli government aimed to provide equal access to all citizens, though very soon a heavy priority was given to agriculture. "The nationalization of water was a very strong management tool: there were no property rights issues. It was a unitary system," explains Professor Eran Feitelson of the Hebrew University in Jerusalem. "In fact you could see it as an integrated water management policy *avant la lettre.*" The Water Law is still applicable, though today the Ministry of Infrastructure, which was created in 1996, has replaced the Ministry of Agriculture in playing the dominant role in water policy making.

The country's land had already been transferred to government auspices, and was centrally managed even before the creation of the state of Israel. The principle of collective land ownership is based on socialist ideas and the biblical tradition that says the Land of Israel was God's gift to the Jewish people. From the early twentieth century onwards the Jewish National Fund started to buy up land in Palestine with the aim of acquiring national ownership of the Land of Israel for the Jewish people. Later, in 1960, the Basic Law was passed, giving "legal effect to the ancient tradition of ownership of the land in perpetuity to the Jewish people," and making 92 percent of the land subject to the principles of collective ownership. This law still applies today and makes private ownership impossible; instead, there is a system of renewable leasehold in which land can be leased for a period of forty-nine years at a time.

Even before the country's land and water resources were nationalized, the government was already working on technical aspects that would enable the redistribution of the country's water resources. After the development of several smaller schemes, the newly established water planning authority, Tahal, put forward a plan for the maximal exploitation of Israel's water resources in 1956. Comprised of a number of smaller projects, the plan included a design for the coordination and integration of water projects throughout the north of the country into a single water supply system. A main conduit was to convey water from the Jordan River to the northern Negev over a distance of more than 200 kilometers. The long-term aim of the plan was to supply water for the irrigation of 3,000 square kilometers of land by 1966 and provide food for a population of 3 million.

Despite the financial, technical and geopolitical problems that the project faced, the National Water Carrier (NWC) was completed in 1964. The network of pipes, canals, tunnels and reservoirs led water westward from the Sea of Galilee and then south along the coast to the northern edge of the Negev Desert. At a cost of $175 million—the equivalent of 80 percent of Israel's investment in water infrastructure for a decade—the problem of water accessibility had been solved. The completion of the NWC, and the establishment of a modern water management system, meant that by the mid-1960s, Israel had the most integrated and efficient water system in the world. It provided two-thirds of the country's water, 80 percent of which went to agriculture.

## Map 7
### Israel's National Water Carrier. Source: Dr J. Chenoweth.

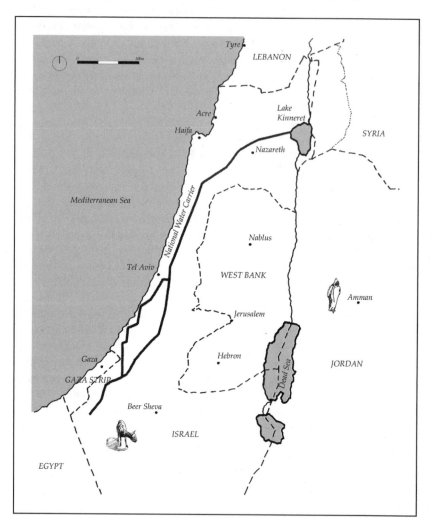

The system has now been in use continuously and effectively for forty years, allowing Israel to overcome regional water imbalances and providing water to the whole country.

But the NWC has also had negative effects, particularly on the country's environment. For as Israel's population and economy have continued to grow, demands on the waters of the Sea of Galilee have continued to rise. Initially, and according to a regional water-sharing agreement, 340 million cubic meters were withdrawn annually. By the 1990s, this figure had risen to 450 million cubic meters. Today, the critical "Red Line," below which the water quality of the lake could incur serious damage, has not only been repeatedly crossed, it has been shifted downward several times. This has led to the shrinking of the Sea of Galilee. The Dead Sea is suffering even more: as a consequence of the diversion of water from the Jordan River to the NWC in Israel, the East Ghor Canal in Jordan and from the Yarmuk in Syria, it has lost a third of its surface area and its level has decreased by more than twenty meters since the beginning of the twentieth century. Water inflow to the Dead Sea is today only 10 percent of its original volume, and the sea's level continues to drop by up to one meter per year.

After the completion of the NWC, it soon became clear that the gap between growing levels of consumption and the limits of the water reserves was still growing. After the occupation of the West Bank in 1967, Israel gained control over the waters of the Mountain Aquifer, which lies almost entirely below the Palestinian West Bank. In doing so they gained limited amounts of additional water supplies; more importantly, their control over the resource made it possible to prevent the Palestinians from expanding their water use, thus securing Israeli water supplies. But even with this additional supply the gap was not filled. While it was obvious that the limits of the resource had been reached, the Zionist drive to develop agriculture and the belief in the power of technology prevailed. Alwyn Rouyer, a political scientist and author, comments: "Instead of a shift towards a more conservation-oriented water policy, desperate attempts were made to prove that the ideological goals could coexist with the practical limitations of water development. Rather than questioning the validity of values giving rise to growing water utilization, Israeli leaders sought to find new technical solutions to the problem of water shortages."

Tal explains that, like most frontier histories, Israel's water experience should have passed through two stages: a first stage in which water resources were developed and made accessible across the country, and immediately after, a second stage during which the limits of the resource were acknowledged and the emphasis would have been placed on conservation and an improvement in efficiency. Tal comments: "The fundamentally ideological approach to water, however, prevented a successful transition to the more mature, sustainable stage." Thus the new solution to scarcity was sought not in conservation but in new technology: desalination, a method that promised unlimited supplies.

Seen as a high-tech solution to the problem of water scarcity facing the region, desalination is in fact a very old method that was already known to the Greek philosopher and scientist Aristotle. He wrote that "saltwater, when it turns to steam, becomes sweet, and the steam does not form saltwater when it condenses." The Roman emperor Julius Caesar also desalinated seawater to quench the thirst of his troops during the siege of Alexandria. The problem had always been cost.

As early as 1956, Israeli Prime Minister David Ben-Gurion emphasized the importance of developing an inexpensive process for the purification of seawater. He said it was "not only vital for Israel; it was a necessity for the world." Inspired by these words, Tahal proposed a fifteen-year $100 million desalination scheme in 1965. But its high cost meant it was never implemented. Requiring high initial investments and high energy consumption, desalinated water was prohibitively expensive. Instead, water policy makers looked into alternative sources such as the treatment and reuse of wastewater. After teething problems that led to a number of health scares and even a cholera outbreak, Israel is today a world leader in the use of treated wastewater for the irrigation of crops: more than 79 percent of Israel's sewage water is treated and purified for use in agriculture.

Since the 1960s, desalination techniques have also come a long way, allowing production costs to be brought down and making it an affordable solution for urban water supply. While it is already the main source of freshwater in countries like Saudi Arabia and Kuwait, it is now also considered to be the long-term answer to Israel's growing water demand. In 2000, the Israeli government approved a large-scale desalination master plan, outlining the construction of seven plants along the Mediterranean coast, which would together supply 315 million cubic meters of water per year, or around 30 percent of the country's water requirement. While the seven plants should have been completed by 2004, internal political wrangling led to serious delays so that today only one of the plants has been completed at Ashkelon. Costing $200 million, the plant—the largest in the world—commenced production in August 2005 and provides an annual 100 million cubic meters of water, or around 5 percent of the country's water needs. Other plants are planned at Hadera and Ashdod. Officials from the Ministries of Finance, Environment and Agriculture have recently criticized the location of the plant in Ashkelon, saying it should have been located nearer to the large urban centers as the water is meant for domestic purposes. Water from the plant is currently mainly transported to agricultural crops in the south, despite the fact that desalinated water lacks a number of essential minerals required for the irrigation of crops.

The continued debate around desalination opposes those who see it as the only solution to Israel's growing water demand and those who believe that water demand management could provide at least as much water at the same cost. In addition, environmentalists and scientists are worried about the environmental impact of desalination on coastal and marine areas. They argue that there has been insufficient research into the long-term effects of returning the highly saline brine that is left over after the desalination process to the sea. The process also remains extremely energy intensive.

### Sitting around the Table with Israelis: The Endless Debate

They say that if you put three Israelis around a table, you will have at least six opinions. It appears that this is also true in the area of water. For every interview

I did, every expert I talked to, every institution I visited, there were new and diverging opinions. Comments like: "It's a hydrological time bomb; at this rate Israel will cease to exist within ten years," were balanced by "Israel has no water problem, any scarcity will be compensated by desalinated water." Some said desalination was a savior, while others saw it as a delusion. And so on. After twenty interviews on the subject of Israeli water management, I still had no idea what to think, the only thing I knew was that there were many versions of reality. And I was not even talking about the issue of how to share water resources with Israel's Palestinian, Jordanian, Lebanese, and Syrian neighbors.

On one thing there seems to be a consensus though: the water problem in Israel is not about availability, it is about management. The question is how to solve it. Particularly as everyone has a different opinion.

Clive Lipchin is an environmental scientist at the Arava Institute for Environmental Studies that is located on Kibbutz Ketura in the Arava Valley. He is firm in his condemnation of current water policies and believes that Zionist ideology continues to have far too great an influence, not just in Israeli politics, but in shaping the public's attitude to the country's environmental resources. "In Israel there is no scarcity, there is a water management problem," say Lipchin. "It's a simple question of budgeting: 60 percent of water goes to agriculture. That can be cut down. Not to eliminate it, but to use only 40 or 50 percent of water for agriculture. Within agriculture there is a whole range of options: you can decrease subsidies, choose different crops, use alternative sources of water…. In the domestic sector on the other hand you don't have these options: the population is growing, there is growing wealth and a pro-natality policy. On top of all that, we are bringing in immigrants from water-rich countries who have even less of a notion of scarcity. There needs to be a realization among decision makers, a recognition of the limitations of the resource. But people have blinders on, ideologically motivated blinders."

Current agricultural and water management policies are still strongly tinted by Zionist ideologies that lend unquestioning support to agriculture despite the obvious limitations in water supply. The 60 percent of Israel's water supply that goes to agriculture today is still relatively low compared to the other countries in the region. However, in Israel, unlike in other countries, agriculture represents only a small portion of the national income. In 2003, it made up only 3.5 percent of the country's GDP, while only 2 percent of the total workforce was employed in the agricultural sector. In addition most agricultural workers in Israel are seasonal workers from Thailand, Africa, and the Philippines. In his research into the influence of Zionist ideology on present-day agricultural and water policy, Lipchin found that only 12 percent of the residents of agricultural communities work in agriculture. Still, the remaining 88 percent that has nothing to do with agriculture benefits from the use of subsidized water allocated to agriculture.

The imbalance in allocations is kept in place by a water pricing system that lends support to agriculture and the provision of water "in the periphery." As it is a public property, water is strictly regulated through a system of quotas and subsidized prices. In agriculture, permits are issued to determine how much water a farmer is allowed to use in a given period. According to Rouyer, this water pricing system blatantly favors agriculture over household and industrial consumers. This is in the first place reflected in the water prices which vary little across the length of the country despite the wide difference in delivery cost. Rouyer comments: "While this policy has generally accomplished its political goal of spreading population and agricultural settlement to remote parts of the country, it has also significantly contributed to the cost of water." The main beneficiaries of this policy are the farmers: the water they use is heavily subsidized, so that they pay much less than users in other sectors.

Israeli farmers pay around 70 percent of the real cost of the water they use. Household users, on the other hand, are charged much higher rates, both by the state water company Mekorot and the municipalities. While farmers paid an average of $0.25 per cubic meter in 2005, household users paid at least twice that price at $0.61-1.27. The water quotas allocated to agriculture are not based on availability or efficiency, but on the type of crops, the ecological zone, the number of residents in a settlement and even the type of settlement. Through their historic importance in the nation's founding myths, kibbutzim therefore receive larger water allocations than other agricultural settlements.

While agriculture is heavily subsidized throughout the Middle East, the motivation for this support is different in Israel: it is a political choice, based on Zionist ideology and geopolitical strategies to settle the periphery. Professor Uri Shamir of the Technion in Haifa explained this: "Agriculture in Israel has a value beyond the economy; it is about settling the land, about having greenery and having populations outside the cities. Agriculture in Israel is not going to be shut down: it is an important element of society." At the same time and in contrast to every other nation in the region, Israel has a very active and very effective environmental movement. Though the movement has not attacked agriculture as such, it has significantly affected agricultural practices and limited the extension of agriculture to new areas.

Still, critics of the current water pricing and agricultural policies are numerous. They point out that the high subsidies for water used in agriculture create a net loss for the national economy and that water-thirsty crops such as bananas and citrus should be imported. But tell the average Israeli that the idea of growing oranges in the desert is ridiculous and environmentally harmful, and they will be almost personally offended. Jaffa oranges have become a symbol of Israel, part of what Israeli's consider quintessentially part of their national identity.

Defenders of Israel's water policies see the pursuit of agriculture as an unquestionable choice, something that will always be part of Israeli identity. They see desalination and the unlimited water supply it promises as the answer to the institutional and political problems. In fact, it is just a way of avoiding the issues and maintaining a system in which household users pay for the water that is used—and because of the low prices, also wasted—in agriculture.

Lipchin argues that any change in this status quo will require the revision of Zionist ideology to match the reality of Israel's arid environment and scarce water resources. "The objectives of Zionism most influential on water and agricultural policy, the rural mode of life and the settlement of territory, have left an indelible mark on the Israeli landscape. Despite the fact that these objectives have never been fully realized, we continue to live as if they have," he says. Indeed, today 90 percent of the Israeli population is urban, and despite massive drives to "conquer the wilderness," 60 percent of the country is desert land, with most of the population clustered around the coastal plain. Lipchin says that to break through the entrenched views of Zionism, the system needs to be more decentralized, allowing for privatization and local-level decision making. In his view this could help reduce the buffer zone that exists between water management and public perception. "Because the public is encapsulated in a centralized system over which they have no control, changing ideological values that actually represent the situation on the ground will prove daunting," he says, adding that it is at the same time a necessity if the country is to confront the regional water crisis.

# 8

# Bitter Waters

*"It's all about politics. With water as well, it is the politics that gets in the way. One political decision would be enough to change everything for Israelis and Palestinians, and that is the decision to accept each other." –Dr Alfred Abed Rabbo, director of the water and soil environmental research unit, Bethlehem University, Palestinian Territories*

### An Afternoon in Bethlehem

Over the phone Jad Isaac tells me he is grounded in Bethlehem. If I am able to cross the checkpoint he will "roll out the red carpet" for me, but he cannot move. We make a tentative appointment for the following Wednesday. The Israelis I ask say I should have no problem crossing, but you never know what happens on the day.

The taxi driver who takes me from the Jerusalem bus station to the Bethlehem checkpoint asks me where I am from. "Holland!" he exclaims. "A wonderful country! Your people like Israelis, right?" I say, yes, but explain that recently public opinion has also been supportive of the Palestinians. "Why?" he asks indignantly. I explain that many Dutch find it difficult to understand Israeli policy towards the Palestinians. The driver is quiet for a while. Then he says: "The Dutch are all Nazis. They wanted to destroy the Jews during the Second World War—did you know that more than 100,000 Jews were deported from Holland in the war?—and now they want to do it again by giving the power to the Arabs. They are all anti-Semites."

The taxi stops at the entrance of a brand-new hangar-like building, a high-security pedestrian crossing to the West Bank. Since 2004, the security fence—or segregation wall, depending on which side of it you are standing—rises to a height of eight meters and separates Bethlehem from Jerusalem. I had of course read about the project and seen photos of it, but it is only when I am standing face to face with the gray mass of concrete that I really understand what it means. It makes my stomach turn. At the checkpoint four soldiers with machine guns are casually chatting. I am directed into the building, where an invisible voice directs me through a maze of steel turnstiles and security checks. At the X-ray scanner there is a long queue made up mainly of men who file along with an air of resignation and boredom. As they shuffle along, they start emptying their pockets and taking off belts and shoes in the hope of speeding up the process. When it is my turn, my EU passport allows me to sail through all scans and checks with expedient smiles from the soldiers behind the bullet proof glass.

On "the other side," it is a different world. Of course. It is the Arab world. Groups of small children come rushing up as soon as I leave the checkpoint, asking for baksheesh, sweets and pens. Two taxi drivers are also waiting by the roadside and ask me where I am going. They promise me "*good price,*" but I decline. "Please!" begs one of them, "Madame, it would be for my pleasure, ten shekel!" I walk on, and within a minute, he has caught up with me by car. "Madame, where are you going? The Church of Nativity? I will take you. No charge. For free. I just want to talk to you. It would be an honor." So I get a free ride to my interview.

The offices of the Applied Research Institute, ARIJ, are housed in a small stone building on the outskirts of town. Founded in 1990, the institute carries out research in the domain of the environment and the conservation of natural resources in the Palestinian Territories. Isaac, an outspoken, sometimes even fierce man with a small goatee and glasses, is the director of the institute. Over the years he has played an influential role as a representative of the Palestinian delegation during joint environmental working groups and multilateral talks. He also advised the Palestinian Negotiations Affairs Department on the Final Status Negotiations of the Oslo Agreements. But recently he has changed his mind about such joint efforts. Isaac is angry. "We had a dream of finding a just and peaceful solution to the conflict. But they have betrayed us," he says bitterly. "We don't want the solution to be dictated to us." He strongly condemns the Palestinian targeting of civilians and believes that this is the main cause for the downward spiral in which the region is caught. "This is not justifiable, not on religious grounds and not in the name of any national movement," he says. But he also says there has to be a willingness from the Israeli side. "The Israelis should see that the occupation is bad for them too. It is also in the best interest of the Israelis not to have hungry neighbors," he says. He sighs and leans back behind his desk.

As he lights a cigarette, he looks at me critically. "So, you are writing a book about all this in the context of water? And who have you spoken to so far? What sources have you consulted?" After I list some names and books, he shakes his head disapprovingly. "You have done very bad research on water issues in Palestine," he says, and immediately calls in his assistant who is sent to dig up a list of ARIJ books and articles. I say that my research in the Palestinian Territories hasn't been made easier by the current conflict and the restrictions on travel in the West Bank, but I feel a bit ridiculous explaining this to someone who has had to deal with daily identity checks, checkpoint closures and travel restrictions for the past thirty-odd years.

He turns to me and sighs. "The conflict is simple and difficult at once. If the rules of international law were applied, then water would be treated and divided as a shared resource over which the parties have a shared responsibility. The problem of water in this arid region cannot be solved individually. It requires joint management," he says. "There should be an equitable distribution of water resources among Israelis and Palestinians, based on population figures: all the water west of the Jordan River should be equally distributed among the people living there. And for the Jordan River, there should be a system of basinwide water management based on justice, needs, equal rights, and all the other conditions of international water law." Immediately he adds angrily: "But this is unthinkable for Israel because they are water-thirsty and they really believe they will starve if the water is taken away from them. It is not true: agriculture is a bad economic deal for Israel. The Palestinians can grow the food for them and sell it to them. But just try telling this to an Israeli..."

Isaac was actively involved in the environmental aspects of the peace talks, and also saw them fall apart. "The peace camp in Israel fell apart in two—those who stuck to their principles, and those who sought quick-fix solutions." He gives me a challenging look and says: "The most important in all this is to not forget your principles. I find that the people who opt for quick fixes end up betraying themselves. I won't do this; I will *not* compromise my principles. I will never let Israel enjoy this by imposing compromises in the agreements. I am not willing to talk to any Israeli as long as they don't accept my rights. Israelis are not the masters and I am not their slave. It is not human." There is a touch of drama in Isaac's voice now. "We have been abandoned by the international community and by the world as a whole. But I will not accept it." Mournfully, he tells me his children have never seen Jerusalem, although it lies only twenty minutes away. I sympathize, but at the same time, I can sense that things are complicated and layered here; truth has many faces when you want to justify your cause.

### The Source of the Problems

To understand the complexity of the Israeli-Palestinian water dispute, it is important to first get a clear picture of the location and quantity of the region's water resources. This is however not a straightforward task: tensions are running high, and both parties have very strong views as to the roots of the conflict and its possible solution. The sharing of the region's water resources has in some cases evolved beyond politics to become entangled with deep-seated feelings of anger, mistrust and frustration. In the conversations I had during the four weeks in the region, I heard Palestinians accusing Israel of being land- and water-thirsty, and of adopting a "cry-baby mentality" when its actions were challenged. Israelis on the other hand described Palestinians as untrustworthy liars who beat their wives. One Israeli even told me the lie detector simply doesn't work on Palestinians: they are so used to lying that they do not respond to the technique.

In this atmosphere, it is hard to form a balanced picture of reality. Judging from the many conversations I had with Israelis and Palestinians, I have come

**Map 8**
**The water supplies in Israel and the Palestinian Territories: the Jordan River,**
**Lake Kinneret, the Mountain Aquifer and the Coastal Aquifer.**

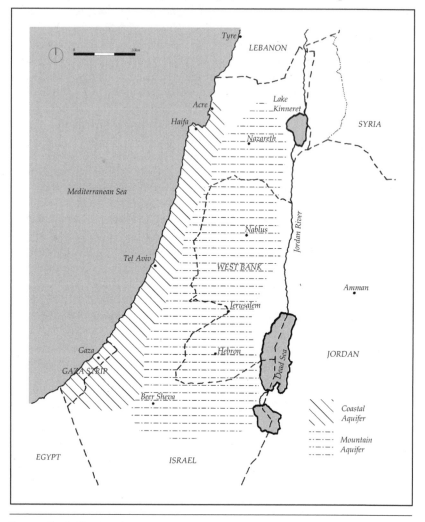

Source: Dr. J. Chenoweth.

to see that there is not one reality, but several versions of it. The Palestinian farmer in the South Hebron mountains, the Jewish-Israeli inhabitant of Tel Aviv, and the Palestinian policy maker in Ramallah all experience the situation in a different way. Despite the fact that they share the same resources and live on the same land, their perception of water is widely different. These communities live only dozens of kilometers apart, yet it is as though they lived in separate bubbles: traveling from Tel Aviv to Jerusalem and on to Bethlehem—a journey of barely an hour and a half—gives you glimpses of three entirely different worlds. This also means that when researching the subject, one comes across a broad spectrum of opinions. From the defiant Palestinian who refuses to compromise his honor, to the Israeli pessimist who says Israel is doomed; and from the Israeli fanatic who believes Israel should aggressively defend its interests and at all cost avoid working with its neighbors, to the optimists on both sides who still believe that a form of joint management can be developed between Palestinians and Israelis.

The resources that are so coveted by all parties come from three main sources: the Jordan River Basin with the Sea of Galilee,[1] the Mountain Aquifer that lies underneath the West Bank and part of Israel, and the Coastal Aquifer that runs from the Gaza Strip to Israel's northern border. Accurate data about the water available from these sources are hard to come by. There is no joint database recording available water resources or the levels of water use in Israel and Palestine. The Israeli authorities have developed a detailed record of all this information, but as water resource data are considered to be an issue of national security, they are not publicly accessible. This in turn leads many Palestinian water experts to question the accuracy of officially released data, which they suspect of having been manipulated and falsified. The Palestinians therefore mainly rely on data from their own measurements, so that there are at least two sets of official figures—one Israeli, one Palestinian and then a mass of other estimates put forward by scientists—recording the water availability in Israel and Palestine.

In his research on Israeli-Palestinian hydropolitics, sociologist Samer Alatout showed that both Palestinian and Israeli experts tend to—most often inadvertently and influenced by cultural and political contexts—choose data that support their own case. Thus Israeli experts tend to estimate shared water resources at a lower level and the exclusively Palestinian resources at a higher level than their Palestinian counterparts. Alatout traced the discrepancy between Israeli and Palestinian estimates to historical, cultural and political motivations. He says that Israelis have since the creation of the state in 1948 lived with the threat of scarcity, not only of water, but also of security, of land and of people. "Scarcity…became more than a technical portrayal of natural conditions; it evolved into both a dominant perception of Israeli experience and an active determinant of Israeli identity," he argues, adding that another facet of this perception of scarcity is the belief, especially prevalent during the 1950s and 1960s, "that the 'other,' in this case the Arab states or Palestinians, live under conditions of abundance." Palestinian experts, who were until 1994 heavily dependent on Israeli sources to estimate water balances, are often suspicious of Israeli figures and therefore tend to adjust the potential of shared resources upwards, while taking lower levels into account for exclusively Palestinian resources.

Having muddled my way through a confusion of contradictory figures, I have chosen to use the figures published by the Israeli Ministry of National Infrastructure, the Palestinian Water Authority (PWA) and the United Nations.

The region's first source, the Jordan River, is about 260 kilometers long and flows from the slopes of Mount Hermon in the north to the Dead Sea in the south. It is used by Israel, Jordan, Syria and Lebanon; Palestinians of the West Bank do not have access to it since 1967. The river is fed by three tributaries in the north: the Dan, the Hasbani and the Banias, which rise in Israel, Lebanon and Syria respectively and provide the main inflow to the Sea of Galilee. Of the approximately 800 million cubic meters of water that the Sea of Galilee receives annually from its upper tributaries and from rainfall, around 500 million cubic meters is extracted by Israel, which obtains a quarter of its water supplies from this source. From the north of the country the water from the lake is pumped into the national network—the National Water Carrier—that transports it to the populated coastal areas for domestic use, and to the Upper Negev for irrigation purposes.

The Jordan River's fourth tributary is the Yarmuk, which flows from Syria and joins the Jordan River just below the Sea of Galilee. While this is the Jordan's main tributary, it is an unreliable source that is fed by seasonal streams so that its flow fluctuates widely from year to year. The flow of the Yarmuk has greatly decreased in the last forty years, partly because Syria diverts much of its headwaters. It does however still form an important water resource for Jordan, which diverts part of the Yarmuk's waters into the East Ghor Canal for irrigation in the Jordan Valley. In addition, Israel also diverts part of the river's flow, further reducing the part that flows south to the Lower Jordan and the Dead Sea. Together, all these diversion schemes have led to a sharp decrease in the outflow of the Jordan River from 1.25 billion cubic meters per year in the 1950s to around 200 million cubic meters per year today. This water is highly saline and often highly polluted with chemical fertilizers, making the Lower Jordan unusable for domestic and even agricultural use.

The reduced flow has also had disastrous effects on the level of the Dead Sea, which has fallen over 20 meters in the last century and continues to decline at a rate of one meter per year. The reduced inflow of water has meant that the sea has lost over a third of its surface area and that the shoreline has receded by one kilometer in places. Today, tourists visiting the seafront hotels and spa resorts on the Israeli shore have to take a make-shift shuttle, a tractor pulling two open-air wagons, to cover the distance between the indoor hot springs at their hotel and the muddy banks of the Dead Sea. The declining groundwater table around the lake has also led to the development of over 1,000 sinkholes along the shoreline of the Dead Sea. These potentially life-threatening holes can reach 10 meters in depth and 25 meters in width, and make the lake's shores unsafe. Thus a campsite near Kibbutz Ein Gedi on the Israeli shore of the Dead Sea was closed down after a worker fell into a sinkhole, while parts of date plantations have also subsided and the sinkholes now also threaten the roads along the lake. Experts believe that the sea will never disappear entirely and that it will eventually stabilize at 100-130 meters beneath its current level of -417 meters and be maintained and replenished by underground springs. But the continued shrinking of the sea will have disastrous effects on the local tourist industry and agricultural activity. Already today, all development plans have been frozen and many agricultural areas have been abandoned because of the risk posed by sinkholes.

One of the proposed solutions to the declining level of the Dead Sea is the construction of a canal between the Red Sea and the Dead Sea, the so-called "Red-Dead Canal," which would replenish the Dead Sea and at the same time generate hydroelectricity. The project, which would cost an estimated $3-5 billion, remains controversial though as environmentalists question the viability of mixing two types of saltwater. The effect of the canal on the Arava Valley that lies between the Dead Sea and the Red Sea coast in the south is also uncertain, as is the local impact on marine life in the Gulf of Eilat/Aqaba from where large quantities of water would be abstracted and pumped northward. Still, Israel, Jordan and the Palestinian Authority are all committed to the project and are raising funds for the $15 million World Bank feasibility study. Critics remain skeptical of the project and argue that instead of seeking a quick-fix solution in another mega-project, a basinwide master plan needs to be drawn up that will also address the declining level and pollution of the Jordan River and regional water use in general.

The region's second major source of freshwater, the Mountain Aquifer, is the cause of considerable tension between Israelis and Palestinians. Situated under the West Bank and part of Israel, the majority of the aquifer's natural recharge area lies in the West Bank, while the majority of its natural discharge area is in Israel. The groundwater underneath the West Bank flows in three directions: west, north and east, dividing the aquifer into three "sub-aquifers." The largest and most heavily disputed of these is the western aquifer which flows into Israel and has a safe yield[2] of freshwater of around 300 million cubic meters per year. In 1951 withdrawal from the western aquifer, primarily by Israelis, involved forty-six wells pumping a total of 24 million cubic meters. By 1971 this had grown to 400 wells abstracting 450 million cubic meters. Over-pumping persisted from the mid-1960s to the 1990s when abstraction rates fell to an average of 350 million cubic meters per year, providing 50 percent of Israel's drinking water.

Since the military occupation of the West Bank in 1967, the water of the Mountain Aquifer has become an important element in Israel's strategic water planning. For while it was able to exploit the water from the western and northern basin of the aquifer before 1967, the occupation allowed Israel to monitor and restrict the Palestinian use of the water of the Mountain Aquifer. It also meant that it could start using the water of the eastern aquifer to supply water to agricultural activity and domestic use of the Jewish settlements, which have developed in the West Bank since 1967.

Until 1967, water administration and legislation in the Palestinian Territories was mostly based on customary law, while it had also been influenced by the legislation of successive regimes—Ottoman, British, Egyptian and Jordanian—that had ruled in the area. According to these laws, water was considered a private resource and many farmers and villages claimed ownership over shallow wells, springs and streams that lay on their land. After 1967, the management of water in the Palestinian Territories was handed over to the full control of the Israeli military authority which established a permit system for the drilling of new wells and fixed pumping quotas on existing wells. From an Israeli point of view, it was essential to maintain and enforce this control over the waters of the West Bank, for any over-utilization or pollution of the water here would have direct consequences for the water withdrawn by Israelis on the other side of the Green Line.[3] However, the Israeli military authority has not interfered with the use of water from the approximately 300 springs in the West Bank, which supply around 60 million cubic meters a year and existing property rights here were left largely unchanged. Some of these springs are very important water sources, such as in Jericho, where the Ein Sultan Spring provides ample water supply to the city's population of 15,000. Still, today Israel controls 82 percent of the groundwater resources in the West Bank.

The restrictions that have been imposed on Palestinian water use in the West Bank have created a wide gap between Israeli and Palestinian consumption levels: while the average Israeli consumes 280 liters of water a day on a domestic level—around the amount that is consumed in European countries and slightly less than is consumed in the United States—Palestinians consume less than ninety liters per day. Problems of leakage due to deteriorating infrastructure mean that the actual water delivered to Palestinian consumers in towns and cities lies even lower at around forty to sixty liters a day. In summer months the water supply to many West Bank towns also becomes unreliable, so that users receive perhaps one day of water a week or less. All Palestinian houses have several water tanks on their roof to store supplies, but even then, during supply interruptions they sometimes have to resort to buying water from water tankers at heavily inflated prices. In one case, during a summer drought in 1998, the areas of Bethlehem and Hebron received no piped water for two months. According to Palestinian sources, Israeli settlers on the West Bank dispose of nine times more water per capita than Palestinians. While aid organizations and the Palestinian Authority try to increase the amount of water reaching the Palestinians, the inequality persists as the military authority continues to control Palestinian use and development of water resources.

The Israeli military occupation of the West Bank has also had severe implications for Palestinian life and livelihood as the restrictions on water use have severely impaired the development of the Palestinian economy. Since 1967

Palestinians have not been allowed to dig or restore a single well without asking for Israeli permission. Permits are frequently refused and if they are granted they come with depth restrictions and meters that monitor the levels of extraction. These restrictive policies limit Palestinian water supply for agricultural use to 84 million cubic meters per year, a figure which has remained constant since the beginning of the occupation according to Palestinian sources. The Interim Agreement that was signed by Israel and the Palestinian Authority in September 1995 stipulates the allocation of between 70 and 80 cubic million meters of additional water resources to the Palestinians, yet to date only around 40 million cubic meters has been made available.

The separation barrier or wall which Israel started building in the summer of 2002 has further impacted Palestinian access to water. While the wall occupies only a narrow strip of land, only 15 percent runs along the Green Line and the rest cuts into the West Bank, isolating both land and water resources. According to calculations by the Palestinian Negotiations Support Unit, which provides legal and policy advice to Palestinian negotiators, 73 percent of the land that has been or will be lost is arable and coincides with a fertile and water-rich area which is commonly known as the breadbasket of Palestine. Thus in the area of Tulkarem alone, thirty wells have been lost, amounting to a loss of 4 million cubic meters of water a year. Many local water supply systems that make use of shallow wells, storage reservoirs and distribution systems have also been disrupted, forcing farmers to invest in the construction of new pipes and reservoirs. The Palestinian Water Authority estimates that Palestinians will lose 5 million cubic meters of water per year due to the wall once it is completed. Tentative Israeli plans to construct a wall on the eastern side of the West Bank, which would isolate it from the Jordan Valley, would further limit Palestinian access to water and agricultural land. Consequently Palestinians have widely denounced the construction of the wall as not only a "land-grab" but also a "water-grab."

The Coastal Aquifer is the third major source of water for the region. Running along the length of the coast from Gaza to Israel's northern border, the aquifer has suffered severe over-pumping in the last sixty years. This has led to the intrusion of seawater and the salinization of wells in some areas, a process which is very hard to reverse, even if withdrawal levels are reduced. Chronic over-pumping in the 1950s and 1980s has created a huge deficit in Israel's Coastal Aquifer that was estimated at nearly 1 billion cubic meters in the early 1990s.

In Gaza the situation is far worse. With an area of 360 square kilometers, it is one of the most densely populated places on earth with an average of more than 3,000 inhabitants per square kilometer and very limited water resources. The portion of the Coastal Aquifer in Gaza has an estimated capacity of 60 million cubic meters of sustainable supplies annually, but present use lies around 140 million cubic meters per year. This massive over-abstraction has led to a sharp lowering in the water table and saline intrusion into local wells. In addition, pollution of the groundwater is a major problem in Gaza as between 70 and 80 percent of domestic wastewater is discharged into the environment without treatment and agricultural and industrial wastewater also seep into the aquifer. The prevalence of waterborne diseases is therefore high among the Gazan population, and gastrointestinal infections and kidney problems are common. According to 2003 UN estimates, only 10 percent of the total aquifer volume in Gaza can be considered as freshwater that is fit for use. One way of reducing the pressure on the aquifer is desalination. Studies by the PWA and US Aid for the construction of a desalination plant on the Mediterranean coast have until now not been implemented though, as politics and the continuing conflict stand in the way of the execution of such large infrastructure projects. An additional way to alleviate the shortage in Gaza and reduce abstraction from the aquifer, is the transfer of water from the West Bank through a "water link." Developed at the beginning of the Oslo process, the idea of the water link was conceived as part of a broader territorial link that would join the West Bank and Gaza. While technical studies have been carried out to explore various routes for this link, no concrete plans have been made. Following Israel's disengagement from Gaza in July 2005, provision was also made for the supply of an additional 5 million cubic meters of water per year from Israel's National Water Carrier. Pipes were laid, but implementation has until now also been delayed. In the meantime though, the Israeli water company, Mekorot, has for the last few years been delivering several million cubic meters of water a year to Gaza City.

## Water Thieves and a Tango with Israelis

The Israeli occupation and its policy of restrictions over Palestinian water use plays a major role in the Palestinian water crisis. However, experts in Palestine and Israel point to the fact that the Palestinian Authority has been very inefficient in the implementation of any comprehensive water policy. "Israel is taking more than its fair share of water, that is undeniable," says Robin Twite of the Israel-Palestine Center for Research and Information. "But at the same time, the Palestinian administration is not perfect: the systems are old and worn out, the pipes are leaking and the Authority didn't take advantage of the lull between 1993 and 2000 to improve systems. So it is definitely not all the fault of the Israelis. The Palestinian Authority has been very slow in implementing change, especially in the treatment of wastewater."

In this context the political scientist and researcher, Dr. Julie Trottier, has carried out extensive research into water management systems in the Palestinian Territories. She says that while the Israeli occupation has certainly had far-reaching consequences for Palestinian water resources, internal political mechanisms also contribute to the current situation of scarcity. Trottier believes that the debate surrounding water availability has been inaccurately reduced to a conflict between Israelis and Palestinians, in which Israelis are blamed for all Palestinian problems.

Trottier describes the case of the village of Dura, where residents received their water from the main water network of the towns of Hebron and Bethlehem. However, they also suffered frequent shortages, forcing them to buy the much more expensive water from water tankers. In 1998 SOGEA, a French company working in the vicinity to detect and repair leaks in the system, found that the Palestinian water salesman of Dura had established an illegal connection to the main pipeline, enabling him to tap almost all the water of the system, take it to Dura, and sell it at inflated prices. SOGEA first attempted to cut off the illegal connection but was prevented from doing so by the Israeli army. Instead, it applied for funding from the American donor US Aid and built a new pipe beside the existing one.

Besides the fact that resolving the conflict would have been cheaper than the laying of new infrastructure, Trottier also believes that it would have had a much more lasting effect. Indeed, with the construction of a new pipe, it seems only a matter of time before the "water thief" establishes a new illegal connection. In addition, Trottier found that many Palestinians she spoke to accused the water thief of being a collaborator. Thus the blame for the Dura water theft was indirectly placed on the Israelis, an attitude which only contributes to maintaining the status quo in the Palestinian Territories. "The idea according to which there is only one conflict concerning water, which is a conflict between the Palestinians and the Israelis seems to be solidly anchored in the prevalent thinking. No other conflict can exist. This complicates the development of efficient institutions on the Palestinian side. Conflicts whose existence are denied, can only be prevented with great difficulty," she comments.

She adds that the ignorance of the Dura villagers also plays an important role, as they had no idea of the cause of the water shortage they were experiencing. They simply assumed that the drilling of Israeli wells had led to a drop in the water table, which had in turn led local wells to dry out. Thus ignorance and a passive resentment towards the Israelis prevented what could have been a straightforward solution to the water shortage in Dura. "Externalizing all difficulties…allows for the perpetuation of the occupation, as it prevents the Palestinians from facing the real problems that are involved in state building," she says.

Dr. Alfred Abed Rabbo, the director of the water and soil environmental research unit at Bethlehem University, admits that the current water shortages in the Palestinian Territories are partly caused by the shortcomings of the Palestinian national institutions. He comments: "I think the Palestinian Authority failed. Many don't dare saying this and admitting it openly, but I don't care, they failed. But I also think Israel made us fail more than we needed to. You see, the peace accord was like a tango, it's a dance you can't dance alone, and Israel did not dance with us." We are sitting in the university's chemistry laboratory, where Abed Rabbo, a gentle, soft-spoken man wearing a white lab coat, teaches and carries out research into water quality in the West Bank. Dozens of students, also in white coats, are milling about, working on experiments and filling in charts. Now and again one of them comes up to Abed Rabbo and interrupts our conversation to ask for instructions or explanation.

After having told three boys to check the details of a chemical formula in the library, he turns to me again. Despite his somber prognosis, he is smiling gently. "It is all about politics. With water as well, it is the politics that gets in the way. One political decision would be enough to change everything for Israelis and Palestinians, and that is the decision to accept each other. The main thing is that we need to be accepted as a country. This was acknowledged in the peace agreements, but the promise was never fulfilled. Peace is sharing resources and living together. The Israeli government thinks it is defending Israel with the wall, but what the Palestinians have tried to make clear is that whatever you do, we will fight back. When I speak to Israeli colleagues, they understand my point of view, but they are academics and they have no power to influence the politics of it. It really is *all* about politics."

## Complete Divorce

It is a cold, dark December afternoon when I visit Professor Arnon Soffer at Haifa University. Perched high over the city, the university campus is exposed to the elements and a chilling wind blows between the faculty buildings as I search for the Department of Geography. Soffer's office is a small cubicle on the second floor. Despite its modest size and appearance, it is here that the professor has been receiving the highest-ranking Israeli military officials and foreign ambassadors in the past years. Soffer—who "taught all the generals in the Israeli army, including Ehud Barak" and was the confidante of former Prime Minister Ariel Sharon—has for years been warning that as the Arab population in the Palestinian Territories and within Israel continues to grow at a higher pace than the Jewish population, the Jewish-Zionist State of Israel is threatened with disappearance. His publications on the subject have been very influential in the formulation of government policy in the last five years. According to Soffer, a recent publication of his, *Israel, Demography 2003-2020, Dangers and Opportunities*, is considered to be the "Bible of Israel," while his ideas about "preserving Israel as an Island of Westernization in a Crazy Region" were of key importance to the construction of the security fence that separates Israel from the West Bank. "I have been preaching this vision for the past twenty years, but it is only with the outbreak of the Second Intifada that politicians have started taking heed," he says.

Soffer believes that the demographic clock is rapidly running out for the Jews of Israel: using simple mathematical forecasting methods, he foresees that by 2020 the Jews will only make up around 70 percent of the population, severely compromising Israel's Jewish-Zionist identity and making it a multinational country. In the Land of Israel—Soffer's term for the land covered by the State of Israel and the Palestinian Territories—there will be a clear majority of Arabs by 2020 and already today, only 49 percent of the population in Israel and the

Palestinian Territories is Jewish. The demographic threat Soffer describes is underscored by the rate of natural increase of Jews and Arabs in the region. For the Palestinian population it lies between 3.5 and 4 percent, while the rate of natural increase among the Jewish population of Israel is 1 percent. According to Soffer such data show that there is an urgent need to intervene.

"I am very clear on the steps that should be taken," he says. "There should be a rapid unilateral separation of all aspects. Complete divorce. The price, of course, will be water, but it is worth it. [Palestine is] a third world country and [the Palestinians] will pollute the Mountain Aquifer and all the resources they have. So let them have it." Soffer believes that Israel can solve its water scarcity problem through desalination and thus provide water for both agriculture and domestic use. Indeed, to Soffer, water is a minor problem compared to the threat of an uncontrolled Arab demography. He is unequivocal: "In my view, without a barrier, a Berlin Wall, Israel will disappear in ten years. There is a great gap between Israel and the Palestinian Territories. Not only in terms of religion and culture, also in terms of economy and incomes."

In a booklet he published since my conversation with him in the context of Israel's disengagement from Gaza, *Israel Demography 2004-2020, In Light of the Process of Disengagement*, Soffer defends disengagement and unilateral separation in unambiguous terms. He argues that separation and disengagement are an existential necessity and that if Israel stays in Gaza and the West Bank it will be the "death knell" of Israel as a Jewish-Zionist State. Internally, separation will allow for the resolution of important national problems which are currently being disregarded. "If Israel returns to reasonable borders and disengages from the yoke of the large Palestinian population, Israeli society can renew the Zionist dream of absorbing Jews under the conditions of an advanced Western society.... A strong society, its face to the West, can also find the resources needed to maintain the quality of life in a dense Israel by going to the sea—land reclamation from the sea, by pushing the population southward toward the desert, and by building upwards, as well as by smart underground design. Problems of transportation, garbage, water desalination, and sewerage are mostly technical problems. With the aid of rational national planning and law enforcement, they are solvable."

Soffer took his message to the Knesset and told politicians that time is running out for Israel. "I talked to them like little children: 'Behave yourselves,' I said, 'and remember these words, there is not much time left.' I hope they understood it." He sees international criticism of Israel's unilateral policy and the construction of the separation fence as a positive sign. Echoing the words of Israel's first Prime Minister, David Ben-Gurion, who said that "It is not important what the *goyim* say, it is important what the Jews do," Soffer says: "In my speech to the government last week, I told them that the fact that all the Arab countries and the EU are against [the fence], shows that we are for the first time doing the right thing."

On a broader regional level, Soffer also has little faith in international coop-eration. In his eyes, everyone should look after their own interests and seek as little regional contact as possible. "I don't believe that the people of the Middle East—after 5,000 years of torturing each other—are ready for collaboration," Soffer comments. "Look at Turkey, Syria, and Iraq: they are not ready for col-laboration. To me, each country should deal with its own problems: Syria should take water from its own dam to provide Damascus. Jordan can do the Red-Dead project. It is a stupid project and very expensive, but they could do it. For Israel, the only answer is desalination. There is no water crisis."

Dan Zaslavsky, a professor of engineering at Haifa's Technion and a former Israeli water commissioner, also has little faith in any form of cooperation be-tween Israel and its Arab neighbors. He says that while there have been attempts at cooperation over water issues between Israelis and Palestinians, there were always many problems. "It is simply a different culture. There are so many com-munication problems between Israelis and Palestinians. There is no trust," says Zaslavsky. He is also "viciously" against any form of peace with the Syrians, whom he describes as pathological liars.

## A Seeping Time Bomb

Opposing Soffer's "complete divorce" and separation camp, there are Israelis and Palestinians who, on the contrary, believe that the only way to address and resolve the regional water crisis is cooperation. Because of the small scale of the countries—Israel and the Palestinian Territories cover an area smaller than Belgium—environmental problems are often shared. Part of the rain that falls on the Palestinian West Bank flows westward into Israel; the water that Israel and Jordan withdraw in northern regions to feed their respective water and irriga-tion systems—the National Water Carrier and the East Ghor Canal—has led to the dramatic shrinking of the Dead Sea and a serious decrease in groundwater levels in Jordan, the West Bank and Israel; and the untreated sewage from the Palestinian villages in the West Bank not only seeps into the underlying Mountain Aquifer, it also flows into Israeli rivers.

This seepage of untreated sewage water not only illustrates the shared nature of the resource, it also forms a serious threat to the Mountain Aquifer, one of the most significant sources of high-quality water for both the Israelis and the Palestinians. In the Gaza Strip the overexploitation of the aquifer at more than twice the annual safe yield has already created a situation in which water poses dangerous health hazards to the population. Many believe that the damage done to the Gaza aquifer is irreversible and environmental scientists now warn that the same could happen to the Mountain Aquifer if adequate measures are not taken.

In a report published in February 2004, the environmental organization, Friends of the Earth Middle East (FoEME), described it as "a seeping time bomb": the sewage of more than 2.5 million people—Palestinians and Jewish settlers—is constantly flowing untreated into the recharge area of the Mountain Aquifer. Highlighting the urgency of the problem, Gidon Bromberg, the director of FoEME in Tel Aviv, says: "The management of the Mountain Aquifer is a critical issue. It is a major source of drinking water for the Palestinians and the Israelis. Yet for the past decade 60 million cubic meters of untreated raw sewage water has been seeping into the aquifer every year. If current quantities of sewage water continue to flow, in ten years the water of the Mountain Aquifer will no longer be fit for use."

The continued pollution of the Mountain Aquifer is tied up in a complex muddle of political and strategic considerations, which are compounded by an atmosphere of mistrust between Israelis and Palestinians. Despite the fact that $230 million has been committed to the construction of sewage treatment plants in the West Bank since the beginning of the peace process, only two have been completed, one at Al-Bireh near Ramallah and one in Tulkarem. It can treat the sewage of 50,000 people; the four other plants in existence are run-down and some of them are completely out of use so that the sewage of the remaining population in the West Bank is left to seep into the groundwater without treatment. In the Palestinian villages, where 61 percent of the population lives, sewage is commonly disposed of in unlined cesspits. In cities and towns, more than two-thirds of the population is connected to sewage networks, but this waste is also left untreated and disposed of in nearby streams. Furthermore, FoEME estimates that only 7 percent of the sewage from Israeli settlements is treated, leaving 15 million cubic meters a year to flow untreated into streams and rivers and seep into the groundwater.

In 2004, Zach Tagar, one of the authors of the report, said that while it had made both sides aware of the facts, it was very difficult to find a way forward. Both sides accused each other of intentionally delaying the construction of sewage treatment plants and levels of trust were very low. "The Israelis claim that the Palestinians are intentionally polluting the resources that flow into Israel. They say the problems in the West Bank have nothing to do with them. One of the ministers we spoke to even called it a 'Sewage Intifada.' And he is convinced it is true: the money is there, so why isn't the plant being built? The Palestinians, on the other hand, say that they don't get the permits and that there are too many constraints and restrictions preventing the implementation of projects."

At the same time, Tagar added, the issue of sewage has been fairly low on the Palestinian agenda. "The Palestinians have more urgent priorities than the construction of treatment plants. They find themselves incapable of long-term planning because they have many more pressing concerns like water supply, food, security, and independence," he said. At a summit of international donors in 2003, the Palestinian Authority detailed its aid requirements, which added up to $1.2 billion. Of this amount only $60 million (5 percent) was requested for sewage infrastructure, with other issues like humanitarian assistance and water supply receiving financial priority.

Tagar said that the conflict was the main obstacle. Since the start of the Second Intifada, donor countries have put most construction work on hold. They claimed that they were incurring significant extra costs—around 25-40 percent of the original cost—because of the stringent Israeli security measures. They also complained that workers, engineers and material are being prevented from crossing checkpoints and that the Israeli military were slow in processing applications for permits. Palestinians also complained that Israel was constantly creating obstacles to Palestinian efforts to implement sewage projects. In response, Israel argued that the extensive security checks were necessary as some of the equipment provided for the infrastructure projects, such as metal piping, could be used to produce weapons.

The report led to some progress on projects. Thus a sewage treatment plant was opened in 2005 in Tulkarem thanks to German funding, while locations have been agreed for several other treatment plants across the West Bank. Sewage solutions have also been sought for the settlement of Ariel in the West Bank. On an official level the Palestinian Water Authority is prioritizing sewage solutions more than in the past, while the coordination between the Israeli security forces and German donors has significantly improved. However, since the election of the Hamas government in the Palestinian elections of January 2006, funding from many Western donors has been frozen and the implementation and completion of pollution prevention and wastewater projects in Nablus, Hebron, Salfit, Jenin, Dir Dibwan, and Qalqilya are under threat. "Water is the most solvable of the five issues that still need to be settled in the final peace agreement," says Tagar. "But if you reduce the resource further, then there is no telling what the consequences might be. This is why it is important to address the pollution of the Mountain Aquifer now, in order to prevent further conflict."

## Sticking to Principles

While there are experts on each side who believe joint management of water resources is possible and who agree that there is enough water for everyone, figuring out how to practically manage and divide this water is trickier. This is where it becomes overwhelmingly clear that politics and history cannot be dissociated from water in the Holy Land. Eran Feitelson, a professor of geography at the Hebrew University in Jerusalem, is an advocate of joint management and believes it is the only viable solution in the long term. "On a regional level, the question is not whether there will be enough; the question is how to manage it. It is not a zero-sum game: the debate should not be framed in terms of who gets how much, but how the resource should be managed."

But the practicalities, Feitelson admits, are not so straightforward and so far joint water management efforts have had limited success. After the start of Second Intifada, the Joint Water Committee (JWC), which was launched in 1994 in the framework of the Oslo Peace Accords, was hailed as the only joint institution that continued to function despite the conflict. However, in 2006 the committee stopped meeting. And even when it was still functioning, the JWC's work had limited impact and negotiations were hampered by a lack of trust between the parties. "The JWC was a failure," affirms Feitelson. "Instead of building of trust, it has led to a loss of confidence. There is no joint coordination: each side has its management and this is brought together in the JWC, but this does not always work well. The Palestinians felt there was an inequality in that anything that was done with 'their' water, the water of the West Bank, had to be approved by the JWC, while Israel could do anything with the water of the Kinneret system[4] without consulting the committee. The way the committee operated and the personalities of the people who worked on it, created lots of problems. The JWC took a long time to clear any requests of project proposals from the Palestinians and the Palestinians felt Israel was intentionally blocking their projects."

Fadia Daibes, a former employee at the Palestinian Water Authority and currently an independent water consultant, confirms Feitelson's views, adding that the difference in experience and training also affected the results of the JWC. "One reason the JWC failed is that Israel's people were all very capable and the Palestinians put technicians in there with no political experience. So Israel decided everything, the Palestinians had no clout at all." Despite having observed the failure of the JWC, Daibes believes the only way forward is cooperation, and more particularly trust-building through joint projects, which could at the same time serve to develop Palestinian knowledge and technical capacities in the area of water resource development and management. She has proposed the creation of a joint database. "It should be done very gradually; time is the main element. It is unthinkable that we would come to any agreement now with Israel. Those who say this are dreaming: if it were to be done now, it would just be a political deal, with no vision for the future, no acknowledgement that we have a real problem with depletion of water resources and pollution. If Israel gave us an amount of water today and the agreement was based on that, it would never work," she says.

Daibes advocates the adoption of a progressive approach which steers clear of the ratification of formal treaties and limits itself to reaching an understanding that will allow the implementation of projects. "The first step is to build trust; then we can proceed to a technical assessment of the situation and the determination of which party has a right to which water according to the standards of international law. Both sides will then be allocated water on a basis of equity."

And this is where principles enter into the debate. For the Palestinians, who have lived under occupation since 1967 and who have not been able to develop any of their water resources since then, the acknowledgment of their right to water is of key importance. In the Interim Agreement that was signed by Israel and the Palestinian Authority in September 1995, Israel recognized this right to water. However, the precise definition of what this right entails was postponed until the Permanent Status Negotiations. Palestinian water experts and officials continue to call for a complete reassessment of the distribution and management of the joint water resources. Using several international laws and conventions to support its argument, the Palestinian Negotiations Support Unit says that Palestine is entitled to "an equitable and reasonable allocation of shared freshwater resources" which should, in their view, be based on "the allocation of equal per capita volumes of freshwater to the various parties." They also demand compensation for "past and ongoing illegal use of Palestinian water resources."

On the other side, the Israelis in favor of joint management tend to criticize the Palestinian insistence on the recognition of their water rights, saying the approach should be more pragmatic and practical and that focusing on the politics of rights is divisive. They advocate the development of new sources such as desalination and the reuse of wastewater, which would dissolve the dispute over the scarce resources and ensure there was enough water for all. The Palestinians see this as a legitimization of the present—in their opinion unjust—distribution of the shared water resources and insist on the definition of their right to water.

In practice, Israelis never feel the water shortage and, while there is an awareness of water scarcity, the average Israeli almost never has his domestic water supply cut off. If there is a severe shortage, it is Israel's commercial farmers who bear the consequences as the Ministry of Water Resources cuts down on allocations to agriculture. In Palestine the situation is very different, as domestic users are regularly confronted with supply interruptions. Sociologist Samer Alatout says that experts believe, and try to convince everyone, that water is scarce throughout the region and that it affects everyone. In his view though, the "technicalization of the discourse of scarcity" and the widely circulated definition of water scarcity of less than 500 cubic meters per person per year are misleading as they distort daily realities. "This technical assessment of scarcity…is inadequate at best because it ignores the fact that within that technical limit, the lived experience of people might and does in fact differ along national–political lines (Israelis have access to substantially more water than Palestinians) and along social-class lines as well (Palestinian rural areas are hit hardest).… The Israeli experience of scarcity, grounded in numbers, is radically different from that of Palestinians, grounded in daily shortages and interruptions," he says.

One of the recent projects which has highlighted the difference in outlook between Israelis and Palestinians was put forward by Israel and proposes to desalinate water on the Mediterranean coast and transfer it to the West Bank for domestic use. Prof Uri Shamir of Technion in Haifa described it as the "only viable long-term solution" for supplying drinking water to the West Bank. But Palestinian critics are incensed at the idea: for besides the fact that few Palestinians would be able to afford the desalinated water which would cost $1 per cubic meter after transport cost, Palestinians feel that desalinated water should be used in the coastal plain to serve the Israeli population and that they should be given access to the water of the Mountain Aquifer below the West Bank.

Dr. Shaddad Atilli, a policy advisor for water and the environment at the Palestinian Negotiations Support Unit, comments: "Desalination is certainly an option for the future to serve the Palestinian population in Gaza, but the West Bank population should be allowed access to its rightful water resources, including the three aquifers and the surface waters of the Jordan River. Israel's historical (and present) appropriation of the water resources of Palestine is altogether in contravention of international law, including the law on belligerent occupation and customary international water law."

Just as progress on formal negotiations over water is currently paralyzed by the broader conflict, the advancement of projects on the ground is also severely affected by the situation. The heightened security measures that have been in place since the start of the Intifada in combination with the measures taken after the election of the Hamas government in Palestine, make life very difficult for those working in the environment and water sector. Nader El Khateeb of Friends of the Middle East in Bethlehem says that work on projects is constantly hampered by the daily reality of checkpoints and closures. Over lunch of hummus, tabbouleh and grilled chicken in his office, Khateeb, an ever-smiling environmentalist, seems resigned about the situation. "Military orders restrict everything. People are dedicated to projects and want to work to improve the situation, but then they can't get the permit and when they want to get together they can't cross over. FoEME staff who want to cross the border from the Tel Aviv office to come to the Bethlehem office can't. And the Israelis can't go to Jordan either, so there are really a lot of barriers now."

In his view, a resolution of the conflict would speed up all aspects of water management and water sharing in Israel and Palestine. "High-level decisions will allow faster developments on the ground. Now we are working with barriers and if they are removed, things could move very fast. Bottom-up measures take much longer."

He quotes a colleague from Friends of the Earth Canada, David Brooks, who recently said that if Israel allocated the equivalent of the cost of two F16 fighter planes to water resource management, the problem of water scarcity in Palestine could be resolved. "Peace can solve the water problem, but water can't bring peace," says El Khateeb, adding that in his view the vast majority on both sides want peace. "There is a willingness to share the resources, but there is a fear of crossing boundaries."

Fadia Daibes also acknowledges that the current situation seems hopeless at times, but remains obstinately optimistic: "There is no instant solution; it is a process that we have to go through with the long term in view. In the end, both Israelis and Palestinians want to preserve the resource. Most importantly though, we have to believe in dreams. Once the first step is taken, it can work."

# Notes

1. The Sea of Galilee is known as Lake Tiberias to the Arabs and Lake Kinneret to the Israelis.
2. The amount of water that can safely be extracted from an aquifer without exceeding the average annual recharge.
3. The 1967 Armistice Line that separates Israel from the West Bank.
4. The Sea of Galilee and the National Water Carrier.

# 9

# War and Visions of Peace

*"Mix politics and public relations with hydrology and science, and I can guarantee you will not get good results."—Professor Nadhir Al Ansari, Al Al-Bayt University, Mafraq, Jordan*

## A Water Fraternity along the Nile

"So how did you come to the subject of water?" Professor Boutros Ghali gives me an inquiring look through his large horn-rimmed spectacles. His voice is a resounding bass and he speaks English with a French accent tinged with Arabic. I look at his pale, slender hands as he clasps them together. When I hesitate, he answers for me; "It was a happy coincidence?" and I nod and smile. The tall Egyptian exudes an air of nobility, and, at the age of eighty-four, he can look back on a full and varied life. Trained as a lawyer, Boutros Ghali started his career as a professor of international law at Cairo University. In 1977 he was appointed to the post of Minister of Foreign Affairs, a function he held for fifteen years until he was elected as the first Arab Secretary-General of the United Nations in 1992. Today he holds an honorary position as ex-Secretary-General of the Organisation internationale de la Francophonie, the organization that promotes the French language around the world.

Our meeting takes places in his offices at the organization, which is housed in a nineteenth-century *hôtel de maître* in Paris' ministerial quarter. Boutros Ghali leans back and looks out the window over the quiet courtyard. Then he starts telling me his water story, a tale of high idealism and grand dreams, and also, ultimately, a tale of failure through mistrust. "I was minister of foreign affairs in Egypt from 1977 to 1991. During this whole period, my main obsession was water. Of course, I was involved with the discussions at Camp David, but the problem of water was always at the forefront of my concerns.

"Water was my main obsession," he repeats once more, staring into the distance as though seeing the events of twenty, twenty-five years ago flowing past his mind's eye. "I tried to raise awareness of the importance of cooperation between riparian states over the sharing of the Nile waters; I wanted to show Egyptians that Egypt's security is related to the south, to Sudan and Ethiopia, rather than to the east and Israel. I created an organization that brought together

143

the ministers of irrigation of the nine riparian states: Sudan, Egypt, Ethiopia, Kenya, Uganda, Tanzania, Burundi, Rwanda, and Congo. We called it Undugu, which means fraternity in Swahili, and our aim was to engender collaboration and consensus on issues related to the Nile," he explains.

An ambitious scheme proposed by Egypt outlined the construction of a series of hydroelectric dams along the Nile, which would create a network of hydropower plants through the region. The generated electricity would then be exported to other regions in exchange for hard currency. An electricity grid extending from Uganda's proposed Inga Dam to Egypt's Aswan Dam would transfer power to the networks of Jordan, Syria, Turkey, and beyond to the European Community. "We held meetings in Khartoum, in Kinshasa, in Addis Ababa," Boutros Ghali remembers, "but right from the beginning there was an atmosphere of mistrust and the upstream countries were suspicious of Egypt's demands. They said: 'If you want to build a new dam, it will flood our villages and displace our people. What will we receive in exchange?' They even said that they would demand one barrel of oil for each barrel of water they gave away." Thus the Undugu scheme slowly lost momentum and eventually disintegrated without leaving any tangible results.

Boutros Ghali has long recognized the gravity of the water question in the Middle East. During his period as Egypt's Minister of Foreign Affairs, he repeatedly witnessed that emotions can run high over the sharing of the region's most precious resource. Thus when President Sadat offered the waters of the Nile to Israel in a bid to open discussions about the West Bank and Gaza, there was public outrage in Egypt and beyond, with upstream countries protesting that the Nile waters were not President Sadat's to distribute at will. Boutros Ghali sees this as just one example of how water can become a political issue. In 1978, tensions over water reached a new peak when President Sadat threatened Ethiopia with military intervention if it embarked on any development projects that might affect the flow of the Nile northwards to Egypt. The incident was not well timed for Boutros Ghali: he had been working to strengthen Egypt's relationships with its upstream neighbors and initiate a dialogue between riparian states.

Boutros Ghali is often quoted for his belief that "the next war in this region will be over the waters of the Nile." As far as he is concerned, this comment, though voiced in 1985, is still valid today. He predicts that explosive population growth and the intensification of agricultural cycles throughout the Middle East and Africa will put great pressure on the already dwindling water reserves of the region—a pressure that could result in armed conflict. Taking the Nile Basin as an example of the difficulties involved in equitable water distribution, Boutros Ghali explains that current use of Nile waters is sure to increase as riparian countries develop their agriculture and their economy. Countries like Sudan and Ethiopia today still rely on rain to water their crops. Once they embrace irrigated agriculture, their downstream neighbor Egypt will inevitably receive less water. If in addition population figures in the region continue to soar, he foresees serious consequences.

"They will all be vying for the same water and the situation will be so dramatic that they will take to arms. Water may not be the apparent reason for the conflict, but it will certainly lie at its origins. If for instance 50,000 refugees cross the border from Ethiopia to Sudan because of drought and they attack a village, then Sudan will attack Ethiopia over this: ostensibly this will not be a conflict about water, but the problem of water will nevertheless lie at the root of this military intervention," he says.

While there has never been an armed conflict over the water of the Nile, there is a long-running tension over its unequal distribution. Today several upstream riparian countries are contesting the contents of a colonial treaty from 1929. The First Nile Water Agreement—which still determines the allocation of Nile water today—was concluded between Egypt and the colonial power Great Britain, which represented the present-day states of Uganda, Kenya, Tanzania, and Sudan. The treaty allocated 48 billion cubic meters of water per year to Egypt and 4 billion cubic meters per year to Sudan. Thirty years on, and in the context of the construction of the High Aswan Dam on the border between Egypt and Sudan, the agreement was altered, increasing the respective allocations to 55.5 billion cubic meters and 18 billion cubic meters per year. As both agreements were made before the other Nile Basin countries—except for Ethiopia—gained independence, they made no mention of the other countries and their water use. Instead, it stated that "once other upstream riparians claim a share of Nile waters, both countries will study together these claims and adopt a unified view thereon." Egypt also reserved the right to "inspect and investigate" the whole length of the Nile to the remote sources of its tributaries in the basin, effectively giving it the power to stop any water development project.

Until recently, no other riparian countries made formal claims to an allocation of Nile water. However, with the pressure from population growth and climate change in the latter part of the twentieth century, countries like Kenya, Uganda, Tanzania and Ethiopia have appealed for the renegotiation of the 1929 agreement. In their eyes it is a relic of a colonial era that no longer reflects the needs and aspirations of the riparian countries. Egypt has over the years repeatedly stated that it considers any change in the agreement as a strategic threat and that it will use all means at its disposal to prevent such violations of the agreement. It is particularly nervous about Ethiopian water development projects, which could seriously affect the amount of water reaching Egypt.

Nicknamed the "water tower of Africa," Ethiopia provides approximately 86 percent of the water that flows down the Egyptian Nile, yet it only utilizes 1 percent of this water. Lack of funding and technical expertise has meant that Ethiopia was never able to develop its own irrigation network. Thus, in a cruel twist of irony, the land that feeds the Nile is unable to feed itself. Ethiopia today remains among the poorest countries in the world, with a population that

**Map 9**
The Nile Basin. The Nile waters are used by the populations of ten countries:
Burundi, the Democratic Republic of Congo, Egypt, Eritrea, Ethiopia, Kenya,
Rwanda, Sudan, Tanzania, and Uganda

suffers from chronic and widespread hunger. With more than 80 percent of the population surviving on less than $2 a day, it is one of the poorest countries in the world; life expectancy is forty-seven years and nearly half the children are undernourished.

It is the same in many other countries in the Nile Basin, where political instability, poverty and conflict continue to hamper development. Five of the ten countries in the Nile Basin are among the poorest in the world, and seven of them are engaged in, or have recently emerged from civil or trans-boundary conflicts. With populations expected to increase from 330 million in 2002 to 450 million by 2015, the situation does not promise to get any easier. And as countries of the Nile Basin continue to develop their economies, the waters of the Nile will become increasingly important to all parties. In January 2004, Ethiopia announced that it would start using water from the Blue Nile for large-scale irrigation projects in the near future. Similarly, Tanzania has plans to draw water from Lake Victoria and lead it through a 150-kilometer pipeline to irrigate dry regions. Kenya too, has called for the revision of the 1929 treaty.

In the hope of relieving the misery that exists in many upstream countries and breaking down the tension that exists around the sharing of the Nile waters, the World Bank and the United Nations launched a new joint water management project for the Nile Basin in 1999. Composed of the ten riparian states—Burundi, the Democratic Republic of Congo, Egypt, Eritrea, Ethiopia, Kenya, Rwanda, Sudan, Tanzania, and Uganda—the Nile Basin Initiative (NBI) aims to foster cooperation and development of the Nile Basin.

Professor Boutros Ghali believes that the NBI could help avert conflicts over water resources in the region. Emphasizing the importance of a foreign mediator, he says a higher body needs to be brought in to play a facilitating role between member states and to ensure the criteria set by the organization are observed. "One of the problems of setting up projects in developing countries is that they are not able to embrace long-term projects; they are only interested in finding short-term solutions," he says. He believes an international organization could provide a solid base on which to build a sustainable and lasting collaboration project in the Nile Basin.

But like its predecessor Undugu, the NBI is wrestling with the long history of mistrust between the ten riparian states. Its initiatives to date have all focussed on confidence building, working on the so-called "win-win projects" that are beneficial to all, and postponing the resolution of key issues to a later date. The question is when these issues will be addressed and whether the institution will be strong enough to resolve the inevitable conflicting interests of member states.

Dr Mauwwia Sheddad, the president of the Sudanese Environment Conservation Society (SECS), places little hope in the potential of the NBI. "The NBI is a way of opening up discussion. For example, Tanzania wants to draw a canal from Lake Victoria to arid farmland: this will *immediately* lead to conflict. In Ethiopia, the Blue Nile runs through deep gorges. Above, the land is dry. So the only way they can utilize Nile water is by building dams; this too, will lead to conflict. The NBI is a nice vision. It looks good on paper, but in reality, water will definitely, I am absolutely sure of this, be a source of conflict if people do not start work *yesterday* on finding solutions."

Sheddad, a Sudanese astrophysicist who is famous in Sudan for predicting the commencement of Ramadan each year, is a larger-than-life character. Tall and broad, he has a mop of bushy black hair and mischievous black eyes that twinkle through his small glasses. Deeply concerned with the state of the Sudanese environment, Sheddad co-founded SECS in the 1980s with the aim of preserving the country's ecology. He says the key to resolving water-sharing issues along the Nile is for Egypt to relinquish its hold over the river's waters. "The Nile will be a very strategic natural resource in the future, not just for Egypt. One always says Egypt is the Nile, but in future the Nile will also be more important for the Sudan and other riparian countries. Egypt will have to get used to this and learn to concede some of the water it lays claim to. Egypt has always claimed it is the Nile. Even in pharaonic times, the invasions southwards were concerned with water resources and control of the Nile. Today, Egypt's political activity in all riparian countries is huge, all to ensure they can keep their share of the Nile waters. But in the meantime Sudan for example wants to use Nile water to generate energy; Ethiopia also has proposals to build dams—Egypt opposes all these initiatives. It needs to move away from this policy of control towards one of negotiation and concession on Nile waters."

Unsurprisingly, the Egyptians do not see things quite the same way. They believe they have a historical right to the waters of the Nile and argue that the water is more important to them, as it is the only source they can draw from, while the upstream countries can rely on supplies from other rivers and rainfall. While they acknowledge the importance of the NBI and its projects, they categorically refuse to discuss any decrease in water allocation to Egypt. Rushdi Said, a professor of geology and an expert on the Nile Basin, believes that any significant reduction in Egypt's allocation of Nile waters could jeopardize the country's very existence. "It is difficult to imagine how Egypt could survive with a lower quota of water, as seems to be the plan under the initiative. Quite possibly this would spell an end to agriculture as a primary activity, for which Egypt has been known since the dawn of history," he says.

Said argues that both Sudan and Ethiopia have ample water resources outside the Nile Basin and that they should focus on the development of these resources instead of "contesting Egypt's sole source of water." But critics of this view, both in upstream Nile Basin countries and elsewhere, say that if Egypt tidied up its own water management system, it could save considerable amounts of water. Modernization of the irrigation systems, the implementation of a comprehensive pricing system and a shift away from the cultivation of water-thirsty crops such as rice, sugar cane and cotton, could go a long way in solving Egypt's water scarcity problems.

Critics also point to the harrowing differences between the welfare in Egypt and the misery in countries like Ethiopia. Egypt has 3.5 million hectares of agricultural land, irrigated by thousands of kilometers of Nile canals, while Ethiopia has less than 200,000 hectares of irrigated land. Although large parts of Ethiopia's highlands are arable, they must rely on sporadic rainfall, which can produce one crop a year at most. Egyptian farmers, on the other hand, can count on a secure and regular supply of water, which allows them to produce two or three harvest seasons a year. Thanks to the Aswan High Dam, Egypt is also able to export power; Ethiopia, on the other hand, produces less than 500 megawatts from a few hydropower dams, providing electricity for less than 10 percent of the population.

Far from envisaging to give up any of their water though, the Egyptians are seeking to increase their supply by digging a canal through the Sudd marshes in southern Sudan and reducing the amount of water lost to evaporation in that region. Covering an area of about 135,000 square kilometers, the Sudd is an extremely flat plain that is composed of a series of swamps and ponds, overgrown with tall grasses and papyrus reeds. Numerous other streams drain into the Sudd, compensating for the enormous amount of water—at least 20 billion cubic meters per year—that is lost through evaporation. Initiated in 1978 in cooperation with Sudan, the Jonglei Canal Project planned the construction of a 360-kilometer canal that would allow for the recovery of 4.8 billion cubic meters per year.

Through the creation of several other such diversion canals at various points in the Sudd, the Egyptians hoped to recover an estimated total of 18.5 billion cubic meters from the White Nile. The work on the first project was interrupted in 1984 when the violent civil war erupted between the local African tribes and the armies of the Muslim north. While a peace deal was signed between the government and the southern rebels in 2005, it is doubtful that the neglected works can be rehabilitated without enormous additional costs. Still, the Egyptians remain keen to restart the Jonglei project as soon as there is durable peace

in the south. Dr Dia El Din El Qosy, a senior advisor to the Minister of Water Resources in Cairo, comments: "We are waiting for the situation in the south to settle, but then there will be more than just the Jonglei Project: there is the Bahr Al Ghazal, the Sudd, many marshes from which we can draw water and implement projects that will save water."

In Sudan there is less enthusiasm for the project and many fear that it will not only destroy a unique ecosystem with its flora and fauna, but also disrupt the lifestyle of local tribes living in the region. Many Sudanese are also wary of giving Egypt more control over the Nile waters. Sheddad believes the project needs further research to assess its environmental impacts. "Fifty percent of the White Nile discharge evaporates over the Sudd. The creation of the Jonglei Canal would allow water to be channeled directly north, but it would have unknown impacts; not only on the local environment but also on rainfall further north in the agricultural belt for example. The land in the south is very flat, so that even if a small percentage were taken from the Sudd, it would be noticeable at a great distance. The water would not reach these lands anymore. There is also the impact on biodiversity: the Sudd harbors a massive supply of genes that have been stored up for millions of years. The stability of this ecosystem might be disrupted by the creation of a canal." Instead of Jonglei, Sheddad says, the Egyptians should look at using water more efficiently. "If they managed water properly in Cairo, not even in all of Egypt, just in Cairo, then it wouldn't be necessary to create this canal," he comments laconically. But the Egyptians insist that the Jonglei Canal could be one of the "win-win" projects that the Nile Basin Initiative encourages.

Despite all the military threats, the Egyptians are increasingly coming to the realization that imbalances such as that between Ethiopia and Egypt only lead to instability in the region. In this context they have started working on an irrigation project in Ethiopia, developing the lands around the Koga River by providing expertise and investment. The project is being presented as a "confidence builder" to show that upstream uses do not necessarily hurt downstream populations. Ethiopian engineers calculated that the irrigation of 6,000 hectares around the Koga River would use less than one-tenth of 1 percent of the Nile flow reaching the Ethiopia-Sudan border. The scheme will provide extra water for crops during the erratic rainy season and a steady supply of water for a previously unthinkable second crop during the long dry season. The NBI thus seems to be bearing its first fruit, and while no one is talking about renegotiating the 1929 agreement, the parties are starting to see the potential benefits of cooperation.

Other joint schemes include the development of hydropower and agricultural trade, and the launch of an environmental protection scheme within the basin. Thus it seems Boutros Ghali's dream of creating a fraternity along the Nile might still come true.

### Saharan Solar Power and Pan-Arab Water Dreams

As soon as the taxi stops in front of the art deco apartment building, I stuff four Egyptian pounds through the window to the driver and run into the marble entrance hall, past the high mirrors and up the steps to the lifts. Thanks to another Cairo traffic jam, I am late to see Mohammed Sid Ahmed, a political commentator and journalist who "has ideas on water," as he put it in a deep gravelly voice over the phone.

I ring the bell and am received by a maid in uniform who ushers me into a spacious hall. The parquet floors are covered with Persian rugs; old black-and-white family portraits hang on the walls. I am shown into an office cluttered with books and papers. Sid Ahmed is sitting behind his computer. "I just have to finish something," he says, looking up absentmindedly and smiling. He points to two Louis XVI armchairs in front of his desk and asks me to sit down. A small elderly man with horn-rimmed spectacles, Sid Ahmed has a wise, grandfatherly air about him. As he sits down in the other armchair, he takes two hearing aids from a small box and fixes them into his ears. "Well now, how can I help you?" he asks when he is hooked up. I tell him about my fascination with water and that I am trying to understand what it means to people in the waterless Middle East. "Ah yes," he says as he recalls our phone conversation. "Well. I don't know much about water, but I can tell you about a dream I had a few years ago. Unfortunately it failed lamentably, but I spent a long time thinking about it and finding ways to make it work."

He leans back comfortably and smiles with satisfaction as he prepares to tell me about his brainchild. "You see, my thinking was as follows: we live in a desert region, water is central to everything here. Living with lack of water has seeped into our traditions. Over time, water scarcity has acquired a cultural and physical presence in our society. I was thinking about this and I asked myself a stupid question: if man can go to the moon to find water, then why should it be so difficult to separate water from salt on earth? And I came up with the idea of taking the Mediterranean, and putting it on the desert," he makes a lifting gesture and places an invisible slab of water onto an invisible expanse of sand.

I look at him with what must be a look of disbelief. He nods and smiles at my incomprehension: "Desalinate the Mediterranean and channel it to the Sahara to turn the desert into a fertile plain. The desalination plants would be powered by solar energy: three rows of concave mirrors spanning from Morocco to the Sinai Desert, all along the North African coast. This would make it possible to produce four times the amount of electricity needed to power Europe! I immediately saw there was great potential here: at the time, in the mid-1990s, it looked like there might soon be a breakthrough in the Arab-Israeli peace process and I thought this could be a joint project. Then, when things turned bitter again, I thought it could be an Arab project that would somehow redress the balance of power between the Arab world and Israel. I had the opportunity to present my idea to President Mubarak for a quarter of an hour. He seemed impressed;

I could see he was thinking like a pharaoh. This could be the grand project he would be remembered for..."

Ostensibly just another mega-project, Sid Ahmed's dream castle was in fact rooted in a desire to create political unity through water. Like Boutros Ghali's Undugu, it sought to reverse the growing enmity over the distribution of this "blue gold" and create a platform for collaboration and innovation between the parties. Unfortunately for Sid Ahmed, the project was doomed to the same fate as Undugu: when he presented his ideas at an international conference in Paris, they were not well received and he grew discouraged.

"Later I heard that Israel was developing a multi-billion dollar project using solar energy to desalinate seawater," he adds. "It completely discouraged me. I had hoped this project could reinforce the Arab status in the Middle East, rectify the equilibrium through peaceful means, and here, instead of redressing the balance, it was being tipped even further in favor of the Israelis." Sid Ahmed wanted to tackle two of the region's major problems in a single, all-embracing project: the physical threat of water scarcity and the political tensions. "I wanted to combine this problem of overcoming the lack of water with a resolution for the Arab-Israeli conflict," he says. "In the twentieth century, we rationalized Egypt's water by building the Aswan High Dam. But I was thinking in twenty-first century terms: I wanted to rationalize water on a larger scale for the whole Arab world," he spreads his arms in a grand gesture.

Now, Sid Ahmed is sombre about the future: "Only 1 percent of all the water on earth is sweet; it is the first time in history that we are draining the non-renewable water sources *in* the earth, instead of the water that flows over it. We are depleting the sources of sweet water. The situation is deteriorating all the time." Like Boutros Ghali, Sid Ahmed believes that control over the scarce resource could lead to conflict in the region: "When you are thirsty, you will kill for water. And we are not even thirsty yet. It is a fundamental issue. The problem is acute. In this region in particular, water could become the epicenter of conflict. Until now land was the cause of conflict. But land is a stable entity; water moves, and this could extend the area of conflict enormously."

Sid Ahmed's bleak forecast reflects a long-running debate around the possibility of "water wars." As populations grow, standards of living rise and water reserves dwindle, competition for freshwater resources in the region is constantly growing. Both in academic circles and in the popular press this has led to the development of an extensive literature on the coming water wars that will, in the eyes of many, certainly occur in the twenty-first century. And because of the volatile political situation in the region, the Middle East and North Africa are often designated as high-risk areas, where armies have in the past already been mobilized and shots have been fired over water.

The arguments in support of water wars are numerous and seem, at first sight, quite logical: because water is vital to all aspects of a nation's survival—from the life of its inhabitants to its economy—water scarcity can lead to great political instability and tension in countries with arid or semi-arid climates. Unlike oil, water has no substitutes. Water also flows across political borders in constantly varying amounts and patterns, making it difficult to manage international watercourses in the framework of classical legal systems and principles.

The 1997 Convention on the Non-Navigational Uses of International Watercourses took twenty-seven years to develop but still does not provide an adequate answer to many water disputes. While it establishes important principles for avoiding and resolving water disputes, including responsibility for cooperation and joint management, it provides few practical guidelines for allocations, the issue that lies at the heart of most water conflicts. An additional consideration is that international law only concerns itself with the rights and responsibilities of states. Thus if the Kurds along the Euphrates, or the Palestinians along the Jordan, would want to claim their rights, they would not be represented. The biggest stumbling block however is that the International Court of Justice will only hear cases with the consent of all parties involved, and no practical enforcement mechanism exists to back up the Court's findings. With so many intricacies and limitations, it is no surprise that the Court has to date only decided one case regarding international water law.

All the above would suggest that water could indeed become the cause of war in the twenty-first century. Indeed, entire bookcases could be filled with the books, academic papers and articles devoted to the analysis of past water wars and the ensuing predictions over the likely hot spots for new water wars.

Besides the Nile Valley, the "water war" debate in the Middle East focuses on the Jordan Basin and the sharing of water between the surrounding countries: Israel, Jordan, the Palestinian Territories, Syria and Lebanon. The third predicted "water war" hot spot is the Tigris-Euphrates Basin, where riparian countries Turkey, Syria and Iraq are entangled in an ongoing dispute over respective water rights and needs from the two rivers.

However, in reality, the hype over the coming water wars is to a great extent an academic construction that has been reinforced by the media. Aaron Wolf, an associate professor of geography at Oregon State University, has done extensive research on "transboundary freshwater dispute" and the discourse around water wars. He found that while there have certainly been tensions and disputes over water resources, there have hardly been any wars. "The actual history of armed water conflict is somewhat less dramatic than the water wars literature would lead one to believe: a total of seven incidents, in three of which no shots were fired. As near as we can find, there has never been a single war fought over water," he says. And in a footnote, he adds: "This is not quite true. The earliest documented interstate conflict known is a dispute between the Sumerian city-states Lagash and Umma over the right to exploit boundary channels along the Tigris in 2500 BC. In other words, the last and only 'water war' was 4,500 years ago."

Wolf points out that much of the confusion around the subject of water wars arises from the vague definition of terms. Thus many authors have written about "conflicts over water" and "water disputes," recording cases that did not involve armed conflict or confrontation. According to Wolf, the most widely cited examples are wars between Israel and its neighbors. Thus many argue that a dispute over water lies at the root of the 1967 Six-Day War between Israel and the armies of Jordan, Syria, and Egypt: in 1964, Syria announced its plan to divert the headwaters of the Jordan River and impound them in a dam. Israel immediately responded with air strikes and ground attacks against the diversion works, thus contributing to the outbreak of the 1967 war. Others argue that Israel's 1982 invasion of Lebanon was motivated by Zionist ideals and a desire to gain control over the waters of the Litani Basin. Wolf comments: "The only problem with these theories is a complete lack of evidence." He argues that while shots were fired over water between Israel and Syria in the mid-1960s, the final confrontation in 1966, in which Israel deployed tanks and aircraft and managed to stop the Syrian construction of the disputed diversion canal, put an end to the water-related tensions between Syria and Israel. Wolf sees the outbreak of the 1967 war as an entirely separate incident.

However, Wolf says, while there may never have been any real "wars" over water, there is considerable evidence to show that a lack of clean freshwater has led to political instability and that acute violence can occur as a result. There are also many cases in which water forms part of a broader dispute over issues as fishing rights, access to ports or river boundaries for example. Wolf concludes that the geographic scale and the intensity of the conflict are often inversely related and that, on a small scale, acute violence can occur.

Conversely, there is a much more substantial history of water dispute resolution. The United Nations Food and Agriculture Organization has recorded more than 3,600 treaties relating to international water resources between 805 and 1984. Most of these deal with issues of navigation. Based on these findings, Wolf has drawn up a database of the 145 treaties signed in the twentieth century that deal with "water per se," excluding those that deal with boundaries or fishing rights. Wolf finds that many of the treaties he studied in the context of his database showed a great elegance and creativity in the ways in which they dealt with this critical resource.

Looking towards the future, Wolf identifies several arguments against the possibility of water wars becoming a reality any time soon. Rather than planting the seeds of war, water appears to induce cooperation. The many treaties over water sharing show that a common waterway brings shared interests. Along the larger rivers, for instance, the best sites to build dams are usually upstream at the headwaters where the valley walls are steeper; prime agricultural land is usually downstream in the alluvial plains. An upstream dam can provide hydropower to the upstream riparian and help regulate the flow for downstream agriculture, thus benefiting both parties.

Furthermore, given the cost of water, and the cost of war, it is simply not worth going to war over water. In this context, Wolf quotes an Israeli defence analyst who was responsible for long-term planning during the 1982 invasion of Lebanon. When asked whether water was a factor in decision making, he said: "Why go to war over water? For the price of one week's fighting, you could build five desalination plants. No loss of life, no international pressure, and a reliable supply you don't have to defend in hostile territory." Wolf thus concludes: "War over water is neither strategically rational, hydrologically effective, nor economically viable."

Other academics too, believe it is time to "debunk the myth of 'water wars.'" Anthony Turton, a political scientist working on water as a strategic issue in southern Africa, believes that by focusing on water wars, attention is being deviated from the real issues such as the management of water scarcity and the resolution of political issues around water management. "'Water wars' are nothing more than a myth," he says. "There is not a shred of evidence to support their existence.... True, there is a lot of conflict, or potential conflict, over water resources. However this does not mean a war over water. Water scarcity as both a necessary and sufficient condition for going to war is an almost non-existent phenomenon." He adds that the water war myth is also being "actively fed into the media, who then propagate the myth as if it were reality." He believes that instead of obsessively reiterating the debate on water wars, the attention of academics and policy makers should focus on other, more pressing areas including the growing water scarcity in certain regions, conflict resolution and mitigation, and the role that NGOs and civil society can play in this. "These issues are the important ones, deserving of our undivided attention. To focus any more energy on 'water wars' will merely dilute those efforts and undermine the long-term need to develop effective coping strategies to ensure social stability in a region facing increasing levels of water scarcity," concludes Turton.

## Peace in a Pipeline

Like Boutros Ghali's Undugu and Sid Ahmed's solar-power-cum-desalination scheme, Turkey's plan to build a "Peace Pipeline" to export water throughout the region was designed to solve problems of trust and water scarcity in one comprehensive move. Launched in 1987 by Turkey's then-Prime Minister, Turgut Özal, the Peace Pipeline Project was designed to supply water from the Ceyhan and Seyhan Rivers in Turkey's southeast to the countries of the Arabian Peninsula and the eastern Mediterranean. The pipeline was to be made up of two branches with sixteen pumping stations, which would transport around 2.1 billion cubic meters of water per year. The eastern branch would cover a distance of 3,900 kilometers to the Arabian states of the Persian Gulf and terminate in Oman; the western branch, 2,650 kilometers in length, would provide water to Syria, Jordan, the Palestinian Territories, and Israel, ending in the holy cities of Jeddah and Mecca in Saudi Arabia.

While Turkey saw the Peace Pipeline as a gesture of concerned goodwill towards its neighbors, the other countries in the region were not so enthusiastic, for besides the technological problems that the project posed, the $21 billion price tag made viability questionable. Many of the Arab Gulf states had already invested heavily in national desalination schemes and serious political and historical considerations also stood in the way of the project's implementation. Both Arabs and Israelis were reluctant to give Turkey such a degree of control over the water they used. The Arab countries in particular accused Turkey of using water as a political weapon; Israel on the other hand was reluctant to become dependent on a source that crossed Syrian territory and could be cut off at any moment.

The Peace Pipeline Project did however generate smaller pipeline projects that focussed on the transportation of water from Turkey to Israel, Jordan, and the Palestinian Territories. The Mini-Peace Pipeline and the Mini-Mini Peace Pipeline were both designed by Israeli water experts and proposed the supply of around 700 million cubic meters of water per year at the more modest cost of $5 billion. However, like their big brother, the implementation of Mini Peace Pipelines was hampered by political considerations.

A fourth scheme, the "Peace Canal" was developed by Boaz Wachtel, an Israeli researcher and consultant, who continues to believe that international cooperation over water issues is the only way to attain regional peace. Thus while others in Israel are focussing all their hopes on nationally managed desalination schemes, Wachtel is critical of this solution. "The Israelis can say that they can desalinate, but this does nothing to advance the situation in the region. In the long term, you can't ignore the plight of the Palestinians," he says. "It is the same with importation of water by tanker from Turkey to Israel[1]: it has very little regional impact. We have to start accepting that this region is hydrologically unstable. Some years there is abundance and other years there is scarcity. With water cooperation, we could stabilize the situation in the region." Developed in the early 1990s, in the hopeful period of the Oslo Agreements, the Peace Canal Project was abandoned after Netanyahu's election and the collapse of the peace process, but Wachtel believes it could one day be relaunched.

We are in Wachtel's home in a green suburb of Netanya north of Tel Aviv. His teenage kids have just gone upstairs after dinner and we are sitting in the living room, Wachtel scouring through the dusty cardboard box that he has just brought down from the attic. He is a tall, exuberant figure with a straggly beard and the distracted air of an artist. "I work on the boundary of water and politics," he says as he hands me various articles and papers he published in the mid-1990s to promote his idea. Describing himself as an autodidact when it comes to matters of water, Wachtel is certainly an unconventional all-rounder. Thus after the collapse of his Peace Canal Project, he redirected his attention to another worthy cause: the legalization of marijuana in Israel. As the founder and chairman of the national Green Leaf Party, Wachtel has spent the last seven years lobbying his cause. At the 2006 election, the third in which it participated, the party again failed to secure a seat in the Knesset, but nevertheless won 40,000 votes.

At the same time, he is hopeful that the Peace Canal Project will one day be implemented. Based on the same principles as the Peace Pipelines, the Peace Canal proposes to transport 1.1 billion cubic meters of water per year from the Atatürk Dam Reservoir or the Ceyhan and Seyhan Rivers to the Golan Heights. From here, it would be equally distributed between Jordan, Syria, the Palestinian Territories and Israel.

What differentiates the Canal from the Pipelines is that it addresses not only the problem of water scarcity, but also deals with the issues of land and Israel's national security. The end of the canal includes a sixty kilometer-long, 750-meter-wide anti-tank barrier that would run over the Golan Heights along the length of the Israeli-Syrian border. "This makes the Peace Canal unique: it combines elements of water security and physical security. The canal on the Golan Heights will form a physical barrier guarded with tanks." Wachtel says the anti-tank barrier will reduce both side's ability to rapidly cross the border and thus induce Israel and Syria to reach a compromise over the Golan Heights. In the east, a replenished Jordan River would serve to delay any attacks from Jordan or further afield. Thus, says Wachtel, the Peace Canal could assure Israel's national security through physical barriers on the ground, and at the same time ensure adequate water supply and peace. At an estimated cost of $2-3 million, the project is less expensive than the pipeline schemes. But critics have found several disadvantages to the Peace Canal. Besides its geopolitical limitations, there are also practical constraints, as a large amount of water would be wasted through evaporation in the anti-tank barrier-canal on the Golan Heights.

Most experts in the region now recognize that water scarcity is unlikely to lead to war in the future. More and more, the squabbling parties are realizing that it is simply not worth it. However, from there to achieving true cooperation over water in an international context, is another matter. Nadhir Al Ansari, an environmental scientist at Al Al-Bayt University in the Jordanian town of Mafraq, says that the increasingly politicized nature of the debate makes it difficult to come to sustainable solutions. "There should be more long-term planning in water. This is a problem in the whole Arab world. It is obvious as far as I am concerned: even though there are government changes and ministerial changes, there should be consistency over water policy. But it is the politics of it that makes it complicated: mix politics and publics relations with hydrology and science, and I can guarantee you won't get good results." Still, Al Ansari believes that in the long term, cooperation over water-sharing issues is the only viable option. "Despite the differences in background and race, I believe people will, in the end, work together. Once there is no other choice anymore, they will. In time, they will come to the realization that water is more than just a commodity; it is the future of our children.

"Of course it is easy to theorize about these issues and say what should change, but to put it into practice you need time and resolve. You see, it's easy to make trouble, but it's not so easy to make peace." He points out the window to the university gardens: "If I go out there now and pick a fight with some students, it's easy—I can do that in minutes. But to make friends with them, that could take months, years… This is the difficulty."

## Note

1.    In March 2004, Turkey and Israel had signed a deal by which Turkey would export water from its Manavgat River to Israel. Yearly, 50 million cubic meters of water were to be shipped from Turkey's southwest coast to Israel. However, failure to find an economical means to transport the water led to the cancellation of the agreement in April 2006. Supporters of the deal argue that transporting the water in large floating bags would be an economic solution, bringing the price of the imported water below that of desalinated water.

# 10

# Relearning the Meaning of Water

*"Working with farmers is very different from working with infrastructure: infrastructure is like a dead body. The farmers give it life by working with it, so it is important that they agree with the methods used. With time, our collaboration with the farmers has got better. We have started learning from them and have learnt to collaborate with them in a productive way."—Engineer Abdallah Doma, Irrigation Improvement Project, Damanhour, Egypt*

In many places in the Middle East, water scarcity is becoming a reality that can no longer be concealed behind reassuring political rhetoric. As a result, governments in several countries are beginning to recognize that to deal with a problem of such magnitude, water users need to be involved. For too long, users were shielded from the impending scarcity, and left to waste the precious water supplies at will. Now, in the context of water demand management initiatives, they are being asked to take responsibility over the water they consume: to use it more consciously and more wisely, and thus, reassess its value.

### How to Use Water: Lesson One for Turkish Farmers

In southeastern Turkey, the GAP project has started addressing the issue of user involvement. GAP, the Turkish abbreviation for the Southeastern Anatolia Project, started as a purely economic power generation project to build twenty-two dams and nineteen hydroelectric power plants on the Tigris and Euphrates Rivers. By 2010 this large-scale and highly ambitious project will provide 22 percent of Turkey's electricity needs and irrigate 1.7 million hectares of new land in the region, enabling agricultural export on a large scale. As the only water-rich country in the Middle East together with Lebanon, Turkey is keen to become the breadbasket of the Middle East, exporting food to water-poor countries like Saudi Arabia and the Gulf States in exchange for money or oil.

Costing more than $32 billion in Turkish and foreign investment, the project has been highly controversial in the West, with environmentalists warning of damage to the region's ecosystems, and human rights activists denouncing the forced displacement of large Kurdish communities. Over the years, this criticism has led to a shift in GAP policies, broadening the scope of the project to include social, cultural, educational and human aspects, and transforming GAP into a "multi-sectoral and integrated regional development project" with a heavy emphasis on social and human development (and also on the very well-oiled PR machine which has re-branded GAP as a humane, sustainable, democratic project and which assails any foreign visitor with a flood of brochures and statistics to prove this point).

Still, when I visited the Atatürk Dam on the Euphrates River, the overriding impression was one of inhuman, alienating hugeness. It is the sixth largest rock-filled dam in the world and details of its construction, capacity and proportions were listed to me during a snazzy PowerPoint presentation given in the slick, 300-seater lecture theater of the Atatürk Dam Visitor Center. Here a young GAP representative enumerated the dam's vital statistics in a staccato of images and diagrams. Reservoir capacity: 48.7 cubic kilometers; embankment volume: 84.5 million cubic meters; power generation: 8.1 billion kWh per year; irrigable land: 110,000 square kilometers; cost $4 billion—figures all so inconceivably large that my mind just went blank.

As I stared out at the dam from the "panoramic balcony," it still felt unreal, like a painted film set that had been mounted in front of the balcony and would be taken down at the end of the day after visiting hours. It looked too pristine, the concrete too smooth, the water too blue and everything so quiet.... The dam's embankment swerved across the valley in a large sweep of concrete and on one side the six long, shining tubes that led to the turbines shimmered in the sun. The only thing that gave me any real sense of its huge scale was the logo of the State Hydraulic Works Directorate, D.S.I., which was mounted on the dam's embankment. The three small, green letters seemed lost on the gigantic slab of concrete, hanging forlornly in the middle of a gray mass. Only the fact that each letter measured forty-two meters in height gave one some idea of just how large the embankment was in reality, and of how much water was behind it.

With a depth of 160 meters, the reservoir's dazzling azure-blue waters are an eerily still and calm tomb for the dozens of villages, houses and mosques, which lie smothered in its depths. The dam's impressive capacity makes it GAP's undisputed centerpiece: it produces enough electricity to provide for a city of half a million inhabitants and the water in its reservoir can cater for an eighth of Turkey's irrigable land, or 725 square kilometres. Afterwards, I was brought to meet the dam's director, Mr. Gülabi Polat, who sat behind a very large desk and proudly declared that he spoke nothing but Turkish. Even through a transla-tor he refused to comment on the impact of the dam on local communities and neighboring countries Syria and Iraq. This, he said, was not his business. He dealt with dams, not politics. Polat's only statement was: "The Atatürk Dam is the symbol of the GAP project. It lies at its heart. GAP is like a living body and without a heart, it cannot live."

The land that is irrigated by the water of the Atatürk Dam is almost all pri-vately owned by local farmers who can hardly believe how their life has changed with the arrival of water. After my visit to the dam, I went to the Harran Plain, south of the main regional town of Şanliurfa. From the Atatürk reservoir, pipelines transport 123,000 liters of water a second over 230 kilometers to the Harran plain, a long rectangular expanse, scorched by the sun in summer and assailed by cold winds from the eastern steppes in winter. Since 1995 when irrigation started, the plain, lined by tall, dry mountain ranges on either side, has become a miraculous carpet of green fertility amidst an otherwise arid and sun-bleached landscape. As we drove south from Şanliurfa along a new road as straight as a ruler, we passed through a Mondriaan landscape of green squares framed by the straight gray lines of irrigation channels. With the large sky and the low horizon, this could have been Holland.

The dusty village of Harran is a last reminder of the waterless days, an island of drought in the midst of this quasi-Dutch landscape. The remains of a large castle lie on a hill in the middle of the village and around it stand the traditional Harran beehive houses with large conical roofs. Heavy stone walls still surround the town but most of the inner precinct is a deserted no man's land. The town's history goes back to the third millennium BC, having played an important role as a university town and a center of scientific, philosophical and political thought in the Assyrian Empire. Today a tall brick tower dating back to the sixth century BC still survives as a testimony to this period: the Assyrian astrological observatory. In those days two rivers, the Jalab and the Daysan, watered the plain and the town, allowing farmers to irrigate crops. When the rivers ran dry in the seventeenth century, farmers had no choice but to rely on sporadic rainfall.

Today, locals call it "cotton land." With more than 200,000 hectares of land now verdant cotton fields, all the villages of the plain are growing and everywhere new houses are sprouting up beside the traditional mud-and-straw houses. The farmers living here still cannot quite believe what has happened. Many of them have spent their whole life in poverty working as seasonal workers and praying for rain. "Before irrigation people were sleeping," one farmer told me. "We waited for the rain and planted one crop a year. Often there was no rain and then we lost all our crops. Now we have several crops a year and we are rich!"

But the management and distribution of such sudden and large amounts of water is not straightforward. One engineer told me that while the GAP project had brought many benefits to the region, it also meant people had to adapt to completely new conditions. "We need education above all. These farmers have never seen water before and they need to learn how to use it. They don't know what to do with it now they have it. It has changed people's lives very suddenly and they need time to get used to it." Sociologists and policy makers at the GAP administration believe the best way to teach the Harran farmers how to use water is to give them the responsibility of distributing and managing the resource themselves, creating a direct relationship between them and the water. Fourteen water user associations have now been created in the Harran plain, each giving the responsibility of local management to the farmers.

The Kurtuluş water user association is housed in a beehive house in Harran. The thick stone walls that taper into large conical roofs protect the interior from the heat of the summer and the cold winds of winter—a sort of fourth century climate control system. Opening the low wooden door, it was as though I had stepped into a fairytale. It was a cross between the House of the Seven Dwarves and a fully wired-up, networked office: from the little entrance hall, four tiny rooms, more like alcoves, made up the whole house, all with wooden floors and crude smudges of plaster on the walls. The light came from small windows and air gaps in the roof. But then cables ran everywhere and the sound of printers, faxes and phones buzzed and whirred in every room as four or five men rushed about the little space, constantly ducking beneath the low door frames.

Seated at his desk in the manager's office, the general secretary, Abdulkerim Dörtkardeş, told me that the association looks after 6,300 hectares of land, which includes 550 farmers and eighteen villages. "Farmers come to the office when they have problems, and our agricultural engineers also go to the field regularly to advise the farmers," he said. He said the water user associations were important because they gave farmers a sense of civic responsibility and influence. "The fact that people are voting and can elect a chairman makes them learn about democracy," he said. "In the general election, the farmers don't really care, they feel it makes no difference to them; it is too far away. But here it really does impact on their lives directly and they know that their vote can affect things around them."

The Harran water user associations are modern versions of the traditional distribution systems I saw elsewhere in the Middle East with regular meetings, elections, and a chairman who settles any disputes and decides on the time allocations of the water. The water that flows to the fields is state-owned, but only until it reaches the individual user associations' channels, then it is theirs to manage and divide equitably. While scarcity needs to be carefully managed, the new system introduced on GAP's Harran Plain shows that abundance also needs to be controlled, and even learnt. As Dörtkardeş commented: "The farmers are learning to use the water. Before irrigation they depended on rain-fed agriculture. Now that they have irrigation they are confused, the agricultural situation has changed and we are trying to find the right way to deal with it. It has taken most farmers at least two years to adapt to the new situation."

At this point Ibrahim Tekdag, the newly elected chairman of the Kurtuluş water user association, came in, dressed in smart trousers and proudly showing off his new mobile phone that was hooked into his belt. A stocky, white-haired man, Tekdag was delighted with his new title. He had just been elected for the next three years and was beaming: not only was he suddenly a prosperous farmer, he was also a chairman with the power to bestow or withhold the new resource. When I asked what he would do for the farmers, he replied that he would grant many wishes, for he had promised fairness in all things. The shape of the Kurtuluş district is long and narrow, he explained, and it is fed by a single channel, making it harder to be equitable and just to all—particularly those at the very end of the channel. Luckily for the others, Tekdag said with a smile, his own plot was right at the end of the canal.

He then hastened to offer me ice cream and cake; he wanted me to stay for a long time, as he liked talking about his new role. "Before irrigation we used to go to Adana to pick cotton," said Tekdag. "On our land we planted wheat and barley and we hoped for rain. Now we have employees coming to work on our land from Adiyaman and Diyarbakir. It is strange for many of us. We were waiting for the water for fifteen years and we thought it would never happen, we never believed it. Some of us still find it hard to get used to."

That evening, as I sat down to write up my notes, I found it hard to distill the significance of all that water in the Atatürk Dam and in the Harran Plain. Surrounded by glossy folders, promotion booklets and pages of notes, I slowly came to the realization that GAP, for all its problems, was gradually laying the link between the grandiose scale of its dam project and the people who used the water. Somewhere between the Atatürk Dam and the Harran Plain, a transition was made that turned the masses of water in the dam's reservoir into one person's water share for the week, scaling down to the human level and making issues of distribution within the local community once again relevant. The traditional system of water legislation and distribution has thus been reinstated, and though it is perhaps dying in the Damascene Ghuta and the Moroccan Ourika Valley, here it is being reborn in a new form on the Harran Plain, as part of one the most ambitious and controversial dam projects of the late twentieth century.

## Building Water Communities in the Nile Delta

In Egypt farmers are also becoming more involved in the management of the Nile waters. The heavily autocratic and hierarchical system of water distribution here is centered on the powerful Ministry of Water Resources. Looming over the Nile in Cairo like an all-seeing concrete-and-steel embodiment of this power, the nineteen-story ministry controls the 55.5 billion cubic meters of water that flows from Aswan to the Mediterranean every year. Surrounded by high fences and manned by dozens of security guards inside and out, the building exudes an eerie totalitarian atmosphere. Inside, all employees and visitors have to pass through security gates, before joining a teeming queue near the lifts. Upstairs, the long gray corridors lead to anonymous offices that are overcrowded with desks, documents, books, and dozens of secretaries.

And yet within this colossus of bureaucratic regulation, things are changing. Instead of staying behind their desks to plan more infrastructural projects, engineers are being sent out into the field to work with farmers on improving the water distribution system throughout the country. Dr Mahmoud Abu Zeid, the Egyptian Minister of Water Resources, explains the policy shift: "Traditionally, this ministry dealt very little with the users, but we are changing that now. By involving them, we give them responsibility, and we show them that the system is theirs, that they have ownership." In a country where the district water engineer was traditionally the all-powerful authority, many engineers are finding this new way of working difficult to get used to. For them, the idea that farmers should be allowed to have their say in the management of land and water and participate in decision making processes, goes against all habits and beliefs. Robert Roostee, a Dutch consultant working on the development of farmer participation projects with the Egyptian Ministry of Water Resources, confirms that change within the ministry is slow. "The engineering wing in the ministry continues to work as always, carrying out engineering studies, designs, and generally focusing on the hard technical side of water management. They seem incapable of integrating human considerations with the pure engineering side of things," he says.

The work with farmers started in 1989 when the ministry launched the nationwide Irrigation Improvement Project (IIP). After initial teething problems and several failed projects in the Delta, the World Bank got involved in the project in 1997. Since then more than 6,000 water user associations have been created throughout the country, each grouping between fifty and 200 users.

Water distribution in Egypt takes place through a fairly straightforward and hierarchical system: all along the course of the Nile there are derivation canals which lead water east and west of the river to the fields. The primary canals lead to distribution canals, which in turn lead to branch canals—all of these are owned and maintained by the government. From the branch canal water flows to the *mesqa*, a smaller side canal that brings the water to the fields of individual farmers. Each *mesqa* is shared by around fifty farmers and irrigates around twenty-five hectares of land. It is at this micro-level that the water user associations function, giving farmers immediate responsibility over how they divide their share of water.

Such collaboration over water—between the farmers, and between the government and the farmers—is unprecedented in Egypt. Before the construction of the High Aswan Dam, periods of drought and flood succeeded each other and when the water came, farmers simply allowed the water to cover their lands. For Jan Bron, the director of a team of Dutch consultants working on the water user association projects with the Ministry of Water Resources, this absence of any kind of structure around water distribution is surprising: "Given that this country has one of the oldest irrigation systems in the world, Egypt actually has surprisingly little experience with collaboration around water. It is strange, but it is lagging behind the whole rest of the world in terms of integration, participation and decentralization," he says.

The first form of collaboration around water came after the completion of the first Aswan Dam in 1902. "When the first dam was built, the rhythm of the flood disappeared. The water no longer rose and fell, and the seasons became muted. Instead of waiting for the water to come to their land, the farmers had to work for it now, lifting it from river level to the fields. They used Arabic waterwheels, so-called *saqqias*, and the Archimedes screw,[1] but as these tools usually had a capacity that was larger than the needs or financial means of the individual farmer, they grouped themselves in so-called "*saqqia* rings" that functioned at the level of the *mesqa*," explains Bron. Water was distributed through a rotational system in which each *mesqa* received water every five to ten days depending on the seasons.

The appearance of small motorized pumps in the 1970s led to the disintegration of most *saqqia* rings as farmers preferred to each own individual hand pumps. This desire for independence among farmers also meant there was little communication. "Even today there is very little social contact along the canals—even from one village to another, people often don't know each other," says Bron.

The IIP aims to reinstate the concept of the *saqqia* ring in the form of water user associations, replacing the many individual motor pumps with a single pump at the head of the *mesqa*. Users of the single pump attend regular meetings and their water needs are managed by an elected *mesqa* leader. Abdallah Doma, an engineer at the National Water Research Center in Cairo, has worked on the development of water user associations throughout Egypt since the early 1990s. He explains that the new system is in fact not very different from the old one. Each *mesqa* still receives the same amount of water that is allocated by the government. The main difference is that water is now distributed more efficiently. "Before, farmers were always worried about water and they never thought they would get enough. They had no information and often didn't know when their next turn would come, especially if their land was at the end of a canal. This meant they often used far too much water, to cover their irrigation needs for ten or fifteen days."

In the old system, the district engineer was the smallest link in the chain of the ministry hierarchy. He managed districts with a surface area of up to 21,000 hectares, in which more than 40,000 farmers worked. Given this large area of jurisdiction, it was impossible for him to monitor the water use of individual farmers and many stole water, which inevitably led to conflicts and animosities over allocations. "Now with the IIP system, the farmers know when they will get water so they are not worried and use only as much as they need. And if something goes wrong, they know they can turn to their *mesqa* representatives for compensation," says Doma. On a technical level, the *mesqa*s have also been improved by the IIP: earthen canals that lost a lot of water through seepage have been replaced by concrete canals or pipelines.

Of course, as with any new system, the IIP has encountered problems. Doma says that there was strong resistance to the project initially, with only 25 percent of the farmers showing any interest in it. He remembers that ministry engineers used to fear their visits to the field: "The farmers would come out with their sticks and chase us away. We couldn't even talk to them. They were very anxious: there is not much land here and they thought that with the new project they would lose both their land and their water," he says. But the engineers also took time to get used to the hands-on approach of IIP. "We had no experience of working with farmers and we didn't know how to listen to them," Doma continues. "Working with farmers is very different from working with infrastructure: infrastructure is like a dead body. The farmers give it life by working with it, so it is important that they agree with the methods used. With time, our collaboration with the farmers has got better. We have started learning from them and have learnt to collaborate with them in a productive way."

The Balaktar Kalaan water user association near the town of Damanhour in the Delta was created in 1990, and after initial reservations, the farmers have now embraced the project wholeheartedly. Doma took me to visit the farmers of the water user association. Traveling through the rural areas of Egypt is like going back in time, and one imagines the scenes of everyday life have changed little in the last 2,000 years: bumpy, winding dirt roads weave their way through fields and villages. It was the time of the onion harvest, and mountains of bright purple bulbs were neatly stacked along the road, waiting to be taken to market. A group of women and young boys sat in a circle cleaning them and throwing them into wicker baskets. Irrigation in Egypt still takes place through flooding and many small plots lay under water. In the distance, two farmers in white *galabiyyas* sat under a willow tree at the edge of a small canal, sheltering from the midday heat. Small channels, canals, and side branches bisected the land everywhere.

We arrived at the *mesqa*, where a young pump operator was opening one of the valves to the fields. Water came rushing out, and several farmers stood by and watched approvingly. The pump operator showed me the ledger in which he recorded the names of members, the incomes and expenditures, and the irrigation fees owed. As we were talking, a farmer in an elegant *galabiyya* and carefully combed silvery gray hair came walking through the field with an almost aristocratic air about him. I asked him whether the association had been good for the farmers on the Balaktar Kalaan *mesqa*: "*Al Hamdu Lillaah*, yes," he said. "After sixteen years we are like a family. There is no conflict anymore and we can manage the land ourselves now. We have saved water, we have saved work, and we have saved our health. It is much better this way. Before, we used to spend three or four hours installing our pumps each time we wanted water. Now we just have to walk over here and talk to this young boy, and we get our water." Doma smiled and said the irrigation department hardly ever came here anymore because things just ran smoothly without them. Of course there was no way of knowing whether everything really ran so smoothly. Despite all the talk of dismantling the old hierarchical structures, it seemed unlikely that Engineer Doma had lost all his authority.

As the success of the water user association is consolidated and more districts join IIP, Bron believes the most important thing now is to ensure the continuity of the project. "This is not a project that can be finished and set up in a few years. The water user associations are seen as the basis for restructuring and decentralizing the water sector and the whole ministry. And it should not stop there. These changes should also impact on other ministries. The country needs far-reaching reforms," he says.

While the use of water user associations may spread to other regions of Egypt, many still question their effectiveness. For while the water user associations and the single pumps at the head of the *mesqa* may increase the efficiency of the water distribution system and reduce conflicts between farmers, it has not saved significant amounts of water.

Prof Mohammed Nasr Allam of Cairo University says that while user participation and privatization of water management are important, the IIP is perhaps not the best way to do it. "We need to encourage the cooperation of users. The government has a shortage of financing and technical capacities. Given that the system is expanding into new regions like the Sinai, the Western Desert and the Toshka region, it is important for the government to transfer water management to other sectors. But the IIP program, which is being implemented in pilot areas, is very slow and its results are not very conclusive in terms of water conservation. It achieves lower costs for the farmer and better production, but no water is really saved. And when you think that the program has only been implemented on a quarter of a million hectares, then it is clear that we will not see the end of this project in our lifetime."

For Bron the reforms should be much more far-reaching. "The most economically sensible option is not necessarily easy to realize though," he says. "Egypt should take its labor force out of agriculture and move to a more modern and large-scale agriculture. Today, the excess labor force of graduates is still being pushed into the agricultural sector, which is totally against any development purposes. There is a graduate scheme aimed specifically at unemployed lawyers and doctors. Logically, they should of course be placed in services and industry, but instead they get put into agriculture. It is like reverse development: instead of becoming more efficient, agriculture is becoming less and less efficient," he says.

Nasr Allam agrees Egyptian agricultural policy needs to change, particularly in the "new lands" that are being reclaimed. "In my opinion we cannot overwrite the agricultural activity in the Nile Valley. There are 30 million people living there and if they start moving to the cities they will destroy the country. But we should certainly not expand agriculture into the desert," he says. He believes Egypt should focus on the development of industry and services, while at the same time making traditional agriculture more efficient. "There is huge potential here, we are the center of the world, but we need to make it easier for foreign investment to come here. I believe Egypt could play a major role in international trade: through its position in the Arab world and its low-cost labor," he says.

## Soap Opera Education in Egypt

Besides the creation of water user associations, the Ministry of Water Resources in Cairo has also started up a special unit to raise public awareness through the media. Since its creation in 1995, the unit has run several awareness campaigns using everything from posters to television and radio commercials and short information films that were broadcast on national television. Ashgan Abou Gabal, who worked on the production of the information films, said that the producers took extreme care in making the script, avoiding overly official vocabulary and anything else that could alienate the farmers. "Farmers usually have doubts about messages from the government or from officials—they don't trust them. This is why more than 80 percent of the interviews and material we used features farmers; we used officials only to answer questions. This is how we gained credibility for the project," she said.

After the success of the first campaigns, the unit decided to push things further and address not only farmers but also their wives and children through the production of a television soap series. This daily program was set in a farming community and focussed on the problems surrounding water distribution and sharing. The first series was so popular among viewers that producers immediately set about writing the second series. Gabal, who also worked on the scripts for these programs, explained that the cast was a combination of engineers, farmers, and actors. "The actors were mainly recruited to act out the story lines—like if there was a love story unfolding between two protagonists. The farmers gave the program added credibility; it showed we were not just making this up, these were real people," she said. "Now we have started a children's program, *Water Carpets*. It looks at water scarcity but also at problems of pollution. I find the work for children very important because they are the future. I work with the hope that in twenty years we will have an environmentally aware society and that people will know how to preserve the environment."

## Putting on the Pressure: Changing Behavior in Jordan

While Egypt tries to make its population aware of the growing threat of water scarcity, Jordan is facing a much more serious situation. Scarcity here is no longer a case of speculation; it is a reality. With 179 cubic meters of water per capita per year—as opposed to 7,407 cubic meters per capita per year in the United States and 2,465 cubic meters per capita per year in United Kingdom—the country is one of the ten poorest in the world in terms of water resources. The reasons behind this extreme scarcity are a combination of limited resources and explosive population growth in the last fifty years. Indeed, the Desert Kingdom did not earn its name for nothing and except for the water from the Jordan and Yarmuk Rivers, which it shares with Israel and Syria respectively, the country relies entirely on scant rainfall and groundwater reserves. The sharp increase in the population in the last fifty years has overstretched these resources: since 1947 the population has grown from 250,000 to 5.7 million in 2005. A high birth rate of 3.3 and the influx of successive waves of Palestinian and Iraqi refugees since 1948 have led to this explosive growth. The situation is worsened by the fact that unlike its eastern neighbors in the Gulf—Saudi Arabia and the Gulf

States—Jordan does not have the financial means to solve its scarcity problem by investing in large-scale engineering projects like desalination.

Together with the Gaza Strip, Jordan is by far the worst off in the region. At the same time, or perhaps precisely for this reason, Jordan seems to be the only country in the Middle East that is facing up to facts and harnessing all its capacities to deal with the situation. As Professor Elias Salameh of the University of Jordan explained, there is no other choice for Jordan today: "We have to develop every drop we have. We can't look at just one aspect or one resource, every option deserves consideration." Besides the construction of a new dam on the Yarmuk River and a new project to extract groundwater reserves in the south of the country, the government is also seeking to increase water use efficiency. Water systems in Jordan's main cities are old and worn out, losing more than 50 percent of the water through leakage. The ministry is now working to rehabilitate urban systems, while at the same time increasing efficiency rates in agricultural water use.

Meanwhile on a domestic level, scarcity is a constant presence in the life of Jordanians. With water rationing in place since the 1980s, users receive twenty-four hours of water a week. This share is pumped into water tanks on the roof of their houses. If it inadvertently runs out before the end of the week, citizens have to buy water from private companies that deliver it in tanker trucks at high prices. "People in Jordan have no choice but to manage water with care and in a very conscious manner. This is not because they want to, they *have* to—otherwise at the end of the week, they run out of water," comments Salameh.

But some believed that Jordanian users could still do better: organizers of a five-year project launched by the American donor organization US Aid, Water Efficiency and Public Information for Action (WEPIA), said awareness on its own was not enough and that behavior and attitudes needed to change. "We don't like the word awareness," said Hala Dahlan of WEPIA. "It is not enough. Of course lots of people are *aware* of the situation but what are they actually doing about it themselves? WEPIA wants to create more than awareness: we want to change attitudes and behavior patterns around water. People's use of the resource has to change fundamentally and lastingly."

To effect this behavioral revolution across all levels of society, WEPIA took a hands-on approach. Between 2000 and 2005 it achieved the amendment of several laws, launched two major media campaigns and designed education programs for everyone from toddlers to university students, women, and even imams.

The core of its work however centered on the dissemination of "water-saving devices" (WSDs), small attachments that can be screwed on to taps, showerheads or installed in toilets to reduce the water flow. Dahlan explained that after the failure of earlier initiatives to introduce WSDs among urban users, WEPIA's first task had been to investigate the reasons behind the lack of success of WSDs. "We found that many domestic users were willing to use them. They were generally aware of the water scarcity problem and wanted to save water, but they didn't know where to obtain the devices, or how to install and maintain them. So we decided we needed to adopt a systematic approach to turn the situation around."

By using a social-marketing technique, the "heating-up approach," WEPIA put the consumer under pressure from all sides and forced him to change his behavior patterns. At home, in the mosque, on television and in the newspapers, the consumer was permanently reminded of the importance of water conservation and sustainable use. Children of all age groups were sent home from school with the task of carrying out a water audit at home, itemizing the quantities of water used in the kitchen, the bathroom and the garden, and seeing in which areas water could be saved. They showed this to their parents and tried to convince them of the savings the household could make using WSDs. As part of the children's education program, WEPIA also managed to obtain a full revision of the school curriculum so that today integrated water use and conservation issues are taught in grades one to eleven in five subject areas.

Women, and particularly women at home, were also targeted, as "an indirect way of getting to the men," as Dahlan explains. "The slogan of the program was 'The Solution is at Your End,' and it was a bit like the American Tupperware party idea: WEPIA trained women to promote water conservation in the home and sell WSDs at social gatherings and women's get-togethers. Besides being useful it also gave them an extra income." The women received a special demonstration kit with a selection of WSDs and a chart that they could use during their demonstrations.

Women were also involved in a separate campaign in which water conservation was taught through the Koran. WEPIA first started work with religious leaders and imams, informing them about water resources in Jordan, the problems the country is facing and methods which could help to save water. Many of them integrated these messages into their sermons and Friday teachings. For Ramadan 2003, the imams produced a booklet on water and Islam with WEPIA, containing special prayers and injunctions surrounding water in the Ramadan period. As part of this project the imams trained women who in turn gave lessons in water conservation to other women at home. And as the imams were not keen to sell the water-saving devices themselves, the women took over this task.

Raising awareness and changing attitudes to water through religion has proved very successful in Jordan, as Dahlan explains. "There is a great receptivity for religious messages in Jordanian society and we have had considerable success through this method," she says. Dr. Murad Bino heads the Inter-Islamic Network on Water Resources Development and Management (INWRDAM) in Amman, which works to increase efficient water use in Islamic countries. He agrees that Islam can play an important role in changing people's attitudes to water and conservation issues. "The government uses the teachings of the Koran about

water to raise awareness among the population. Because of the importance of religion in many people's lives, they accept the message readily and are open to the teachings," he says.

To monitor the success of its programs, WEPIA kept a permanent tab on WSD sales' rates: by keeping in close contact with suppliers, it saw whether sales were rising or falling. As soon as negative results were registered, WEPIA knew that part of its message to society was not coming across and it investigated what part of its work needed to be adapted.

Parallel to its targeted education programs, WEPIA disseminated its message through television, radio, newspapers and magazines, with campaigns in 2001 and 2002. The central character of both campaigns was Abu Tawfir, "Father Conservation." He was portrayed as a typical average Jordanian: a government employee who lived in an urban setting with his wife and son. Abu Tawfir was shown cleaning out his water tank, installing WSDs around the house and making sure none of his taps leaked.

An important aspect of WEPIA's media campaigns was the involvement of local NGOs and several private companies. Together with the newly created water demand management unit (WDM) at the Ministry of Water Resources, these NGOs took over WEPIA's work when its mandate expired in October 2005. Since its creation in 2002, the WDM unit has worked on several campaigns, both with WEPIA and independently. Rania Abdel Khaleq, the unit's director, says that while their awareness campaigns and education programs have been largely successful, there are challenges ahead. "The negative content of our message makes it difficult to get people to listen: people don't want to hear what we are saying, so we have to try to make the message as positive as we can. For example, 'conservation' was seen as a negative word: people felt it pressurized them and that it implied a drop in their standards of living. Now we use the term 'efficiency' instead," she says.

Khaleq and Dahlan also admit that despite their work, many people still feel it is the government's task to solve scarcity. "People blame the government for the water problem. They say there should be more resource development and water projects. They don't realize that the resources are all being stretched to the limit already," says Khaleq. The greatest challenge for Jordanian NGOs and the ministry's WDM unit is to ensure the durability of WEPIA's work, not only perpetrating its education and media projects, but also making sure that the general public doesn't forget WEPIA's core message: "The Solution is at Your End."

## Looking after a Shared Resource in Israel and Palestine

In Israel and the Palestinian Territories, the question of awareness is more complex. The continuing political tension and conflict mean that on both sides there is little space for concern about the environment. And while there is a continuing struggle for access to additional water resources, little attention is paid to the sustainability of this quest.

Traditionally, and compared to other nations in the region, Israelis have a more keen sense of environmental awareness. Many Israelis I spoke to recall growing up in the 1960s and 1970s, and being constantly reminded of the threat of water scarcity in their country. When washing hands, they were always taught to turn off the tap while using the soap and turn it back on to rinse. Popular songs also reflect this connection to water: in the poem "Love of the Land," the popular twentieth-century poet Yehuda Amichai wrote: "And the land is very small/ I can encompass it inside me./ The erosion of the ground erodes my rest, too/And the level of Lake Kinneret is always on my mind." Indeed, the rising and falling of Lake Kinneret is closely observed by many Israelis, and during the rainy season the daily fluctuations are recorded on the front pages of national newspapers beside the weather report.

However, in everyday life the efficiency of the Israeli water distribution system has led to a complacency and all too often the water that runs from the tap is taken for granted. As it only rarely becomes tangible, water scarcity can be largely ignored. The present political situation also contributes to this sense of indifference towards issues of water scarcity and environmental pollution. Since the start of the Second Intifada, the economic situation in Israel has seriously deteriorated and people live with a constant security threat. In the face of such immediate and tangible concerns, the environment almost inevitably takes second and third place. "The instability in the region and within the government makes it very difficult to accomplish anything in environmental spheres," comments Ayala Levy of Friends of the Earth Middle East (FoEME) in Tel Aviv. "Right now, it is easier to raise awareness about poverty. In the last five years, unemployment and poverty levels have risen and people are really feeling it. Several charities are working to help the poor and they have more of an audience. There are few projects that focus on the environment. In the case of water, this is because the scarcity is not tangible in Israel."

On the Palestinian side, the occupation, the political tensions and the threat to security have had an even more severe impact on the collective morale. Fadia Daibes, a Palestinian water consultant and former advisor at the Palestinian Water Authority, explains that because many Palestinians believe that Israel controls all the water resources in the Palestinian Territories, they have adopted a negligent attitude towards water. "The political situation has damaged Palestinian values. Expectations are very low," she says. "As the Palestinians have lived under occupation for such a long time, their perceptions are skewed. They think that when they are 'stealing' water from the system—illegally tapping water for example—they are stealing from the Israelis. They don't realize that they are in fact stealing from the Palestinian village down the road. Water isn't valued in Palestinian culture today. Like many other things, it has lost its meaning." Alice Nassar, who works at the Bethlehem offices of FoEME, also believes that since the start of the Second Intifada, it is more difficult to reach out to water users. "Farmers often feel they can't bring about change, that things have been taken out of their hands. They want to act, and they feel the water scarcity, but then at the same time, there is apathy. There is a willingness to work over borders, but many people feel other issues are more urgent."

FoEME, a non-governmental organization with projects in Israel, Jordan and the Palestinian Territories, is working on several fronts to change attitudes towards the environment in all three countries. Besides campaigning for the protection of the Mountain Aquifer and the preservation of the Dead Sea, the organization has also launched a joint environmental project involving Israeli, Palestinian and Jordanian communities, to rehabilitate the quality of the region's rivers. The Good Water Neighbors (GWN) project is being implemented at eight locations, involving seventeen communities—seven in Israel, six in the Palestinian Territories and four in Jordan. "The project is designed to show people that we have a shared responsibility over water, that long-term solutions will require a collective initiative," says Levy who managed the Israeli part of the project in 2004. "Water has no boundaries, it doesn't respect political borders. This is why problems of pollution and sewage can only be resolved through cooperation and joint initiative."

As the name implies, the project is being implemented in neighboring communities and communities that share a water source. Through work with the municipalities, teachers, schoolchildren, and civilians, the project aims to restore water's value in the communities. Levy cites the example of the Palestinian town of Tulkarem and the adjacent Hafer Valley in Israel. A sizable town with a population of more than 100,000, Tulkarem relies entirely on the water from ten wells for its water supply. Its sewage system is old and only covers part of the municipality, so that much of the city's waste seeps into the rivers and the groundwater that flows westward to Israel. In addition, Tulkarem's only waste disposal site is an open-air dump and hazardous materials can easily infiltrate into the groundwater. The waste from Tulkarem therefore flows straight into the Hafer Valley, most visibly in the Alexander River, which springs near the Palestinian city of Nablus and flows west past Tulkarem into Israel. Since 1995 there have been efforts to restore the quality of the water of the Alexander River in Israel, but this cannot be achieved without working with the Palestinian Authority. Through the GWN project, schoolchildren on both sides of the border have become involved in the restoration project, working to clean up the riverbanks. Besides such rehabilitation initiatives, the GWN project has also created "wise-water buildings" in each of the communities, public buildings such as schools or community centers that served as models for sustainable water use in the community. In each school involved in the project the principal, teachers, students and even the janitor helped design a model system—for instance, a simple device to catch rainwater from the roof of school buildings, or a structure to collect wastewater from drinking fountains that could be re-used for the flushing of toilets or the watering of the school garden for instance.

Both Levy and Nassar say that the conflict has made it more complicated to implement projects like GWN that involve communities on different sides of the border or political divide. "It requires a lot of patience and a lot of perseverance," says Levy. "The political circumstances make it difficult to build relationships between the communities as they can never meet face to face. Instead, we are forced to work through websites and online petitions." The project, which is currently funded by the EU Partnerships for Peace program and the Richard and Rhoda Goldman Foundation, was launched in 2001. Following the success of the first phase, the project received further funding for a second phase in which more communities were involved and activities expanded.

The problem with all these projects that aim to raise awareness of water scarcity and change behaviors towards water, is continuity. The water user association projects in Egypt and Turkey, WEPIA's media campaigns in Jordan, the GWN project in Israel, Palestine, and Jordan are all laudable initiatives. The question is how long their message will be remembered. With all these projects, the money and help of aid agencies will one day be discontinued, leaving local governments, NGOs and individual users to take over. In many of these communities there is however a very low environmental awareness, so that the hard-won results of these projects may be lost, allowing old habits to resurface.

The perseverance required for the implementation of such community projects once again shows the appeal of large-scale engineering projects: building a dam is perhaps more expensive, but certainly easier than attempting to change attitudes to water on a long-term basis. By building a dam, one provides a short-term, large-scale solution to the problem of water scarcity. Long-term policies that seek to improve water management mechanisms, raise awareness and involve users, are on the other hand fraught with difficulties, complications and, inevitably, political intrigue. Here, one is not dealing with concrete and steel, but with people: with the conflicting interests of the farmer and the city dweller, with deep-seated tradition and ideology, and sometimes—like in Israel and Palestine during the Second Intifada—with situations where saving water is the last thing on people's minds. And yet, while such projects may be more difficult to implement and sustain, they are important. Even if no water is saved in the Egyptian IIP project, and even if the water of the Alexander River in Palestine and Israel becomes only marginally cleaner, these projects make users think about their water and reassess its value. And then maybe, in coming generations, users will not only think, but also act to conserve their water.

## Note

1.   The Archimedes screw is a device for raising water. Essentially, it is a large screw, open at both ends and encased lengthwise in a watertight covering. When one end of the screw is placed in water and the screw is elevated at an angle and then turned, water trapped in the air pockets between the threads rises from the open lower end, up the length of the screw, and is released through the open upper end. Developed over 2,000 years ago by the Egyptians for irrigation, the Archimedes screw is still in use today.

# 11

# Four Stories of People and Water

*"It was like a miracle: after months of frustration, the sight of water bubbling up from the depths of this desert land—even if it was muddy and warm—was like an act of God. Everyone went crazy, people were crying and laughing at the same time."—Father Paolo dall'Oglio, Monastery of Mar Musa, Syria*

## Feeling It in Your Gut

"Water is everything for us," says Father Paolo dall'Oglio in a gruff voice, "it is what our future depends on. Finding and not finding water really gets to me." He points at his stomach: "Here, in the middle of me, in my gut. It affects me a lot; too much even. Every drop of water, I care about and I can feel inside me." The Italian r's roll off the tip of his tongue like marbles; one immediately sees that this is a subject that deeply touches the Jesuit priest. As the founder of a religious community in the Syrian Desert north of Damascus, he has for years been learning to live with the small amount of water collected from rain and wells.

Father Paolo would not strike you as a priest: he wears baggy trousers, a red-and-white checkered *kheffiyeh* is draped loosely around his neck, and wraparound sunglasses protect his eyes from the glaring desert light. He keeps his eyes on the road as we speed along in his pick-up truck; we are driving to the Monastery of Mar Musa. The landscape is desolate: steep, barren hills that rise over burning plains of rock and sand. It is vast and elementally empty, a biblical wilderness devoid of any life. At least that is how it appears at first sight. But look closer, and the land reveals a rich and layered history. Roman roads and staging posts; the crumbling remains of a summer palace that belonged to the flamboyant Princess Zenobia of Palmyra; ancient irrigation systems used by Roman garrisons and Byzantine monks... And, hidden away at the end of a small valley, the sixth-century Monastery of Mar Musa al Habashi, St. Moses the Abyssinian.

Abandoned at the end of the nineteenth century, Mar Musa was rediscovered in 1982 by Father Paolo, then a young Jesuit priest who had come to Syria's Qalamun Mountains for a spiritual retreat. Today it houses a growing community of ecumenical monks and nuns from around the Middle East and Europe. Active on many fronts, the community dedicates much time to promoting dialogue and understanding between religious communities, focusing on the relationship between Christians and Muslims living in the direct vicinity of the monastery. They are also working on the restoration of the frescoes and woodwork in the eleventh-century church of the monastery.

Life in these arid surroundings is not easy though. Traditionally, man always lived in harmony with the inhospitable desert environment here, until the nineteenth century when the balance between humans and their environment gradually deteriorated. The resulting problems—desertification and pollution in particular—increased dramatically in the twentieth century. The valleys around the monastery have, until now, been largely spared and they remain a sanctuary for plants and animals. However, an increase in population, together with a return to farming, has put further pressure on the already frail environment in the region: water resources are stretched to the limit and overgrazing is leading to growing desertification.

Lack of water, which drove the religious community away in the nineteenth century, is still a serious problem. Father Paolo explains that when he discovered the abandoned monastery and decided to restore it, water was his first concern. "When I first came to the monastery there was nothing, just a system that the monks had used for catching rainwater in their caves in the fifteenth century. We lived like medieval hermits," he says. He believes that it was by living with this extreme scarcity that they came to value water. "Through its scarcity water became the center of our life. We developed a hierarchy. Water was no longer just water: there were different levels of water. Water that had been used for washing hands and face could be used for washing feet. Water that had been used for washing feet could be used for flushing the toilets. It was a whole system of use and reuse."

Since then, two wells have been dug near the monastery, a project that inadvertently turned into a perilous adventure, as a drill-head got stuck at a depth of 460 meters in one well, and a pump was lost at the bottom of another well. "We made several attempts at digging wells, we dug one and failed; there was not enough water. We lost all the money from the grant we had received and we had to start again. We dug another and another. It was desperate; I felt almost physically affected by the process. My thoughts were 500 meters underground, at the bottom of the well, trying to *feel* the water," he says with passion.

"The fourth attempt was successful: on a dark March night in the middle of an electric storm and driving rain, we finally found water. It was like a miracle: after months of frustration, the sight of water bubbling up from the depths of this desert land—even if it was muddy and warm—was like an act of God. Everyone went crazy, people were crying and laughing at the same time. We slaughtered a ram on the spot to celebrate, and as it roasted, the water continued to flow and became clear and transparent. Since then, we can irrigate our fruit trees," he says, smiling at the memory.

To supplement the water from the wells, a small retaining dam has also been built at the top of the valley. The scarce rain that falls in the Qalamun

Mountains can thus be collected and used on the various projects at Mar Musa. For besides restoring the monastery itself, the monks are working to revive the barren environment around the monastery, starting with the valley they live in. Working with the Syrian government, local farmers, shepherds and international NGOs, the Mar Musa community is rehabilitating the degraded and infertile land, which has suffered from heavy overgrazing and desertification. "Improved transport means farmers no longer pay attention to the limits of the land," Father Paolo explains. "They let their animals graze until they have taken the last bit of vegetation and then they transport them by truck to a new place."

Using only local plant species, the monks are now restoring the traditional flora: pears and peaches are being grafted onto wild almond trees that are notoriously resistant to heat and drought. The region was also famed for medicinal plants, which are now gradually being reintroduced. At the monastery itself, the priests keep goats and bees, producing cheese and honey together with local farmers. The ultimate aim of the project is to not only restore the environmental balance in the area, but also to improve the livelihoods of the local population and thus counter migration—particularly of Christian families who have been leaving the region in growing numbers recently—to the large cities or abroad. In a way, caring for the environment at Mar Musa was not a choice; it was the only way for the community to survive. Ignoring the decline in biodiversity, the growing pollution and the threat of desertification would in the long term have made life at the monastery impossible.

The biodiversity project at Mar Musa is linked to an ecotourism project and the construction of national park, a visitor center, a hostel and a museum of the environment in the valley near the monastery. This part is more problematic to the members of Mar Musa. In 2001 an asphalted road was built to the monastery, and visitor numbers immediately shot up. Father Paolo is resigned. When asked what he thinks of the road he shrugs his shoulders. With French intonation he says: "*Boff.* There is not much to say about it. It's a road, that's all. It ruins our view completely but we have to play the game: the government is planning to turn our monastery into a tourist attraction and we have little say in the matter." He says Fridays are the worst; there are so many tourists that the quiet and meditative atmosphere that is so important to monastic life is completely drowned out by the crowds of people.

Father Paolo now seeks to strike a balance and encourage a kind of spiritual ecotourism that will respect Mar Musa as a place of silence and meditation. At the same time, the fact that there is so much interest for the spiritual center from both Muslims and Christians living in the vicinity, gives hope to the community which preaches tolerance and mutual understanding.

In a broader context, Father Paolo's main concern is still the growing water scarcity in the region. In his eyes wastefulness is one of the greatest culprits; he says people have no respect for the resource and therefore squander and pollute it without thinking of the consequences. He tells of the nearby village of Nebk where people only receive water once a week: "Even in this situation of extreme scarcity, they still waste water. As soon as it arrives, they throw it in the streets, they splash it through their houses, and they let the tap run until their reservoirs are filled." Towards such attitudes Father Paolo is unequivocal. "The solution to the water problem is to either make it expensive, or to make it scarce. When water flows freely from the tap, it is taken for granted."

The project at Mar Musa is one of several small-scale initiatives I visited throughout the Middle East and North Africa. While all different in nature—some are government projects, some are grassroots initiatives; some involve the revival of traditional techniques, some, on the contrary introduce modern water-saving technologies—these projects have one thing in common: they all acknowledge that water, and therefore the problem of water scarcity, cannot be considered separately from the people who use it and the environment in which it is used. The local nature of these projects automatically means that they have a very limited impact on the broader problem of water scarcity in the Middle East. On the other hand, the local focus makes it possible to involve users more directly in the management and use of water, while specific ecological and climatic conditions can also be taken into account more carefully.

Through their holistic nature these projects tackle the problem of water scarcity as part of other ecological, social, and economic problems such as desertification and salinization of poor soils, the migration of rural population, unsustainable urbanization and education.

## Rebuilding an Underground Heritage

While Father Paolo is trying to improve conditions in the area of Mar Musa through a combination of spirituality and ecology, Dutch anthropologist Joshka Wessels is trying to achieve the same goal in a more down-to-earth, hands-on way. In an effort to revive the use of traditional water systems in Syria, she has spent the best part of three years wading through the muddy waters of the country's qanats, working on the restoration of these ancient underground water networks with a team of specialists.

Having completed a first pilot restoration in 2000 in northern Syria, she has been supervising restoration works at two other sites around the country. One of these sites is in Qara, a small village 100 kilometers north of Damascus at the foot of the Anti-Lebanon Mountains. This is where I accompany her to: we drive up from Damascus, Joshka fearlessly navigating her way through the anarchy of Syrian traffic in a huge four-wheel drive jeep. Wearing a pair of mud-covered mountain boots and with her blonde hair pulled back in a ponytail, she is a combination of ultra-cool girl-power and a very Dutch no-nonsense mentality.

On the way, Joshka explains that there are ten qanats in Qara. Only six of these are still in use and they are all seriously neglected, their flow decreasing every year. Called "qanat romani" by locals, they are thought to date back to Roman times. In Qara, they have always been the main source of water for local farmers. Now the Aïn El Taïbeh qanat—literally "the source of good water"—has dried up, and the Aïn El Ameh has decreased in flow despite restoration in 2002. The largest qanat in the village, Aïn El Baïdeh, is being maintained by a rich farmer so that its flow remains abundant. The water of Aïn El Taïbeh, a qanat that consists of three branches, also used to provide water to the Lebanese Christian Monastery of St. Jacques le Mutilé, which lies on the outskirts of Qara. Recently restored, the brand new spaces of the monastery lie deserted: everything now depends on the return of the water. "Without water we can't do anything," says one of the sisters at the monastery. "Everything is on hold until the water comes back." Dozens of new bedrooms that have been built for the novices remain uninhabited. In the meantime, the seven nuns who now make up the community with the reverend mother, Soeur Agnès de la Croix, have to rely on the delivery of expensive water supplies from tanker trucks.

Joshka explains that the flow in the Aïn El Taïbeh decreased quite suddenly. "When we first came here, farmers were irrigating their land from it and the water was being managed by a guard, the *natur*, who divided the water shares. It was a system that worked. But when we came in 2002, the whole thing had come to a standstill: the guard had gone and the reservoir was empty." Joshka says the drying up of the qanat is a tragedy for the monastic community. "Without water it will be impossible for them to survive. They have tried to dig a well, but it brought very little water and it was brackish." Joshka first became involved in qanat restoration through the International Center for Agriculture Research in Dry Areas (ICARDA), a research center based near the Syrian town of Aleppo that hired her to assess to socio-economic feasibility of the project as an anthropologist. Since completing her contract at ICARDA, Joshka has produced three films about qanat restoration.

As soon as we arrive, Joshka grabs her hard hat—which she will need to crawl through the low tunnels—and her digital camera, and we head off to the site. Having lived in Syria for three years, she is fluent in Arabic and she jovially greets the workmen, cracking jokes as though she were one of them. The workmen for their part regard her with a mix of respect and friendliness. One of them even openly expresses his appreciation for her, saying: "I wish my wife were more like you. She just sits at home and eats, and I need to go out and earn the money."

The restoration team is from the nearby village of Maaloula, one of the few places in the world where Aramaic, the language of Jesus, is still spoken. As the supervisor shouts down orders to the men in the tunnel, Joshka is lost: "I don't understand a word of it, it sounds nothing like Arabic." The workmen laugh and help us down into the tunnel with a mechanical pulley system. Down below, one of the workers shows how they have cleared away the fallen debris that blocked the flow of water. In places they have had to consolidate the walls and airshafts with concrete and wooden beams. Joshka explains: "They are taking off the debris with a drill; it has been accumulating for years and years and it's really hard, like cement." Qanat restoration is no easy job; the workmen wade around in the muddy water collecting the rubble and lifting it into small baskets that are hauled up with the electric pulley. Samer Zeynab, the work supervisor, comments: "It's not just anyone who can go down and work in a tunnel like this; you need experience, knowledge and guts."

As we wade upstream through the muddy water, we get nearer to the mother well and see the water seeping from the walls: qanats do not flow from a single source, they tap the hidden sources all along the course of the tunnel, so that many small tributaries feed the main canal. "This is a very sustainable way of using groundwater because it doesn't use mechanical means. It relies on gravity and on the natural flow of water," explains Joshka.

As the largest landowner in the village, Abdel Hakim Zeyn is very pleased with the results of the restoration project. "It's excellent, we are just waiting for God's mercy to send us rain. But already, the water level is double as high as before," he says. "When the flow of the qanats drops, farmers leave and look for work elsewhere: they go to Lebanon to work in the apple and cherry orchards. Maybe, if the flow starts again, people will start coming back." The restoration of the qanats in Qara is being combined with the introduction of drip irrigation systems in all the fields, allowing farmers to save water and increase efficiency.

The complexity of Joshka's work is underscored when we visit the second branch of Aïn El Taïbeh, which dried up in 2001. Some of the villagers blame lower rainfall levels for the interruption in the flow in this branch, others simply call it God's will, but Joshka suspects one of the farmers of having dug a well on his land that is sucking away the water from the qanats. "Pumping lowers the groundwater levels. That's the technical reason for the drying up of qanats," she explains. But it is difficult for her to be sure and—as she knows from her vast experience of working with small farming communities in Syria—it is not wise to go pointing fingers before you are certain of your case. But then, on the second day of our stay in Qara, she speaks to a farmer who tells her that in the last two years, hundreds of wells have been sunk over the border in Lebanon. Suddenly she is dealing with a problem of quite a different magnitude: it is no longer just local; it is regional and even international. It is a poignant illustration of the inescapable effects of modernization: while Joshka's work focuses on local problems of water management, external factors like this can never be ignored.

The restoration project at Qara is part of a broader project in which a first "pilot qanat" was restored in 2000 in the northern Syrian village of Shallalah Saghirah, or "Little Waterfall." The village, which is made up of about twenty households, has no electricity and relies on the water from the ancient qanat system for most of its water supply. In talking to the villagers, the researchers from ICARDA found that the qanat, which dates back at least to Byzantine times, was gradually decreasing in flow. Joshka explains that it was mainly a question of maintenance: the qanat had not been cleaned out or reinforced in years and the villagers appeared to have forgotten how to do it. "We saw how important this water was to them: if they could no longer rely on it, they would leave the village and go to the city," she says.

The ICARDA team therefore decided to initiate a restoration project, involving the villagers themselves in the building work. However, the team was almost immediately confronted with the intensity of village politics. Joshka explains that the whole village is in fact one family, the descendants of Musa Oqla Hariri, a farmer who moved to the region from Syria's southern Hawran Plain at the end of the nineteenth century. He bought the land on which the village now stands and started cultivating it with his five sons. "The villagers today tell the story that one day Musa started cleaning out the well he had found near the village. While he was cleaning it, he found a tunnel which he followed; then he found another airshaft and cleaned it out. Gradually he cleaned out the entire tunnel and found himself at the mouth of the qanat in the village, with water flowing plentifully from the qanat."

Today the village community is still divided into five main households, named after Musa's five sons. Seven village elders decide on all the village affairs; they hold the land and water rights for their extended families. But long-running disputes also divide them and these had to be resolved before the restoration work could start. "You have to look at the social system surrounding this kind of tunnel," Joshka explains. "It's not only a technical issue." She says that besides ensuring that the geological and hydrological conditions warrant the restoration work, social conditions around the qanat's management also need to be good. Thus, among other things, the community must be willing to invest in future cleaning and maintenance work; there needs to be a strong social cohesion within the community and a well-established system of rights needs to be in place to ensure smooth management of the water.

And, of course, conflicts need to be resolved before anything can happen. "In the beginning it wasn't that easy, but eventually the conflict was resolved and we were able to start on the restoration," she says. Funding was obtained from the Dutch, German and Swiss governments, enabling extensive works to be carried out. "Fortunately most of the young people in the village had experience with construction work in cities like Aleppo and Beirut. It took us three months to clean the tunnel; one of the things that delayed the work were two fifteen-meter wells that had to be cleaned out," she says.

While the restoration at Shallalah Saghirah was a great success on a technical level—there has been a marked increase in the water flow—Joshka says life in the village remains tough. "It doesn't make them self-sufficient; the young men still have to work in the construction industry to provide for the family. From that point of view, you can't escape the fact that you are dealing with a modern society, in which urbanization is inevitable. You can't deny that." Only time will tell whether the project is really sustainable, whether villagers will keep up regular maintenance work, and whether the increased flow from the qanat will keep the young people from moving away to the cities.

One of the ways in which the use of the qanat could become more profitable is to combine its use for agricultural purposes with ecotourism. Thus the restoration in Shallalah Saghirah has attracted tourists from Lebanon, who came to see the tunnel and experience traditional village life. "It brings a small revenue and it also reaffirms the value of the tunnel for the villagers: it's their cultural heritage."

After the successful restoration at Shallalah Saghirah, the research team undertook a survey of the remaining qanats in Syria, documenting the geographical, socio-economic, and hydrological characteristics of forty sites. They identified ninety-one qanats, of which thirty are still flowing. Overpumping and the use of diesel motors to extract groundwater are seriously affecting the water tables throughout Syria, which in turn leads to the drying up of the qanats. As a consequence, more and more farmers are abandoning their land and moving away to the large cities; the knowledge about the construction and maintenance of qanats is thus rapidly being forgotten. Joshka believes that the restoration of Syrian qanats and, more importantly, the involvement of the local population, can help reverse this process. Beyond the value of the technology itself as a sustainable method of water collection, Joshka points to the traditional social organization around the qanat, which could serve as a model for local water management elsewhere.

In the months after our visit to Qara, the team from Maaloula continued work on the three galleries of the Aïn El Taïbeh, completing the restoration in March 2004. By this time, more than 850 meters of underground tunnels had been explored and twenty-five tons of mud had been removed. During the work, eight subterranean springs were found and connected to the system. The gradient of the tunnels was restored to increase the water flow, while the casing, walls and vaults were repaired using original material and traditional building methods. The inauguration of the qanat in April 2004, which was attended by members of the local communities and European embassy delegations, was covered on national television. After the renovation was completed, the monastic community reported in May 2004 that the qanat's flow had increased threefold; the *natur* went back to work to regulate the division of Qara's water, and farmers returned to their land to start irrigating again. After the heavy rains in 2004/2005, the mother of the monastic community sent this e-mail to Joshka:

> Good news! The Ain al Taibeh Qanat is RUNNING AGAIN!! It reaches now half of its former volume: more than 300m³ per day ! Now Qara is asking if we could not use the same technique to renovate the Ain al Qass Qanat. We will invite the three ambassadors to make a new proposal. God bless you, dear Joshka. Without you, this dream would not have been possible.

## Bringing New Water to the Waterless Region

Another way of addressing scarcity on an agricultural level, is to differentiate between types of water, reserving high-quality freshwater for domestic purposes and using lower quality—brackish, saline, and treated wastewater—for agriculture. In these arid regions where an average of 80 percent of the water resources go to agriculture, the use of such "alternative sources" is becoming increasingly widespread, allowing for the creation of a more sustainable agriculture.

Leading the region in the use of treated wastewater in agriculture, Israel and Tunisia have been practising this technique for more than thirty years now. Thus in Israel 25 percent of agricultural water used in 2000 was treated wastewater from the metropolitan areas. By 2020 this figure is set to increase to 46 percent. In Tunisia, treated wastewater is used for irrigation of crops that are not eaten raw such as fodder, cotton and cereals. Golf courses, parks and orchards are also kept green through this technique. In Jordan, 12 percent of water used for agricultural purposes is treated wastewater. In addition, much of Amman's treated wastewater is blended with the freshwater in the reservoir of the King Talal Dam at the head of the Jordan Valley to be used for irrigation of a variety of crops in the valley.

Near the ruins of Petra in southern Jordan, the technology is now being applied to treat the wastewater from Petra's many tourist facilities and provide water to local farmers. Thus Petra not only brings an income to the tourist business, but also, indirectly, to the agricultural sector. The Wadi Musa Reuse Project—a joint initiative of the Jordanian Ministry of Water Resources and the American donor agency US Aid—produces 1.25 million cubic meters of agricultural water per year, providing freshwater for the irrigation of 107 hectares of land. Initiated in September 2002, the scheme is already bearing fruit, with local farmers cultivating a wide variety of crops including barley, sorghum, and vegetables.

Her Highness Sharifa Zein Bint Nasser, the head of development for the Royal Hashemite Court and one of the project's initiators, explains that this is the first time any such initiative has been undertaken in the Middle East. "This is a groundbreaking project: it is the first time that treated wastewater is being used by local Bedouin tribes. We very much hope that the project will serve as an example to the whole country," she says.

Near the main site there is a small demonstration area where a wide variety of plants, trees, and flowers are being grown; they were all selected to resist the arid climate of Wadi Musa and are irrigated by drip irrigation, ensuring efficient water use. HH Sharifa Zein says that it was partly thanks to the creation of this demonstration area that the local Bedouin tribe, the Ammariin, embraced the idea of using treated wastewater for irrigation. "In the beginning they all saw the wastewater treatment plant as an awful and ugly thing, a building that stank. And the treated wastewater that flowed from the plant through the valley was left untouched; the farmers wouldn't even let their livestock drink it.... To them the water was impure and *haram*, and they believed that any animal that had drunk it would become impure and be unfit to sell at the market," she says.

She recalls that it took "hundreds of cups of tea and coffee, and night upon night of sitting in tents and discussing the project with the community," before the local farmers of the Ammariin tribe accepted the idea of treated wastewater.

"We showed them examples in which treated wastewater had been successfully used for the irrigation of crops in Tunisia. And we were also able to show them a fatwa that had been issued by scholars at Al Azhar University in Cairo, approving the use of treated wastewater for the irrigation of crops. Once they saw the results of the demonstration site, they were really convinced: now we have managed to make them see that water is valuable, that it is not just a commodity to be looked down upon, and that even this treated water is a precious resource."

HH Sharifa Zein has been working with the Bedouin in this area for twenty years and she emphasizes the importance of knowledge of local customs and inter-tribal relationships when implementing such a project. Thus the choice of the site for the construction of the treatment plant was already a sensitive issue: first none of the tribes wanted the plant built near their village; they said it was a dirty, ugly thing that they wanted nothing to do with. The government subsequently chose a piece of land that is today government-owned, but that historically belonged to the Ammariin tribe. The plan was to build the plant and let the tribe members participate in the scheme. "As soon as the locals started seeing the benefits of the project, they suddenly all put a claim to the land, all the villages started coming with stories. The most unlikely things like: 'My grandfather once had a picnic here.' I kept quiet because I could see this was a touchy question. In Arabic there is a saying: 'Your land is your honor.' When they started quoting this, I saw it was no light matter."

A team of anthropologists was brought in to study the ownership rights and they conclusively showed that the land belonged to the Ammariin. Still, to keep the peace with the other tribes, and to ensure that the Ammariin would still be able to sell their produce to their neighbors, HH Sharifa Zein proposed to give a small part of the land to the army veterans' club, which is composed of members from each tribe. "It was purely to keep the peace. I had put a precondition into the contract: no 'foreign workers' were allowed to work the land. This practically ensured that all the land would go to the Ammariin, because the veterans themselves don't have the capacity to develop the land."

The Ammariin have now been organized in a cooperative of 200 members, with men and women partaking as equal shareholders. "The fact that women are given equal say in the day-to-day management and running of the project is another unique feature of the project," says HH Sharifa Zein. She explains that the tribe elders were initially reluctant to allow women to participate in such a manner, but they have now also come to see the benefits.

Ismail Twaissi, the agricultural engineer in charge of the project, is very pleased with the results at Wadi Musa. "We really hope to change the lives of local farmers with this project. Before they had to wait for rain; with this project they know they will have a reliable and steady supply. Already now we can see the difference," he says. The area around Petra has always been extremely arid; already 2,000 years ago, the Roman historian Diodorus Sicilus described it as the "waterless region." Survival in this harsh climate depended on the ingenuity and inventiveness of the local population. Part of the strength of the powerful Nabataean civilization that thrived from the sixth century BC to the third century AD lies in their refined water management system which made use of every drop of water that fell from the sky. Today, thanks to the new technology, the Ammariin no longer have to wait for rain.

Still, the new conditions of relative abundance also take getting used to and, besides having to tackle the concept of treated wastewater, Twaissi explains that the farmers have a lot to learn. "The farmers often don't know how to deal with the new crops they are planting," he explains. "They don't know when to sow and when to harvest; how to apply the right amounts of fertilizer. They also needed help with the use of the drip irrigation system; they had never used this before."

While animal fodder is the principal crop now, Twaissi points out that a variety of trees have also been planted, both in the demonstration site and on the individual plots. Native trees such as juniper, pistachio, almond and olive have been reintroduced, with the aim of restoring plant diversity and combating desertification.

After a year and a half, members of the cooperative are already so pleased with the results that they are starting to take initiatives to increase the value of the project. Thus the farmers had the idea of selling their produce, mainly animal fodder, to farmers from other tribes. They are now planning to build a storage facility on the site and hold weekly market days to sell their crops in the area. Since the end of 2003, there is also a small greenhouse in the demonstration area. Here four women tend to a variety of cut flowers, which are sold to the larger hotels in Petra and Aqaba, generating an additional income for the cooperative. Amal, one of the young women working in the greenhouse, is very pleased with her new job. "Before this I never worked; with this new job I feel I am learning a lot. My work is also useful, both to the community and to my family," she says.

"Already now the wastewater treatment project is generating spin-off projects. Over time, all these projects will start generating their own income and become sustainable," comments HH Sharifa Zein. But she cautions: "We have to beware that we don't spread ourselves too thinly; the projects must be built up gradually." Nevertheless, she already has ideas for the next project: the cultivation of herbal plants. The valleys around Petra harbor many rare species of medicinal plants and herbs, and HH Sharifa Zein believes that this could be another project for local women: the development of a herb garden which could form an additional tourist attraction in Petra and at the same time provide a source of income to the Ammariin cooperative.

Despite its local nature, the project at Wadi Musa could serve as a model for similar projects around the country. By offering small communities a new, sustainable source of water, it allows them to pursue a rural lifestyle. Their direct involvement in the project also changes their perception of water and makes them see it as a precious resource rather than a mere commodity.

## The United Nations of Trees

"This is the Tree that Started it All," says Elaine Solowey, pointing to a sprawling and contorted acacia that stands in the middle of the orchard like a majestic grandfather. "When they were preparing the terrain here, flattening the dunes to set up the date tree plantation, the workers wanted to raze this tree too. But I refused. It was such a beautiful tree that I couldn't let it be cut down. It must be at least 350 years old. So I stood in front of it and just said: 'Not this one.' So they left it. Now it's at the heart of everything," she says proudly, as she leans against one of the low branches. Solowey, a small, sturdy Israeli woman with large orange-lens sunglasses—they offer better protection from the glaring sun—and a small sunhat, is like a walking botanical encyclopedia. As we walk through the gardens at Kibbutz Ketura in Israel's southern Arava Valley, she fires off the Latin and English names of all the trees we walk past, adding the main characteristics of each type in a rapid staccato. Having more or less created the gardens at Kibbutz Ketura from scratch, she knows all the trees here personally: their origins, whose clone they are, their teething troubles and their particular needs.

Solowey has lived at the kibbutz since the 1970s and in this time she has developed her own vision of a desert agriculture that is suited to the fragile ecosystem of the Arava Valley. Now she heads the sustainable agriculture research team at the Arava Institute for Environmental Studies, an environmental research institute that is also located at Kibbutz Ketura. The Arava Valley, which runs through Israel and Jordan, has an extremely arid climate: the average atmospheric humidity is 14 percent, and the only source of water consists of two saline aquifers, which are used by the kibbutzim and for agriculture. The kibbutz is equipped with a small desalination unit that provides freshwater to the inhabitants, but crops are all irrigated with saline water that is extracted from deep wells. "What I am looking for are crops that don't need a lot of water and that are salt-tolerant," she says. "And I am looking everywhere."

And when she says everywhere, she means it: in the orchard there are plants from Chile, the Mexican Highlands, the Philippines, and the Australian outback; there are Barbados cherries, plums from the Kalahari Desert, mustard capers from the Sinai Desert, cactus apples from Peru... and the list continues. "It's like the United Nations of Trees here," Solowey comments cheerfully, "the only difference is that unlike people, trees coexist very well. They all get along with each other."

The aim of Solowey's United Nations is not just to grow the trees, but also to see whether they could be commercially viable and provide small-scale agricultural communities in the Middle East with a stable source of income that does not damage the water and land resources. The work is part of a cooperation scheme between Morocco and Israel, which aims to develop a new kind of sustainable agriculture, focusing on the cultivation of salt- and drought-tolerant plants. Solowey explains that in Morocco such crops could support whole families, while at the same time providing a legal alternative to the cultivation of marijuana; in Israel, they could offer commercial possibilities for the cultivation of sustainable crops. She hopes to soon start working with Jordan, where indigenous fruit trees and medicinal plants are to be reintroduced in the desert wadis of the Jordanian Arava Valley, and Afghanistan, where she has been asked to work on the development of alternative cash crops that could replace the poppy.

So far, Solowey has been most successful with the marula, a tree from the mango family that is used for its fruit, and the *argania spinosa*, a tree from Morocco that is used for its oil-rich nuts. The argania, which can survive on very little water, has a long history in the southwest of Morocco where it was traditionally grown by the Berbers in the Draa Valley and the Jewish community around the coastal town of Essaouira. The nuts of the argania are renowned for producing high-quality oil; the process of its production is even recorded in the Talmud, although the production method that was adopted by most Moroccan Jews is considered unkosher. The nuts were traditionally fed to goats and the pits were collected out of the dung and processed to be made to oil. Solowey has now grown several argania trees and wants to try to extract the oil "without the goats." Fifteen of the argania trees standing in the Ketura orchard were a personal gift from King Hassan II of Morocco. Another set of trees comes from the Rothschild family who brought them to Mikve Israel, the first modern agricultural school in Israel, in the beginning of the twentieth century. The trees are growing well, but Solowey has yet to find an effective way of extracting the nut from the hard kernel. The oil of the argania is one of the best in the world, and Solowey believes there is a market for it, first of all among the 750,000 Moroccan Jews living in Israel. The tree has also been reintroduced in parts of Morocco, where the Berber population strongly identify with it.

Solowey started looking into drought- and salt-tolerant trees and crops in the 1980s. At the time the kibbutz was planting traditional crops like tomatoes and aubergines, crops that were in fact totally unsuited to the conditions of the Arava Valley. "It was making an ecological mess, because we were planting crops that needed a lot of water and fertilizer. It was damaging the fragile soil." As all the fertilizer and packaging had to be imported from the north of the country at high cost, the community was also hardly making any profit. The last straw for Solowey was that as a kibbutz member she had to do her daily shift in the vegetable fields, an exhausting task after she had already spent eight hours working on the date plantation that she was creating. "I always think I should be awarded some sort of medal for giving birth to six sons during that period," she says dryly.

So while the tomatoes were still being grown and picked down the road, Solowey started her own "little investigations," and looked into crops that could be commercially viable without damaging the environment. "I started by looking at biblical stuff: I figured if our Father Abraham managed to grow those crops, we should also be able to," she says. Solowey started experimenting with the

Seven Species, the crops that are named in the Book of Deuteronomy in the description of the Land of Israel—wheat and barley, vines, figs and pomegranates, olives and dates. She also tried growing the four trees that are associated with the Jewish celebration of Sukkot, the Festival of Ingathering: citron, willow, palm frond and myrtle, known as the Four Species. "I tried all of these, some with less success than others," she says. Thus citron, "the granddaddy of the citrus fruits" as she describes it, grew well, but was not commercially viable; wheat and vines on the other hand, needed too much water and were not suited to the arid climate of the Arava Valley. Dates were probably the most successful of all, as the impressive 3,000-tree orchard shows. Planted in the 1980s, the trees now rise to a height of twenty meters, yielding an average of 250 kilos of dates per tree. Harvesting is done with tractors equipped with hydraulic ladders, after which the dates are packaged for export.

After the biblical species, Solowey started looking more broadly at drought-tolerant plants. As she traveled to international conferences and workshops, she gradually collected her United Nations, which include many rare medicinal plants.

It is obvious that the problem of water scarcity facing the Middle East and North Africa cannot be resolved through small-scale projects like these. Dams, but more importantly, desalination plants, must be part of the solution to water scarcity. However, Joshka's qanat restoration project and Elaine Solowey's impassioned quest for salt- and drought-tolerant plants, represent a new way of looking at water and at the environment at large. Instead of exploiting water resources to their limit and beyond, and instead of seeking to transform the arid landscapes to suit the image of a greener, and therefore implicitly more prosperous land, these projects seek to maintain the fragile ecological balance. In doing so, they also restore water to its true value in these desert lands.

# Epilogue:
# The Smell of Rain

The Otel Uğur in the center of Sanlıurfa was listed under "bottom end" in the accommodation section of my guidebook and as soon as the owner opened the door to the room I knew why: a wave of stagnant, heavy heat streamed out of the small space. He showed off the benefits of the room: "Two beds, a fine view," he said with a generous grin as he waved at the window and the darkness beyond. "No fan?" I asked tentatively. "Fan?" I motioned to the ceiling and made a turning movement with my hand. "Ah, fan," he nodded happily, "no fan, no. No need fan. Urfa not so hot," he laughed gaily as he shuffled back to his receptionist sofa and the late-night Turkish comedy I had interrupted.

I thought Urfa was quite hot: it was nearly midnight and the temperature was still above 30 °C. It was the kind of heat that called for cold showers, or air-conditioning, or just plain getting out of there, but as none of these were options, I took the airless room. It was the middle of July and I had been traveling and writing for four years; this was my sixth and last water journey to the region. Since January 2001, I had passed through thirteen countries, crossed seven deserts, and, in a haphazard fashion, covered more than 7,000 kilometers from southern Spain to Turkey.

I had set out to discover what water means to people in the Middle East today, and how their perception of water differs from the Dutch perception. Along the way I had heard many water stories, from the Moroccan Ourika Valley to Egypt's Western Desert and Syria's dying Ghuta Oasis. Together, these stories formed a dizzying amalgam that revealed the many meanings and values that are associated with water in the Middle East today.

Before setting off, I had expected the beliefs, attitudes and traditions surrounding water to be very different from perceptions of water in the Dutch climate I had grown up in. I imagined people had more respect for the resource, used it more sparingly and valued its presence more highly than we did in our damp marshlands. Yet in most places I found water was an unquestioned resource that was taken for granted like the air people breathed, and few seemed to cherish it to its true value. Only those who experienced acute scarcity at a physical level—the Sudanese farmers who sent their daughters to fetch water three hours walk away every day; the Amman housewife who had to run her

**The ponds of the holy carp, Urfa. According to an ancient Muslim legend this is the place where God saved Abraham from a burning stake by transforming the fire into water and turning the burning wood into fish.**

household on a ration of twenty-four hours of water a week—seemed to fully acknowledge the value of its presence.

In the eyes of many, water is still an abundant resource. And in places where scarcity is a daily reality, few feel any sense of responsibility to resolve the problem. As I traveled through the region, I became increasingly aware of the gap between public perception and the reality of water scarcity. I also became convinced that these perceptions are just as important as the plain fact that water is running out. Perceptions are perhaps even more important than the truth because the facts of hydrology, demography and meteorology are often only known and fully understood by scientists, politicians and policymakers, whereas the perceived truth is what the Moroccan nomad, the Israeli farmer and the Cairene businessman act upon.

The attitudes and beliefs of the general public however also influence political decision making—or the lack of it, which makes it possible to uphold the status quo. Strongly tinted by religion, ideology and tradition, these beliefs are so deeply rooted in Middle Eastern societies that they have the power to thwart any far-reaching change. Thus in Egypt where approximately 85 percent of the water goes to agriculture and water scarcity forms a serious threat, agriculture is still being expanded. Desert land is being reclaimed while unemployed law graduates are being put to work as farm hands.

More than anything, politicians in the Middle East are eager to maintain stability in their country. Confronting the imminent threat of large-scale water shortage and the inevitable social and economical reforms that go with it obviously does not fit into this political program. As long as it is still possible, it is much easier to gloss over the harsh facts and reassure the public, thus in effect reinforcing their false perception of abundance.

The fact that it is possible to delay and avoid decisions on an issue that is so primordially important, reveals a strange paradox: it is as though water is so fundamental to our lives, that we cannot imagine it running out. It is such a basic need, that life without it is unimaginable, and so we do not imagine it; instead, we imagine everything will be all right in the end. And indeed, compared to the abstract threat of water scarcity, many other things appear more urgent and real: poverty, unemployment, terrorism; these issues seem more pressing. Given that water scarcity is not conspicuous on an everyday basis in many places in the Middle East, this is perhaps true.

In the long term however, clean and sufficient water supplies are more important than anything else. But this is a difficult message to convey to populations who are often poor and under-educated, and always misinformed. As I have discovered for myself too, water is a complicated subject. To many, it is just something that should be available; it is something we are owed—by God, or the Government, or Mother Nature. Because it is such a basic need and at the same time so invisible—for most of us, it comes from an invisible source, through hidden subterranean pipes, to our taps, where we see it appear like a miracle—it is difficult for governments to convince us of the need to save water. As one journalist in Beirut told me, after the end of the war in 1992, the government launched large-scale reconstruction works, repairing the roads, public buildings and the old city center, but leaving the run-down and damaged water supply and sewage system in a state of disrepair. Water is not a glamorous affair and it does not bring instant results; politicians prefer to focus on projects that bring visible results in the short term.

Water scarcity may still be invisible to many, but that is no reason to pretend it is not a problem. The combination of the high population growth rates throughout the region, the continuing emphasis on agriculture, and the limited water reserves, mean that the problem is only going to get worse. This is an issue that will not resolve itself with time. It needs to be confronted, by politicians but also by the population at large, because it has severe implications for life and livelihood in the countries of the Middle East and North Africa in the coming fifty years.

This is also why it is important to implement change before disaster makes it necessary. By anticipating the consequences of water scarcity, one can pre-empt the large-scale population migrations that some predict. Instead of waiting for farmers to massively move to the large cities as environmental refugees, opportunities should be created for them to change their lifestyles and source of income. By acting now, disaster can be avoided in the future.

Without being able to put it into words exactly, I felt I had internalized the water issue in this hot and dry land. I sensed the inactivity, the sluggish response to the threat and I understood the attitude. The immense water problem loomed like the huge waves when you swim in deep sea. They lift you and let you down gently, rock you around at a slow pace. Until you get too close to the shore, where the breakers will wash you to the beach with irresistible force.

For now though, I was still in Turkey. I was nearing my final destination, Istanbul, but I still had two weeks to go, one of which would be spent in Urfa interviewing people and visiting the GAP project. All my appointments were set up, the visits had been scheduled and the interviews arranged; I knew I would do it all, but I felt very tired and, for the first time perhaps—and although I would not admit it even to myself—a little homesick. I never thought it possible, but I yearned for the damp Dutch summers, for the watery sunshine of a July morning on the waterfront, for a magnificent rain shower that surprised you on the bike and left *nothing* dry, and for cool night breezes that blew in from the sea...

The morning of my last interview in Urfa I rented a car and drove east. The heat was unrelenting: one could almost see the grass burn as the midday sun shone down from a sky of steel. The air hardly moved. The vast plains stretched wide and flat to the horizon, sweeping across the Syrian border in the south and towards the Iranian deserts in the east. Everything about the scenery here was big; I could almost picture the Mongol hordes of history books charging ferociously to the conquest of the Turkish Sultanate.

To the north, the gray silhouette of the Mardin Mountains marked the limit of the plains. As I reached the Christian hill town of Mardin, the road climbed out of the plain and it grew a bit cooler. I continued eastward, towards the Syrian-Orthodox monastery of Mar Gabriel. The narrow road snaked through a deserted landscape of dry trees and shrubs. And then something happened. There were clouds. Large, gray clouds, heavy with rain, were angrily forming on the horizon.

Mesmerized, I watched and realized that these were the first real clouds I had seen in months. They were voluptuously stacked upon each other like castles of whipped cream with turrets and all. I was spellbound by their growing blackness that presaged rain. But before the rain, there was the smell: the overpowering smell of rain on hot earth rushed towards me, rich and fragrant, releasing a scent of fertility and greenness that I had forgotten existed. Then large, silent drops started falling from the sky. Slowly first, with a certain deliberation, and then fiercer, until I was driving through a true downpour. I turned off the road and drove towards the gates of the monastery that loomed at the top of the hill. It was a forbidding sight: on the top of the hill stood a large walled precinct with big black gates and several church towers. Past the gates, I drove through pistachio orchards and came to the entrance. I stepped out of the car into a deluge. The rain was pouring down like a sheet from the sky, even though the sun was shining on the other side of the valley. There was something symbolic about this rain: after having looked for water for all this time, and after having found it in so many forms, here it came to me in an abundance that I recognized without having to think for an instant. It was under my skin.

# Bibliography

## Prologue: Abundance

Van Veen, J. *Dredge, Drain, Reclaim, The Art of a Nation*. The Hague: Nijhoff, 1948.

Schama, Simon. *Landscape and Memory*. London: Fontana Press, 1995.

Schama, Simon. *The Embarrassment of Riches*. London: Collins, 1987.

## 1. The Death of the Garden of Eden

Broadhurst, R.J.C., transl. *The Travels of Ibn Jubayr*. London: Jonathan Cape, 1952.

Degeorge, G. *Damas, des Origines aux Mamluks*. Paris: L'Harmattan, 1997.

Degeorge, G. *Damas, Des Ottomans à nos Jours*. Paris: L'Harmattan, 1994.

Elhadj, E. *The Household Water Crisis in Syria's Greater Damascus Region*. Occasional Paper 47, SOAS Water Research Group. Consulted on 15 July 2006 via http://www.kcl.ac.uk/kis/schools/hums/geog/water/occasionalpapers/AcrobatFiles/occ47.pdf.

Keusséoglou, A. *Le Vieux Damas qui s'en va, 1930--Images et "Cris" de la Rue*. Damas: Dar Tlass, 1996.

Kinglake, Alexander. *Eothen*. Evanston, Ill.: The Marlboro Press/Northwestern, 1996.

Thubron, Colin. *Mirror to Damascus*. London: Penguin Books, 1996.

Tresse, René. "L'irrigation dans la Ghouta de Damas." *Revue des Etudes Islamiques*. Vol. 3, 1929: 459-573.

## 2. A Gift from God

Abdel Haleem, Muhammed, transl. *The Qur'an*. Oxford: Oxford University Press, 2005

Abdel Haleem, Muhammed. *Understanding the Q'ran*. London: I.B. Tauris, 1999.

Buitelaar, M. & Van Gelder, G.J. *Het Badhuis, Tussen Hemel en Hel*. Amsterdam: Bulaaq, 1996.

Cheyne, A.G. *Islam and the West: The Moriscos, a Cultural and Social History*. Albany: State University of New York Press, 1983.

Dalley, Stephanie, transl. *Myths from Mesopotamia*. Oxford: Oxford University Press, 1992.

Dalrymple, William. *From the Holy Mountain*. London: Flamingo, 1998.

El Bokhâri. *Les Traditions Islamiques, traduit par O. Houdas et W. Marçais, tome 2ème*. Paris: Imprimerie Nationale, 1906.

Graves, R. & Patai, R. *Hebrew Myths, The Book of Genesis*. New York: Doubleday & co, 1964.

Hagg, Marti. "Water uit de Hof, een verhandeling over het mikweh." MA dissertation in theology, Soest, The Netherlands, 1988.

Herodotus. *The Histories*. London: Penguin Classics, 1972.

Hilgard, Peter. *Der Maurische Traum*. Kassel: Verlag, Winfried Jenior, 1997.

Isaacs, R.H. *The Jewish Sourcebook on the Environment and Ecology*. Northvale, N.J.: Jason Aronson Inc, 1998.

Kaplan, A. *Waters of Eden, the Mystery of Mikvah*. New York: NCSY, 1982.

Leroy, B. *L'Expulsion des Juifs d'Espagne*. Paris: Berg International, 1990.

Russell, Bertrand. *History of Western Philosophy*. London: George Allen and Unwin Ltd, 1961.

Said, Rushdi. *The River Nile*. Oxford: Pergamon Press, 1993.

Sasson, J.M., ed. *Civilizations of the Ancient Near East* (vols. III & IV). New York: Simon & Schuster/Macmillan, 1995.

Slonim, R., ed. *Total Immersion, A Mikvah Anthology*. Northvale, N.J.: Jason Aronson Inc, 1995.

Tal, Alon. *Pollution in a Promised Land*. Berkeley: University of California Press, 2002.

*Tanakh: The Holy Scriptures*. Philadelphia: Jewish Publication Society of America, 1985.

*The Holy Bible, King James Version*. Nashville, Tenn.: World Publishing, no date.

Toelle, Heidi. *Le Coran revisité: l'Air, le Feu, l'Eau et la Terre*. Damas: Institut français d'études arabes de Damas, 1999.

## 3. Fading Traditions

Beaumont, P., Bonine, M., & McLachlan, K., eds. *Qanat, Kariz, Khattara*. Kent: MENAS Press, 1989.

Goblot, Henri. *Les Qanats: une Technique d'Acquisition de l'Eau*. Paris: Mouton Editeur, 1969.

Jaubert, P.A., transl. *La Géographie d'Edrisi (1154)*. Amsterdam: Philo Press, 1975.

Mazaheri, Aly. "La Civilisation des Eaux Cachées. Muhammad Al-Karagi, traité de l'exploitation des eaux souterraines." Ph.D. dissertation, Université de Nice, Institut d'Etudes et de Recherches Interethniques et Interculturelles, 1973.

Perennès, J.J. *L'Eau et les Hommes au Maghreb*. Paris: CNRS, Editions Kartala, 1993.

## 4. *Chafa* and *Chirb*, The Laws of Water

Caponera, Dante A. *Water Laws in Moslem countries*. FAO for the UN, 1973.

El Bokhâri. *Les Traditions Islamiques, traduit par O. Houdas et W. Marçais, tome 1er*. Paris: Imprimerie Nationale, 1906.

Faruqui, N., Biswas, A. & Bino, M. eds. *Water Management in Islam*. New York: United Nations University Press with IDRC, 2001.

Glick, Thomas. F. "Hydraulic Technology in Al-Andalus." In *The Legacy of Muslim Spain*, edited by Salma Jayyusi, 974-985. Leiden: E.J. Brill, 1992.

Glick, Thomas. F. "Irrigation in the Fifteenth Century Huerta of Valencia." In *Irrigation and Hydraulic Technology, Medieval Spain and its Legacy*, edited by Thomas Glick, 1-7. Aldershot: Variorum, 1996.

Hillel, Daniel. *Rivers of Eden*. Oxford: Oxford University Press, 1994.

Mallat, C. "The Quest for Water Use Principles: Reflections of Shari'a and Custom in the Middle East." In *Water in the Middle East: Legal, Political and Commercial Implications*, edited by J.A. Allan and C. Mallat, 128-137. London: I.B. Tauris, 1995.

Monod, Théodore. *Méharées, Explorations au Vrai Sahara*. Paris: Terres d'Aventure en Collection Babel, Actes Sud, 2000.

Ouhajou, L. "Espace Hydraulique et Société, Les Systèmes d'Irrigation dans la Vallée du Dra Moyen, (Maroc)." Ph.D. dissertation, Université Paul Valéry, Montpellier III, France, 1986.

Perennès, J.J. *L'Eau et les Hommes au Maghreb*. Paris: CNRS, Editions Kartala, 1993.

Tresse, R. "L'irrigation dans la Ghouta de Damas." *Revue des Etudes Islamiques*. Vol. 3, 1929: 459-573.

## 5. The Value of Water

Allan, J.A. *The Middle East Water Question: Hydropolitics and the Global Economy*. London: I.B. Tauris Publishers, 2001.

Attia, B., Baroudi, Ellysar and Lahlou, A., eds. *Managing Water Demand: Policies, Practices, and Lessons From The Middle East And North Africa Forums*. Cairo: IDRC, 2005.

Bazza, M. & Ahmad, M. "A Comparative Assessment of Links Between Irrigation Water Pricing and Irrigation Performance in the Near East." Paper delivered at the Conference on Irrigation Water Policies: Micro and Macro Considerations, organised by the World Bank, Agadir, Morocco, June 2002.

Brooks, David B. "Fresh Water in the Middle East and North Africa: Source of Conflict/Base for Cooperation." In: *Integrated Water Resources Management and Security in the Middle East,* edited by Lipchin, C., Pallant, E., Saranga, D. and Amster A. The Netherlands: Springer AK/Nato Publishing Unit, forthcoming.

Brooks, David. *Water, Local-level Management*. Ottawa: International Development Research Centre, 2002.

Faruqui, N., Biswas, A. & Bino, M. eds. *Water Management in Islam*. New York: United Nations University Press with IDRC, 2001.

Frazer, J. *The Golden Bough, A Study in Magic and Religion* (vols. I & II). London: MacMillan and co, 1951.

Griffiths, J.G. *De Iside et Osiride*. Cardiff: University of Wales Press, 1970.

Hillel, Daniel. *Rivers of Eden*. Oxford: Oxford University Press, 1994.

Robenbeck, Max. *Cairo, The City Victorious*. London: Picador, 1998.

Said, Rushdi. *The River Nile*. Oxford: Pergamon Press, 1993.

## 6. Myths of Concrete and Steel

Alghariani, Saad. "The Sweet Seas of Africa and the Re-direction of the Congo River towards the Great Sahara." Translated by Salem El-Maiar. *Al Arab*, no date.

Bulloch, J. & Darwish, A. *Water Wars*. London: Victor Gollancz, 1993.

Hodge, Trevor. *Roman Aqueducts and Water Supply*. London: Duckworth, 1992.

Ley, Willy. *Engineer's Dreams*. Amsterdam: Elsevier, 1961.

Pearce, Fred. *The Dammed, Rivers, Dams and the Coming World Water Crisis*. London: The Bodley Head, 1992.

Said, Rushdi. *The River Nile*. Oxford: Pergamon Press, 1993.

Vandewalle, D., ed. *Qadafi's Libya 1969-1994*. London: Macmillan Press, 1985.

## 7. Making the Desert Bloom

Hillel, Daniel. *Rivers of Eden*. Oxford: Oxford University Press, 1994.

Lipchin, C. "Report from the Field: Perceptions of Water Use in the Arava Valley of Israel and Jordan." *Journal of the International Institute*, vol.8, no.2, 2001.

Lipchin, C. "Water, Agriculture and Zionism: Exploring the Interface between Policy and Ideology." Paper delivered at the Third International Water History Association Conference, June 2003, Alexandria.

Perennès, J.J. *L'Eau et les Hommes au Maghreb*. Paris: CNRS, Editions Kartala, 1993.

Rouyer, A. *Turning Water into Politics, The Water Issue in the Palestinian-Israeli Conflict*. London: Macmillan Press, 2000.

Swaeringen, W. *Moroccan Mirages: Agrarian Dreams and Deceptions, 1912 – 1986*. London: I.B. Tauris, 1988.

Tal, A. *Pollution in a Promised Land*. Berkeley: University of California Press, 2002.

## 8. Bitter Waters

Alatout, Samer. "Water Balances in Palestine: Numbers and Political Culture in the Middle East." In *Water Balances in the Eastern Mediterranean*, edited By Brooks, D. and Mehmet, O., 58-84. Ottawa: IDRC, 2000.

Brooks, David & Lonergan, Stephen C. *Watershed, The Role of Fresh Water in the Israeli-Palestinian Conflict*. Ottawa: International Development Research Centre, 1994.

Daibes, F. *Water in Palestine, Problems, Politics, Prospects*. Jerusalem: PASSIA, 2003.

Hillel, Daniel. *Rivers of Eden*. Oxford: Oxford University Press, 1994.

Phillips, D.J.H., Attili, A., McCaffrey, S. Murray, J.S. "Factors Relating to the Equitable Distribution of Water in Israel and Palestine." In *Proceedings of the 2nd Israeli-Palestinian-International Conference Water for Life in the Middle East*, edited by Shuval, H. and Dweik, H., 250-263. Jerusalem: IPCRI, 2006.

Rouyer, A. *Turning Water into Politics, The Water Issue in the Palestinian-Israeli Conflict*. London: Macmillan Press, 2000.

Soffer, A., Bystrov, E. *Israel Demography 2004-2020, In light of the process of Disengagement*. Haifa: Reuven Chaikin Chair of Geostrategy, University of Haifa, 2005.

Soffer, A. *Israel, Demography 2003-2020, Dangers and Opportunities*. Haifa: Centre for National Security Studies, University of Haifa, 2003.

Tagar, Z., Keinan, T. Qumsieh, V. *Finding Solutions, Pollution of the Mountain Aquifer by Sewage*. Investigative Report Series on Water Issues No. 2. Friends of the Earth Middle East, 2005.

Tagar, Z., Keinan, T., Bromberg, G. *A Seeping Time Bomb: Pollution of the Mountain Aquifer by Sewage*. Tel Aviv: Friends of the Earth Middle East, 2004.

Trottier, J. *Hydropolitics in the West Bank and Gaza Strip*. Jerusalem: PASSIA, 1999.

UNEP. Desk Study on the Environment in the Occupied Palestinian Territories. United Nations Environmental Programme. 2003.

## 9. War and Visions of Peace

Hillel, Daniel. *Rivers of Eden*. Oxford: Oxford University Press, 1994.

Raphaeli, N. "Rising Tensions over the Nile River Basin." *MEMRI*, no. 165, 2004.

Said, Rushdi. "Cold Water Wars." *Al Ahram Weekly* (26 April-2 May 2001).

Turton, Anthony. "Water Wars: Enduring Myth or Impending Reality?" In *Water Wars: Enduring Myth or Impending Reality?* edited by Hussein Solomon & Anthony Turton. Africa Dialogue Monograph Series No. 2 (June 2000): 165.

Wachtel, Boaz. "The Peace Canal Project: A Multiple Conflict Resolution Perspective for the Middle East." In *Water and Peace in the Middle East*, edited by Jad Isaac and Hillel Shuval. Amsterdam: Elsevier Science B.V., 1994.

Wachtel, Boaz. "The Sad Facts and Dire Politics." *Link*, no. 57, 1996.

Wolf, A. "Conflict and cooperation along international waterways." *Water Policy*, Vol 1 #2, 1998: 251-265.

## 10. Relearning the Meaning of Water

Antonius, R. "Irrigation et Pouvoir Social en Egypte." Ph.D. dissertation, Université du Québec Montréal, Canada, 1991.

Boutet, A. "La question de l'eau au Proche-Orient." Ph.D. dissertation, Université d'Aix-Marseille, France, 1991.

Brooks, David. *Water, Local-level Management*. Ottawa: International Development Research Centre, 2002.

## 11. Four Stories of People and Water

Wessels, J. & Hoogeveen, R.J.A. "Renovation of Qanats in Syria." Consulted on 15 July 2006 through http://www.inweh.unu.edu/inweh/drylands/Publications/Wessels.pdf.

Wessels, J.I. "Community Water Management in the Middle East; dimensions of collective action for the sustainable management of ancient water tunnels (qanats) in Syria," Ph.D. thesis, University of Amsterdam, The Netherlands, forthcoming.

Additional statistics and data from United Nations Environmental Programme (UNEP), United Nations Development Programme (UNDP), United Nations Population Fund (UNFPA), the Food and Agriculture Organisation (FAO) and AQUASTAT, the FAO's global information system of water and agriculture.

Translation of all French, German, and Dutch texts and quotations by the author

# Index

Abed Rabbo, Dr Alfred, 123, 133-34
Abu Zeid, Prof. Mahmoud, 93, 163
Africanus, Leo, 7
Agriculture: 75-80; comparative advantage and food security, 75, 95, 137; economic reorientation, 78-79; subsidies, 75; use of saline water in, 188-90; water-intensive crops and scarcity, 76, 79. *See also* Desert, Treated wastewater, and under individual country
Aïn el Fijé (Syrian river), 12, 14, 19
Al Ansari, Prof. Nadhir, 81, 157-58
Alatout, Dr Samir, 127, 140
Al-Bukhari, 36-37
Alexander River (Israel), 174-75
Algeria, water legislation, 63-64
Alghariani, Prof. Saad, 85, 93-100
Al-Ghazali, 35
Al-Idrisi, 49
Al-Karagi, Mohammad, 42-46, 48
Allan, Prof. Tony, 79
Ammariin tribe (Jordan), 185-87
Applied Research Institute Jerusalem (ARIJ, Bethlehem), 124
Aqueducts, 83-85
Arava Institute for Environmental Studies (Israel), 119, 188
Arava Valley (Israel/Jordan): 129; desert agriculture (Israel), 188-90; public awareness of scarcity in, 81
Aswan Dam (Egypt): 86-90, 93, 100, 144-45, 149, 152, 164; public awareness of scarcity and, 68-69
Atatürk Dam (Turkey), 157, 160-61,163
Ateibeh Lake (Syria), 12, 14
Awaj (river, Syria), 9-21, 64

Banias, (tributary of the Jordan River), 13, 128
Barada (river, Syria), 9-15

Bathing culture, Middle East, 34-35
Ben-Gurion, David, 110, 114, 118, 135
Bethlehem (West Bank), 123, 127, 130, 133, 141, 173
Bible, 25-26, 37, 54, 69
Bino, Dr Murad, 170
Birth rates, *see* Population growth
Blue Nile, 74, 147
Boutros Ghali, Prof. Boutros, 143-47, 150, 152
Brackish water, for agricultural use, 50, 78, 181, 185. *See also* Desalination, Salt-tolerant plants
Bromberg, Gidon, 137
Brooks, Dr David, 70-72, 78, 80, 141

Cairo, 23-24, 39, 67, 69, 72, 77, 92-93, 150, 163, 167-68, 186
Ceyhan (Turkey), 155, 157
*Chafa*, 54
*Chirb*, 54
Christianity: 23, 25, 39, 68, 72, 78; body and soul, 27, 34; Calvinism, 4; deluge, 37; purity/impurity, 32-34
Climate change, 50, 72-74, 79, 96, 103, 145
Coastal Aquifer (Israel/Gaza Strip), 71, 113, 127, 131
*Code des Eaux* (colonial France), 63-64
Conflicts/wars about water: 123-58; the Nile and, 143-50; arguments for and against, 153-55; between Israel and the Palestinian Territories, 123-41; preventing, 156-57
Congo River: 85; dam project, 97-100
Creation stories, 25-26

Dahlan, Hala, 169-70, 172
Daibes, Fadia, 139, 141, 173
Damascus (Syria): 9-22; agriculture around, 14-15, 18-21; drinking water supply, 14-15 ; environmental impact

201